An Ideal Prison?

An Ideal Prison?

Critical Essays
on Women's Imprisonment in Canada

Edited by Kelly Hannah-Moffat and Margaret Shaw

Fernwood Publishing • Halifax & Winnipeg

Editing: Kim Goodliffe
Cover image: Gayle Horii
Design and production: Beverley Rach
Printed and bound in Canada

A publication of:
Fernwood Publishing
32 Oceanvista Lane, Black Point, NS, B0J 1B0
and 748 Broadway Avenue, Winnipeg, MB, R3G 0X3
www.fernwoodpublishing.ca

Fernwood Publishing Company Limited gratefully acknowledges the financial support of the Ministry of Canadian Heritage and the Canada Council for the Arts for our publishing program.

Canadian Cataloguing in Publication Data

Main entry under title:

An ideal prison

ISBN 1-55266-024-9

1. Woman prisoners -- Canada. 2. Female offenders -- Rehabilitation -- Canada.
I. Hannah-Moffat, Kelly, 1967- II. Shaw, Margaret.

HV9507.I33 2000   365'.43'0971   C00-950050-2

Table of Contents

Acknowledgements...7
Contributors 8

Introduction
Kelly Hannah-Moffat and Margaret Shaw.................................*11*

Section I—Systemic Concerns **29**

Re-forming the Prison—Rethinking Our Ideals
Kelly Hannah-Moffat *30*

Prison Reform and Incorporation:
Lessons from Britain and Canada
Stephanie Hayman *41*

Aboriginal Women and Correctional Practice:
Reflections on the Task Force on Federally Sentenced Women
Patricia Monture-Angus *52*

Women, Violence and Disorder in Prisons
Margaret Shaw..*61*

Section II—Therapeutic Concerns **71**

Dependency Discourse as Social Control
Shoshana Pollack...*72*

Psy-ence Fiction:
Governing Female Prisons through the Psychological Sciences
Kathy Kendall *82*

Feminist Therapy with Women in Prison:
Working under the Hegemony of Correctionalism
Gillian Balfour *94*

Section III — Experiencing Imprisonment **103**

Processing Humans
Gayle Horii *104*

The Prisoning of Women: Meeting Women's Needs
Elizabeth Comack *117*

Women in the "Hole": The Unquestioned Practice of Segregation
Joane Martel *128*

Personal and Political Musings on Activism: A Two-Way Interview
Karlene Faith and Kim Pate *136*

References..148

Acknowledgments

Attempting to put down and draw together the events and ideas in this book was not an easy task. It seemed a simple idea to ask a number of women who had been thinking and working and living with these issues over the past ten years or more to write about their views and experiences. It was quite another to put together a book which did justice to their work, to the lives of women in prisons and to the complex events which have taken place in Canada in this period. It was an even greater challenge to do so for readers who might know little about that history and the issues of women's imprisonment and penal reform, and in a (very) small and introductory book.

We owe an enormous debt to all our contributors who, in the midst of their immensely busy and productive lives, had put up with our initially vague requests, our comments and our tough e-mail deadlines, and had to reduce wonderfully rich and detailed accounts to much smaller versions. We thank them all for not giving up and for their commitment to the project. Many other people, far too many to name, with whom we have worked or talked over the past years have enriched our understanding of women's imprisonment and we thank them for their support. This includes many of the staff and policy makers who have worked to develop the new women's prisons.

We would especially like to thank Wayne Antony at Fernwood Publishing for his interest, encouragement, insightful advice and help in the editing process. We appreciate the insights and constructive commentary of Dorothy Chunn, the external reviewer. We also thank Kim Goodliffe for her attentive and painstaking editing.

We owe a special debt to Dawn Moore and Kellie Leclerc, who have helped us keep some order in our lives among the flood of manuscripts, and to Madeleine Weiler for her help in amending and checking the many draft versions. We would also like to thank our families for their continued support, and particularly Alexandra Hannah-Moffat whose birth and first year has paralleled the project and reminded us why we need to write things down.

Most importantly, we would like to thank all those women over the years who have helped us understand a little of what it means to serve a prison sentence. As a society, we are collectively responsible for the conditions under which a sentence is served, whatever the reasons for that sentence, and this book is an attempt to ensure that we do not forget our responsibility. We have asked that all the royalties from this book be donated to organizations working with women in conflict with the law.

Finally, we would like to dedicate the book to the memory of Jo-Anne Mayhew who had agreed to write a chapter but who died in November 1998.

Margaret Shaw and Kelly Hannah-Moffat

Contributors

Co-editors

Kelly Hannah-Moffat is Assistant Professor in the Department of Sociology, University of Toronto at Mississauga. She worked as a researcher and policy advisor for the Commission of Inquiry into Certain Events at the Prison for Women in Kingston. She is a past-president of the Toronto Elizabeth Fry Society, a halfway house and organization that works for and on behalf of all women in conflict with the law. Her publications include: *Punishment in Disguise: The Governance of Canadian Women's Federal Imprisonment*, (forthcoming), "Moral Agent Or Actuarial Subject: Risk and Canadian Women's Imprisonment" (1999) and "Prisons that Empower: Neoliberal Governance in Canadian Women's Prisons" (2000).

Margaret Shaw is a sociologist and research and policy advisor. She had taught in the Department of Sociology and Anthropology at Concordia University, Montréal for the past ten years. Prior to coming to Canada she worked as a criminologist at the Home Office, England. She is a board member of the Société Elizabeth Fry du Québec and of CAEFS. She has undertaken a substantial amount of research on women's involvement in lawbreaking and imprisonment. Recent publications include "Is there a Feminist Future for Women's Prisons?" in R. Matthews and P. Francis (ed.) *Prison 2000: An International Perspective on the Current State and Future of Imprisonment* (1996) and "'Knowledge Without Acknowledgment': Violent Women the Prison and the Cottage." (1999). Her current work is on penal policy, and on risk and classification.

Additional Contributors

Gillian Balfour is currently working on her Ph.D. in sociology at the University of Manitoba. Her dissertation research is a comparative study of the narrative accounts of women convicted of violent crimes and the narratives told by police and trial documents. She teaches in the Department of Sociology/Justice and Law at the University of Winnipeg. She has presented the following papers: "Surviving Prison" at the Congress of the Social Sciences and Humanities for the Canadian Law and Society Association (June 1998) and "From Advocates to Experts: Feminist Therapy with Women in Prison" at the American Sociological Association meetings (August 1998).

Elizabeth Comack teaches in the Department of Sociology at the University of Manitoba. Her publications include: *Locating Law: Race/Class/Gender Connections* (1999), *Women in Trouble* (1996), *Feminist Engagement with the Law* (1993), two editions (with Stephen Brickey) of *The Social Basis of Law* (1986 and 1991) and several articles and book chapters. Her current research is in the area of women's violence.

Karlene Faith has been a community activist for human justice since the mid-1950s and began her work with women in prison in 1972. Completing her Ph.D. in History of Consciousness at the University of California in Santa Cruz in 1981, she joined the Criminology Faculty of Simon Fraser University. Her publications include work on prison education, the "female offender," Ras Tafarians, Michel Foucault, women's music, and media images of "criminal" women. Her most recent book is *Unruly Women: The Politics of Confinement and Resistance* (1993).

Stephanie Hayman is a Research Officer at Goldsmiths College, University of London, having previously worked at King's College, London, where she edited *Criminal Justice Matters*. She received her M.Sc. in criminal justice policy from the London School of Economics and Political Science (LSE) and is presently completing her Ph.D. at the LSE. Her thesis critically examines the development of the new federal prisons for women in Canada, following the implementation of *Creating Choices*. Her Master's dissertation, *Community Prisons for Women— A Comparative Study of Practice in England and the Netherlands* (1996) was published by the Prison Reform Trust.

Gayle K. Horii, in 1995, was a co-founder (with four additional sister-prisoners and three social activists) of the non-profit Strength in Sisterhood (SIS) Society whose aim it is to provide a support network for women in prison, past and present. The aims of SIS encompass the encouragement and development of services for women on various forms of release while also promoting the fair, dignified and lawful treatment of women inside through both the elimination of all forms of discrimination against women and the necessity of public openness and accountability of the authorities in all places where women are incarcerated in Canada.

Gayle also serves on the board of the 1992 West Coast Prison Justice Society (WCPJS). Some of their aims are to inform prisoners about recent legislation that may affect them and to provide a venue for dialogue through monthly newsletters, to encourage the application of the Canadian *Charter of Rights and Freedoms* inside prisons and penitentiaries and to promote the provision of legal services to people incarcerated. Gayle has written for various publications including the *WCPJS Newsletter*, the *Journal of Prisoners on Prisons* and the *Accord*. She presented at the 1995 Arbour Inquiry and at various forums, both governmental and non-governmental over the past seven years and continues to speak to classes at Simon Fraser University in Burnaby, B.C. about the realities of incarceration.

Gayle's chapter replaces one intended by her sister-inside, Jo-Ann Mayhew, who died from ALS on September 15, 1998.

Kathleen Kendall is a lecturer in the medical school at Southampton University, United Kingdom. Before moving to England, she worked both as a program evaluator and as a special advisor on female offenders for the Correctional Service of Canada. She also worked as a researcher on forensic issues in a position funded by the University of Saskatchewan and the Regional Psychiatric

Centre, Prairies. Kathy has taught sociology in both Canada and the United Kingdom. She has published a number of articles and reports related to female prisoners, including *Program Evaluation of Therapeutic Services at the Prison for Women in 1993* (1993), and "Beyond Grace: Criminal Lunatic Women in Victorian Canada" (1999). She is currently continuing her research on "mentally disordered" female offenders and is working on issues related to Iranian women prisoners with Soheila Sadeghi Fassaei.

Joane Martel has been an Assistant Professor of Criminal Justice and Critical Criminology at the University of Alberta since July 1996. Her research interests center on the sociology of criminal law, on punishment regimes as well as on the place of women in normative systems, mainly within the Criminal justice process. In the past, she has worked in various agencies of the criminal justice apparatus, such as probation, the judicial, and group homes for young offenders. She is currently a member of the Program Citizen Advisory Committee at the Edmonton Maximum Institution for men. Joane Martel has published on topics such as the media reconstruction of wife-battering in nineteenth-century Canada, psycho-social intervention within the criminal justice process, the transformation of criminal law relating to assisted-suicide and women prisoners' experiences of segregation in federal and provincial prisons.

Patricia Monture-Angus, a tenured Associate Professor in the Department of Native Studies, University of Saskatchewan, is a citizen of the Mohawk Nation, Grand River Territory. She currently resides on the Thunderchild First Nation in Saskatchewan with her Cree partner and five of their six children. Patricia was a member of the Working Group of the Task Force on Federally Sentenced Women. Her books include *Thunder in My Soul: A Mohawk Woman Speaks* (1995) and *Journeying Forward: Dreaming First Nations' Independence* (1999).

Kim Pate is the executive director of the Canadian Association of Elizabeth Fry Societies and a long-time advocate for prisoners' rights and social justice in Canada and internationally. Prior to her current position, she worked for the John Howard Society. She has published in the areas of women's imprisonment and social justice.

Shoshana Pollack, teaches in the Faculty of Social Work at York University. Shoshana spent five years working as a psychotherapist at the Kingston Prison for Women, where she also conducted a program evaluation of a prisoner–peer counselling program. Her current doctoral research examines issues of empower-ment and agency in the lives of women in conflict with the law, particularly in relation to race, class and gender locations.

Introduction
Prisons for Women—Theory, Reform, Ideals
Kelly Hannah-Moffat and Margaret Shaw

> Forming a vision which truly represents an alternative to the status quo
> is the core of social change. Struggling for changes which transform
> the lives of all women is the concrete, constructive core of feminism."
> (Dobash and Dobash 1992:288)

In 1990, the Canadian government published a remarkable report called
Creating Choices (TFFSW 1990). It set out a new philosophy and set of principles for the construction and operation of five new women-centred prisons.
The report was the outcome of the Task Force on Federally Sentenced Wom-
en (TFFSW), which was established in 1989 to consider the future of women's
imprisonment in Canada for those serving sentences of two years or more.
Canada is in a unique position as one of the first countries to have attempted
to develop a new prison regime for women that incorporates feminist principles, as well as recognizing the need to respond to the extraordinary experiences of Aboriginal women.

Apart from stimulating considerable interest in other countries, the report
also influenced some provincial governments to rethink their policies for
women's prisons. For example, the provincial government of Nova Scotia set
up its own task force on women's imprisonment. Their report, *Blueprint for
Change* (Solicitor General's Special Committee on Provincially Incarcerated
Women 1992) was modelled on TFFSW and argued for the virtual ending of
imprisonment at the provincial level in Nova Scotia (i.e., for all those women
serving sentences of less than two years).[1] Similarly, Ontario established a
Women's Issues Task Force in 1993, whose more restrained report, *Women's
Voices, Women's Choices,* appeared in 1995.

The millennium marks the tenth anniversary of *Creating Choices*. The
anniversary is an excellent time to reflect on and re-evaluate changes in
women's imprisonment. This book is about women in prison, about the effects
of punishment and penality on those women, about the impact of feminism
on the lives of women prisoners and the systemic barriers that limit prison
reform. It takes as its starting point the publication of *Creating Choices*. The
report serves as a vehicle for analyzing the difficulties of reforming carceral
institutions, and the role of prisons in our society, the intersection of gender
with race and class, and the particular problems faced by women prisoners.
While the focus is on the current period, we argue that it is essential to place
the penal system in a historical context in order to understand the present. In
a short and introductory text, it is not possible to give a detailed account of all
the issues facing women prisoners or penal reform. Instead our objective is to

stimulate a reflexive and analytical discussion of women's imprisonment that goes beyond a description of events or individuals.

Feminism, Reform and the State

The feminist agenda has always been concerned with bringing about social change, with improving women's lives (although not exclusively). This relates to all shades of feminism (Daly and Chesney Lind 1988; Comack 1999) and feminist engagement with the state and theoretical analyses and debate (Harding 1987; Rafter and Heidensohn 1995). Yet working for change in the justice system seems to have been more difficult than in other areas of social policy, in part because of the authority and power of the law and its ability to co-opt feminist concerns. Feminist criminologists have raised concerns about the role of state intervention. Many critical and reflexive analyses question the wisdom of relying too heavily on the state; in fact, a number of writers have argued that such engagement can make things *worse* for women (Smart 1989; Snider 1990, 1994; Los 1990; Comack 1999) and that rather than empower women the state contributes to women's oppression. For example, many feminists have documented that male violence against women persists despite numerous well-intentioned state initiatives directed at remedying the problem. The state's response to male violence against women has not remained true to the original feminist agenda. While demands for reform and state action (legislation and policy) have had some immediate advantages for women, such as funding of shelters, feminist structural analyses of this problem is often ignored, misinterpreted and misrepresented. The governments individualize and psychologize (syndromize) the experiences of battered women rather than address the broader concerns about men's behaviour and the structural inequality of women in society.

The impact of feminism in criminology was first felt when Frances Heidensohn in England (1968) and Marie Andree Bertrand in Canada (1969) "awoke criminology from its androcentric slumber" by drawing attention to the omission of women from general theories of crime (Daly and Chesney-Lind 1988:507). Feminist thought, however, has changed considerably over the past twenty years in Canada and elsewhere. The following three areas capture the central components of the initial feminist critique of criminology and criminal justice practices. First was an acknowledgment of systematic neglect of women/gender in criminological theory. Traditional mainstream criminology, like most academic disciplines, had largely ignored women despite increasing evidence that crime was gendered. Those few theories that attempted to explain female crime provided stereotypical and biologically based constructions of women's offending which pathologized, infantilized, demonized and sexualized women's crime and deviance (see Morris 1987; Naffine 1987). These studies reinforced stereotypical views about the nature of females (and males), while ignoring the substantive differences in their social status and economic position. Most traditional sociological theories, including strain theory, opportunity theory, learning theory, subcultural theory and social-control theory, failed to question why women were much less likely to be committing crime than men. Instead, they were concerned with activities of men and boys. Similarly, early versions of critical theories, like labelling and class-based conflict theories failed to address gender difference in offending or in the administration of the criminal justice system. Feminist recognition of this "collective amnesia" resulted in broader theoretical concerns about the *generalizability* of theories of crime based on men and boys to the experiences of women and girls, and about the failure of existing theories to explain why women and girls appear to commit *far fewer* crimes than men and boys.

Second, before 1970 little was known about the nature of women's crime or the qualitative or quantitative differences between male and female offending. Early feminist critiques of criminology challenged traditional explanations of female crime (Klein 1973; Smart 1976; Heidensohn 1985) and stressed the importance of examining women's experiences from their standpoint, of contextualizing women's offending, of analyzing institutional and interpersonal power relations, and of the gendered nature of social controls. These feminist theoretical analyses evolved into a more substantive critique of traditional criminological methods and positivistic claims of scientific objectivity and neutrality.

Feminist scholars also began the daunting task of redressing the significant gaps in our knowledge about women's "everyday" experiences in the criminal justice system. Feminist research in this area includes studies of the dynamics of female crime (sometimes referred to as feminist empiricism) and of the *experiences* of women in the criminal justice system—either as law-breakers, victims or practitioners. Many of these studies clearly document the discrepancies in the treatment of males and females by the criminal justice system and in some extreme cases an institutionalized sexism. This research inspired rights-based litigation and policy claims for equality of treatment for women and men

Third, the feminist critique prompted a re-examination of the assumptions underlying the law and the administration of the criminal justice system. A parallel critique of feminist legal scholars identified the male-centred nature of law, and showed how family law, and criminal law in particular, played a major role in gender oppression. Some feminist scholars remain skeptical about the capacity of legal reform to alter the material conditions of women and instead argue for a decentring of the law in favour of other more systemic changes (Smart 1989).

More recently, North American and Western European feminism has been criticized for its failure to adequately theorize race and socio-economic status (Rice 1990; Carlen and Worrall 1987; Simpson 1991; Hester, Kelly and Radford 1996). The universal category "women" and the proselytizing of feminism by predominantly white and middle-class women, is seen as a form of elitism that ignores the impact of racial and cultural experiences, age, ability and sexual orientation on different women's lives. The category "women" is contentious in that it highlights only one dimension of a "fractured identity." Some postmodern legal scholars argue for a more integrated analysis that considers the *intersection* of multiple forms of oppression (Crenshaw 1992; Razack 1994; Bannerji 1995). Others argue that feminist inquiry has to be expanded to include analyses of masculinity as well as femininity (Newburn and Stanko 1994; Daly and Maher 1998). There has also been a recent critique of feminism's portrayal of women primarily as victims, who neither act nor resist but merely submit to violence (Bosworth 1999), as well as its neglect of women's capacity to perpetrate violence (Heidensohn 1992; Shaw 1995).

In the course of the past thirty years feminism has undergone considerable development, and its ideals and visions for change or reform have included a wide gamut of approaches. These range from trying to reform the mainstream institutions of the state through policy and law reform to rejecting reform, preferring instead radical grass-roots activity and radical social change because "the system" cannot adequately address the concerns of women as a group.

The Neglect of Incarcerated Women

Where does feminism now stand in relation to women in prison? As Rafter and Heidensohn (1995:7) have pointed out, it is ironic that while "feminists began their criminological critique with the neglect of women as *offenders*, their greatest achievement has been developing new theories about and policies for women (and children) as *victims*." Until recently, much feminist research has focused on the treatment of female victims of sexual assault and domestic violence. In the same way, feminist advocacy has concentrated primarily on dispelling the myths and misconceptions surrounding violence against women, and on improving women's access to services and the response of the criminal justice system to victims. It has been suggested that feminist criminologists gave greater attention to women's victimization rather than their lawbreaking because it is more easily linked to patriarchal relations of power (Daly and Chesney-Lind 1988). In short the issue of victimization appears to be more consistent with the feminist project, and it was perceived as a more pressing social problem. With the exception of women accused of violence against intimates, and the acceptance by the courts (in some cases) of the "battered women's defence," the impact of feminist research and activism on offending women has been much more restricted (Ursel 1991; Comack 1993; Noonan 1993; Bertrand 1994). There is little evidence of changed regimes, correctional agendas or sentencing practices for women offenders in most countries. There has been relatively little focus on the lives of women who come into conflict with the law and even less on imprisoned women. The characteristics and condition of women prisoners remain depressingly familiar, with considerable deterioration in conditions in some countries. In the United States, for example, the number of women in prison has risen from some 12,000 in 1980 to more than 60,000 in 1995, an increase that includes primarily non-white women sentenced for minor offences (Chesney-Lind 1995; see also Bloom, Lee and Owen 1995). A recent comparative account of women's prisons in North America and some European countries reaches the conclusion that they still feature excessive security, fail to classify appropriately, restrict access to children and families, and lack a range of suitable programs for women (Bertrand 1998).

Part of the explanation for the limited impact of feminism on the lives of women prisoners lies in the ambivalence many feminists feel about acquiescing in the correctional treatment of women, or asking the criminal justice system to become, as Snider puts it, "an equal opportunity oppressor" (1994:83). There are other factors which have contributed to the reluctance to engage with such issues, apart from concerns about the theoretical, structural or practical feasibility of doing so, like loss of public interest, which accompanies the post-sentence stages of the criminal justice system. With the exception of a few key women whose situation or sentence rouses public interest, most attention is focused on the drama of the court process up to the sentence itself (Shaw 1995) and that too is where much feminist interest has stopped. The secrecy associated with correctional regimes is another factor that protects those regimes from the public eye. Secrecy presents real barriers to investigation and research (Snider 1994; Doyle and Ericson 1996). Overall, therefore, not only has feminism taken longer to affect the lives of women in conflict with the law than in other areas of social policy, but there has been even less analysis of or engagement with women's prisons. This is what makes Canada's attempt to draft a new and feminist-based prison system so unusual.

Studies of Women's Prisons

In the wider criminology literature—as within feminism—there has been extensive analysis of penality and the role of the prison in society. Views on changing penal trends are divided. Some argue that the emergence and development of the penitentiary in the nineteenth century was progressive, humanitarian and positive. Others—who are referred to as the *revisionists*—contend that those changes led to more pervasive and totalizing forms of social control (Foucault 1977; Ignatieff 1978; Rothman 1980; Cohen 1985). Such works have almost without exception ignored the situation of women prisoners and women's prisons.

In most countries, critical studies of the imprisonment of women emerged only in the past twenty years. Concerns about male power in terms of repression and social control dominate many of these accounts. Most of these studies outline the patriarchal oppression of women prisoners at the hands of their (usually) male keepers, from the seventeenth to the twentieth centuries, while some also consider the impact of class, race and issues of women's resistance (e.g., Freedman 1981; Rafter 1992; Carlen 1983; Zedner 1991). Dobash, Dobash and Gutteridge (1986) for example, show how penal and therapeutic techniques of governing women prisoners amount to gender-specific forms of disciplinary regulation. They trace the development of punishment and prison regimes, and discuss the role of criminological and expert knowledge in the formation of those regimes. Thus, their work offers a valuable critique of the revisionist analyses of men's penality (Ignatieff 1978; Rothman 1980; Foucault 1977) for failing to consider the role of patriarchal and gender-based assumptions in the development of modern prisons.

More recently, Howe (1994) has shifted the emphasis. She claims that the introduction of gender into the study of women's imprisonment has not advanced feminist theory, and that "gender-sensitive penal analyses do not seem to have realized that a consideration of gender cannot be reduced to a study of women" (Howe 1994:158). She argues that feminist analyses of penality must also consider the role of masculinity in the development of men's prisons, as well as incorporating the insights of non-feminist critical analyses of penality. Thus, Howe advocates an approach to the study of women's "penality" that does not focus explicitly on the prison, but rather on wider strategies of regulating women. However, her assertion that many feminist histories of punishment have been *atheoretical* in nature clearly misses the importance of feminist contributions that document (and in some cases do theorize) the experiences of women prisoners and reformers.

In her work on women's penality, Kelly Hannah-Moffat (1997, 1999, 2000 forthcoming) builds on Howe's study and on recent analyses of "governmentality"[2] as they relate to the problem of crime and its management. She argues for a more complex analysis of how power is exercised over individuals, particularly prisoners. She suggests (1997; 2000 forthcoming) that the analysis of relations of power between prisoners and their managers must be extended beyond an analysis of disciplinary power and patriarchy. Changes in contemporary organization of prisons cannot be viewed in isolation from past strategies of governing. Using this method she argues that recent risk discourses are gendered and racialized and thus differentially affect incarcerated men and women (Hannah-Moffat 1999; Shaw and Hannah-Moffat 1999).

As with other countries, the literature on women in prison in Canada is scarce, and most of it was written in the past fifteen years.[3] Some accounts look at the historical treatment of women prisoners (Backhouse 1991; Cooper 1993; Hannah-Moffat 1997; Oliver 1998). Others examine specific institutions such as the Andrew Mercer Reformatory, the first prison specifically for women in Ontario (Strange 1985; Berkovits 1995), or that established by the Soeurs du Bon Pasteur in Montreal in 1876 (Hamelin 1989). A few studies focus on the struggle to reform the imprisonment of federally sentenced women and the infamous Prison for Women (e.g., Cooper 1993; Berzins and Hayes 1987). Others examine more recent history, including the conditions under which women serve their sentences and the social controls over them (Berzins and Collette-Carrière 1979; Watson 1980; Adelberg and Currie 1987, 1993; Hamelin 1989; Woodrow 1998; Shaw 1991; Frigon 1999). There are some comparative studies that examine conditions in women's prisons in other countries as well as Canada (Axon 1989a, 1989b; Shaw 1991; Faith 1993a, 1993b; Bertrand 1998).

There are surveys of women prisoners' needs and experiences based on interviews with them, and accounts of the impact of imprisonment on them in the context of their lives—of separation from their children and families, of prison programs and of punishment and segregation (Walford 1987; Sugar and Fox 1989; Shaw et al. 1991, 1994; Kendall 1993; Sommers 1995; Comack 1996). There are also analyses of the impact of feminist engagement with the prison (Hattem 1990; Biron 1992; Kendall 1993a, 1994a, 1994b; Shaw 1993, 1996b; Hannah-Moffat 1994, 1995; Faith 1995; McLean 1995; Bertrand 1998). Kathy Kendall and Shoshana Pollock, for example, undertook extensive analyses of the development of programs based on feminist principles at the Prison for Women in Kingston in the early 1990s (Kendall 1993; Pollack 1993). These studies fill an important gap in our knowledge of women's imprisonment in Canada and reveal the many failed attempts to reform the conditions under which women serve their sentences.

Who Are the Women in Prison in Canada?

Canadian women's prisons are unique in part because of the political and social development of the country as well as its physical characteristics (including its enormous size, the relatively small and widely spread population, and the existence of significant language and cultural differences). Unlike many other countries, Canada has a two-tier correction system. The 1867 constitution divided responsibility for imprisonment between provincial and federal governments, and parallel institutional systems developed for men and women (Friedland 1988). Those who receive sentences of under two years, referred to as *provincially sentenced,* serve their sentences in a provincial correctional institution or jail. In some provinces and territories, such as Manitoba and Saskatchewan, provincially sentenced women are housed in the province's single women's prison. In others, for example Quebec, there is more than one women's prison but for the most part women serve their sentences in small sections of prisons housing much larger numbers of men. Ontario, for example, has for many years imprisoned women in jails and detention centres throughout the province, often in very inferior conditions (Shaw et al. 1991; Shaw 1994a).[4] An exception is British Columbia where both provincially and federally sentenced women have been housed at the Burnaby Correctional Centre for Women since 1990.

Women sentenced to two years or more are referred to as *federally sentenced* and serve their sentences for the most part in a single federal penitentiary. Institutions for men are dispersed throughout the country and offer a variety of programs and facilities as well as security levels. For women until 1995, in part because of their small numbers, there was only one federal prison, the Prison for Women in Kingston, Ontario. Unlike prison systems in some other countries, there were no minimum-security facilities, no facilities for mothers with babies nor even specific psychiatric facilities for women serving long sentences.[5] And even those who come from Ontario, the same province in which the prison is situated, might still be up to 1000 miles from home. From the 1970s some federally sentenced women were able to stay in provincial prisons under exchange of service agreements, so that they could receive services in French, in the case of women in Quebec, or be closer to home.

Provincially sentenced women form the larger group, most of them serving very short sentences.[6] In 1991, for example, almost 10,000 women were admitted to provincial prisons under sentence, and a further 8,500 on remand, compared with 141 women admitted on a federal sentence (Johnson and Rodgers 1993). Compared with men, however, women represent a very small proportion of those sentenced to imprisonment. Provincially sentenced women comprise about 7 percent of all prison admissions, and at any given time there are some 900 women serving provincial sentences across Canada. At the federal level the discrepancy is even greater. In 1998 the total federally sentenced population was about 14,000 but only some 360, or 2.5 percent, were women. While the smallness of the female prison population has contributed to their neglect, such a small population could be seen as an advantage and an opportunity to do something unique and different. First Nations peoples are disproportionately represented in federal and provincial prisons. Up to 25 percent of the federal population in prison are Aboriginal; however, in some provincial prisons the proportion is considerably higher. There is also evidence of increasing numbers of Black women in provincial and federal prisons. For example, the tough policy on drug offending in Ontario has particularly affected the Black population, and women more than men (Commission on Systemic Racism in the Ontario Criminal Justice System 1995).

Overall, only 18 percent of all criminal code offences are committed by women. For both women and men minor property offences predominate, but women are much less likely to be convicted for serious offences and violent crimes (Johnson and Rodgers 1993; Boritch 1997). Only 12 percent of all offences classified as violent are committed by women. Women in prison are most likely to have been convicted of property crimes (theft and fraud), drug offences and "other" offences including prostitution and crimes against the person, especially at the provincial level (Trevethan and McKillop 1999). Two thirds of the small population of federally sentenced women, however, are sentenced for offences classified as violent, including murder or manslaughter, attempted murder, serious assault and robbery, and over a quarter of them for drug offences. In both federal and provincial prisons, Aboriginal women are more likely than non-Aboriginals to have been convicted for offences classified as violent, reflecting the huge disparities in socio-economic status, levels of alcohol use and systemic racism experienced by those women. In spite of popular conceptions, however, reported female crime has decreased, not increased, since 1992, while violent crime has either remained stable or decreased (Dell and Boe 1998).

There are a number of factors that women prisoners share with men in prison (Statistics Canada 1999):

- aged between 25 and 34;
- poor, often unemployed and with very limited income and resources;
- have little formal education or certified job skills—grade nine education or less;
- offences usually included high levels of involvement with alcohol and drug use;
- Aboriginals are over-represented.

On the other hand, there are also a number of distinct differences (Shaw 1994a, 1994b):

- two thirds of women in prison are mothers, and are far more likely to be primary or sole care-givers than men;[7]
- women's health needs are different and often greater than those of men;
- Aboriginal women are even more over-represented than Aboriginal men;
- women's criminal histories are generally less extensive and serious than men's;
- women are less likely to be reconvicted and are generally seen as better "risks" than men;
- women have higher reported levels of physical, sexual and emotional abuse as children and adults than men;
- overall, women have lower education and job-skill training than men, and more poverty and welfare dependence;
- women are more likely than men to be diagnosed as having mental health problems.

Apart from these "factual" differences, women also *experience and respond to prison* quite differently from men. Women tend to feel the "pains of imprisonment" more than men, and to express their feelings in different ways (Liebling 1994). For women, relationships with their children, family and friends are central, their relationships in prison are more intimate than men's (Shaw 1994a, 1994b). In general, there is less overt violence in women's prisons, but a greater likelihood that women will slash or injure themselves or attempt suicide. There is a long history of controlling women in prison with medication (as there is outside prison), and a greater use of disciplinary proceedings for minor infractions which would not be pursued in a male facility. They are often regarded as being "more difficult to handle" than men, and more verbal and emotional.

In summary, while there is some overlap in the kinds of offences for which women and men are convicted, there are also considerable differences, and the context of their offending and their experiences outside and inside prison, as well as their reactions to imprisonment, are both quantitatively *and* qualitatively different from those of men. These differences underline the importance of considering women's imprisonment independently of men's. Still, changes in prison practices must also consider the differences *between* women in terms of their own experiences of racism and poverty, as well as the possibility that changes to women's regimes could benefit men's institutions.

The Task Force on Federally Sentenced Women and *Creating Choices*

Up to the mid-1990s, there was only one penitentiary for federally sentenced women in Canada. In 1934, a single separate facility for all federal women, the Prison for Women (P4W), was opened in Kingston to replace the existing structure inside the walls of the Kingston Penitentiary. P4W was built as a maximum-security institution according to nineteenth-century penitentiary architecture—with ranges and cells, each with bars reaching from floor to ceiling. Since its opening, there have been numerous calls for its closure. Four years after its completion, the 1938 Archambault Report found conditions at P4W to be inferior to those in men's prisons, and recommended its closure and the transfer of all women back to prisons in their home provinces under provincial authority (Cooper 1987). Since the Archambault report, numerous subsequent government and private sector reports have expressed concern that women suffer more hardship than men by being incarcerated so far from their homes and families, and that the provision of programs and facilities does not take into account the needs of women, nor match those available for men (Berzins and Hayes 1987; Cooper 1987; Biron 1992). These reports have variously recommended the replacement of P4W, its enhancement or its closure, and the dispersal of federally sentenced women back to their home provinces.

In 1980, frustration with the lack of progress led to a formal complaint to the Human Rights Commission of Canada on behalf of federally sentenced women. This complaint was launched by a group of feminist reformers called Women for Justice (Berzins and Hayes 1987). This was a turning point in Canadian women's prison reform. The Human Rights Commission upheld their complaint and declared that "federal female offenders were discriminated against on the basis of sex and that in virtually all programs and facility areas, the treatment of federal women inmates was inferior to that of men" (Cooper 1987:139). They argued that the state had a legal and moral obligation to provide women with programs and facilities "substantively equivalent" to those provided for male inmates.

The case was sent to conciliation but resulted in little change to the programs and conditions for prisoners at P4W, and Women for Justice withdrew from the process (Berzins and Hayes 1987). In 1987, the Women's Legal Education and Action Fund (LEAF) (Razack 1991) began a similar *Charter of Rights and Freedoms* challenge against Correctional Service of Canada. With the appointment of the Task Force on Federally Sentenced Women (TFFSW), however, the case was postponed and never reached the court.

In part because of the pressure from women's groups such as the Canadian Association of Elizabeth Fry Societies (CAEFS), LEAF and Women for Justice, by 1988 the federal government was more receptive to the needs of federally sentenced women and was willing to re-open the issue. There had been a number of suicides at P4W, most of them by Aboriginal women, which had raised public awareness of the problems at the prison (Kershaw and Lasovich 1991). The Task Force on Federally Sentenced Women, appointed by the Solicitor General in 1989, was unusual in that it included both voluntary sector and government members as well as representatives of Aboriginal and minority groups, and women who had themselves been in prison. Many of the members of the TFFSW used a feminist perspective, a perspective which does not favour a "sameness" approach, feeling that traditional correctional approaches based on the male population were not appropriate for women prisoners. They emphasized the extensiveness of violence in women's lives and their unique social and economic barriers, and the need for a "women-centred" approach for new facilities, regimes and programs. The TFFSW was careful, however, to use the term *women-centred* rather than *feminist*. Aboriginal women on the TFFSW made a considerable impact, arguing for recognition of their experiences of racism and oppression as well as violence (Sugar and Fox 1989). In the end, however, the final report represented a compromise between government, voluntary groups and Aboriginal members.

The report of the TFFSW, *Creating Choices* (TFFSW 1990), recommended the closure of P4W, and the construction of five new regional facilities and a healing lodge for Aboriginal women, as well as the parallel development of a community-release strategy. The report set out five women-centred principles on which the new facilities and policies were to be based: 1) empowerment, 2) the provision of meaningful choices, 3) treating women with respect and dignity, 4) the provision of a physically and emotionally supportive environment, and 5) the sharing of responsibility for women's welfare between institutional staff, community members and the women themselves.

The report argued for not just new buildings, but for fundamental changes in the way the new facilities should be run and staffed (Shaw 1993). The new regional facilities were to be situated on several acres of land with cottage-style houses accommodating six to ten women each. There were to be independent living areas and facilities for women to live with small children and for family visits. Staffing levels were to vary according to the needs of the women, but the emphasis was to be on high levels of staffing and support rather than on physical security measures. One cottage in each facility was to have enhanced security for women who felt the need for a more structured environment on a temporary basis, but the facility as a whole would not require a fence, unless there was a need to keep people *out*. A core area would provide educational, recreational, daycare and spiritual facilities, as well as flexible space for programs. All staff were to be carefully selected for their sensitivity to the circumstances of federally sentenced women and given mandatory training in counselling, communication and negotiation skills. To help them develop a broader understanding of the backgrounds and experiences of women prisoners, new staff would be trained in cultural differences and educated about racism and sexism.

Programs were to be *holistic*, to deal with the "interrelated nature of a woman's experience" (TFFSW 1990:105) and to reflect the wishes and needs of individual women. Community groups and agencies, or local authorities outside the correctional system in the case of educational or health services, would provide such programming. It was envisaged that each facility would provide core programming which included individual and group counselling for family violence and incest survivors, as well as training in living skills, stress reduction and relaxation. Health care, mental-health services, addiction programs, education, vocational training and recreational, spiritual and cultural programs were all to be provided. Each of these programs was to be designed specifically for women prisoners.

The healing lodge was to be built in the prairies to serve Aboriginal women from across Canada. It was to be developed, staffed and run (primarily) by Aboriginal peoples, governed by an Elder Council and linked to a nearby native community.

The second part of the TFFSW plan was the development of a range of community-based resources for women that would provide them with continuity of programs and support on their return to the community. These were to include halfway houses, satellite apartments and supported accommodation, residential addiction centres for women and community-release centres.

Initial Implementation of *Creating Choices*

The recommendations of *Creating Choices* were accepted by the federal government and fifty million dollars allocated for their implementation. But while accepting the main recommendations, the Solicitor General rejected the proposed implementation process. The volunteer sector, most notably CAEFS, which had a role on an external advisory committee to oversee the implementation, felt it was not consulted or informed about crucial decisions until they were a *fait accompli*. Such decisions included the selection of sites for the new institutions and the appointment of wardens. These events effectively, in the eyes of CAEFS, excluded those outside government from the process (Shaw 1993) and eventually led to the withdrawal of CAEFS support.

Furthermore, the government failed to provide funds for the development of community services, seen by *Creating Choices* as a crucial aspect of the new regional facilities. Other subsequent changes included alterations in the architectural plans for the facilities themselves, with the development of secure facilities, the erection of fences and, in at least one prison, the elimination of certain key components, such as the daycare centre or the gymnasium. These decisions were made by the government on a variety of grounds including cost, public pressure from local citizens living near the proposed sites, considerations of employment and job creation, and perhaps, in the aftermath of the withdrawal of CAEFS, the desire to locate far away from local Elizabeth Fry Societies who might prove too critical (Hannah-Moffat 1995). The new prisons in Truro, Nova Scotia; Kitchener, Ontario; Edmonton, Alberta; Joliette, Quebec; and the Okimaw Ochi Healing Lodge at Maple Creek, Saskatchewan, were finally opened between the end of 1995 and the spring of 1997.[8]

The Context: Parallel Events and the Responses

As the implementation of the TFFSW report proceeded, events both inside and outside the Correctional Service of Canada continued to have an impact on the initial vision. Public anger emerged over the location of some of the new prisons with local residents developing powerful campaigns to prevent prisons being built near them. In part, anger was fuelled by the publicity surrounding the horrendous disclosures in the arrest and trials of Paul Bernardo and his wife Karla Homolka.[9] For the press and public, the case underlined the stark reality that women—as well as men—can be violent, something *Creating Choices* had largely avoided. It was also fuelled by resentment based on the public's perception that *prisoners* would be offered facilities that those living outside prisons did not have.

In April 1994, an event inside P4W heightened this change in attitude. This incident involved a fight between six prisoners and a number of guards, six of whom were injured, which resulted in a consequential chain of actions: segregation of the inmates; continued disturbances by those women; well-publicized strip-searching and shackling of the women by a male emergency response team; the removal of these women into isolation for up to eight months; eventual disciplinary hearings; and further punishment on their release back into the population of the penitentiary (Faith 1995; Arbour 1996). In 1996, a series of slashings, escapes, a suicide (now an alleged murder) and a cell-smashing occuring in two of the newly opened prisons put to rest any notion that the new regimes and institutions *in themselves* would eliminate most of the difficulties experienced in the old penitentiary.

The public responded to these various events with increasing fear and outrage. They demanded fences (or higher fences), cameras and tougher security measures in the new institutions—now perceived as places which would not house passive victims of abuse, but violent and dangerous women from whom society must be protected. The Correctional Service of Canada (CSC) responded by increasing security measures and doubling the provision for secure accommodation in the new prisons. The mother and child program was put on hold. On the recommendation of the internal report about the April 1994 incident, and in spite of the planned closure of P4W in 1996, additional segregation cells were built at the prison at a cost of some $500,000. In September 1996, a decision was made to exclude all women classified as maximum security from the new prisons. Instead, they were to be housed in men's maximum-security institutions, including Kingston Penitentiary, from where they had been removed early in the century. Within the CSC, there were more frequent discussions about separating the "difficult" women (those designated as "violent and disruptive" or "difficult to manage," or those thought to have "borderline personalities" or to suffer from "identity disturbance" or "personality disorders") from others.

The Arbour Commission of Inquiry

In the midst of these development, however, was a further event with wide-reaching implications. Claims of injustices, relating to the April 1994 event and its handling, from women prisoners, community workers and lawyers, were generally ignored or dismissed by the correctional authorities. Even though a 1995 report by the Correctional Investigator reinforced the validity of those claims, it was the broadcast by the Canadian Broadcasting Corporation in February 1995 of a videotape of the strip-searching that finally brought that incident to the public's attention. The Solicitor General immediately announced an independent inquiry. The report of that inquiry, headed by Madam Justice Louise Arbour, was made public on April 1, 1996. The Arbour inquiry found a flagrant disregard for the rights of prisoners and a culture of defensiveness in the correctional system. As Madam Justice Arbour concluded on the basis of introductory submissions by the CSC to the Commission: "these comments brought home to me the realization that, despite its recent initiative, the Correctional Service of Canada resorts invariably to the view that women's prisons are, or should be, just like any other prison." (Arbour 1996:178).

Madam Justice Arbour, after a careful review of the events and a series of public consultations on the future regime for federally sentenced women, made fourteen recommendations which were designed, among other things, to create legal safeguards and a "culture of rights" within the CSC. She commended the approach developed in the healing lodge as well as endorsing the overall philosophy in *Creating Choices*. The Commissioner of Corrections who had been in office during the period of the April 1994 incident and the Inquiry, resigned when Arbour's report was published. To date only a few of the recommendations made in the Arbour report, one of which was the creation of the position of Deputy Commissioner for Women's Corrections, with responsibility for overseeing federally sentenced women[10] have been implemented.

The decision to exclude all maximum-security women from the new prisons was not revisited until three years later, when the Solicitor General made an announcement in September 1999 (*Globe and Mail* 1999).[11] Those maximum-security women, half of them Aboriginal, have been housed in men's prisons across the country during this period. In Ontario, they have remained at P4W (now scheduled to close in 2001) even though additional maximum-security units for women have been built at the new regional prisons.

The healing lodge, intended to be available to all Aboriginal women, is still not an option for those Aboriginal women classified as maximum security.

The Future of Women's Penality

As suggested earlier, *Creating Choices*, and the events which have followed, provide a vehicle for examining the issues of punishment and reform in women's prisons and, maybe, all prisons. A number of important questions are raised: What happens when governments implement grass-roots plans? What happens when women are constructed only as victims and we fail to confront their use of violence? What happens when Aboriginal ideals are blended with white European technologies of punishment? Can prison be reformed? What good is feminism able to achieve? What should we do now? What does the future hold for incarcerated women? What is the future role of their advocates?

Clearly, the ideals embodied in *Creating Choices* were theoretically and practically limited. There was, and continues to be, a transformation of the original (feminist) vision to fit public, government and correctional agendas, and co-optation of Aboriginal notions of healing and feminist notions such as empowerment by the correctional system. Without a doubt, the physical conditions in the new facilities are a considerable improvement, but as the remaining essays will make clear, problems persist. Minimum-security women, who constitute a sizable proportion of the population, are still in far more secure conditions than those available to male federal prisoners. For women classified as maximum security, or with mental-health problems, and who have been housed in isolation in men's institutions, conditions have arguably been worse than they were at P4W.

There has also been a deterioration in conditions for women in some provincial prisons over the past ten years. Nova Scotia has not carried out the recommendations of its task force. Ontario is about to close it's only women's prison. In British Columbia both federally and provincially sentenced women are housed in maximum-security conditions. Manitoba's prison is overcrowded and its programs are in disarray.

Yet it is easy just to be critical. It is easy to underestimate the energy of well-intended interventions. Many of the women, within both the correctional system and the federal government, who have been part of the developments over the past ten years, entered into the implementation of *Creating Choices* with tremendous sincerity and great energy. Many have put themselves "on the line" and experienced negative reactions from the established and male-dominated correction system. While their situations are not comparable to that of women prisoners, it is important to recognize the struggles of women working to change the correctional system. Future work around prisons should pay greater attention to power dynamics within, and the role of, prison admin-istration and staff, and the constraints under which they work (see, for example, McMahon 1999a).

One of the biggest dangers of engaging with prison reform has always been that by focusing on the prison, other possibilities are ignored. Some argue that prison should be *abolished*,[12] that most women prisoners could be accommodated in the community because they do not need the excessive and costly controls imposed by prison.[13] CAEFS advocates greater use of community sanctions for women rather than prison, and has taken an abolitionist position. A moratorium on the use of prison for women, for example, may be a way of forcing us to think about *what else* can be done to deal with the troubles that women become involved in (Carlen 1990b, 1998).

The Issues in the Book

The following essays look at different aspects of the post-*Creating Choices* world of women's prisons in Canada, both provincial and federal, and at attempts to create an *ideal prison*. Some look at the problems implicit in the *Creating Choices* model itself and question whether we can ever conceive of a prison as *ideal*. Some consider the processes of implementation and how feminist ideas can become co-opted or changed to meet the requirements of the public or the correctional system; thus illustrating the dangers, yet importance, of feminist engagement with the state. Other essays show how racial discrimination and class intersect with being female, and pose the question, do women in prison *really* have choices in their lives? They go beyond a dichotomous view of women as *either* victims *or* offenders and try to examine the context, to situate women both historically and currently in their own experiences by showing the complexities of prisons, the ways they govern and control, and the ways in which these activities are always gendered and racialized.

Notes

1.   The number of women receiving provincial sentences in Nova Scotia is small, around 100 to 130 a year, reflecting the population of the province, with an average prison population in the Halifax Correctional Centre of 24 women. *Blueprint for Change* recommended that the women be housed in four small community residences for five to twelve women dispersed throughout the province. The provincial government has accepted the recommendations of this report, although they have so far not been carried out.

2.   Governmentality is a term that refers to studies of governance. Briefly, these studies rely on Foucault's notion of government, which draws "our attention to the variety of ways of reflection and acting which aim to shape, guide, manage, or regulate the conduct of persons—not only other persons but also oneself—in light of certain principles or goals" (Rose 1993:287).

3.   The first Canadian book to bring together essays on women's involvement in the justice system including prison was *Too Few To Count* (1989) edited by Ellen Adelberg and Claudia Currie.

4.   Ontario, the largest province in Canada, admits some 3,500 women to prison a year, and the average population on any given day is about 360 (Ministry of Correctional Services, Ontario 1992). In the 1960s, Ontario opened Vanier Correctional Centre, designed specifically for the treatment of women. This institution is now

to be closed, and women will be housed with men, though in a separate section, in the new Milton "super jail."

5. Following the completion of the 1990 Task Force on Federally Sentenced Women, a minimum-security facility for eleven women was opened opposite the Prison for Women. One or two provincial prisons have had very limited facilities for babies to live in for short periods.

6. Canada appears to use short sentences for women (and men), often a few weeks, far more than do most countries (Shaw 1990a).

7. Not only do more women in prison have children than men, around half of them were primary care-givers prior to their sentence. Overall, few men need to make specific arrangements for the care of their children at the time of their sentence (Shaw 1994).

8. British Columbia was initially to be included, but renewed its Exchange of Service agreement with the federal government in 1990. A new, but traditionally designed, women's prison was built in Burnaby to house both federally and provincially sentenced women. To a large extent Burnaby has remained apart from the new developments for federally sentenced women.

9. This well-publicized case involved the kidnapping, sexual abuse, torture and murder of two teenaged school girls and involved graphic testimony and video tapes of the victims taken by Bernardo.

10. Nancy Stableforth was appointed Deputy Commissioner for Women's Corrections in 1997. Another recommendation made was for a review of the employment of male staff in the prisons. For further information, see the reports of the cross-gender staffing monitor project (LaJeunesse and Jefferson 1998, 1999).

11. In 1997, a group of women classified as maximum security at P4W challenged their proposed transfer to Kingston Penitentiary. In 1999, csc announced that all women would be housed in the new regional facilities by 2001. They have developed an intensive intervention strategy that will create new, enhanced, secure units for women who are classified as maximum security, and structured living environmental houses for women with serious mental-health needs.

12. For example, the International Conferences on Penal Abolition (icopa) was founded in 1983, and their ninth conference will occur in Toronto in May 2000.

13. In her comparative study, Bertrand (1998) argues that 85 percent of women sentenced to imprisonment in countries visited by her and her colleagues do not need to be housed in closed prisons.

Section I
Systemic Concerns

Introduction

This section is concerned with some of the theoretical and systemic problems underlying the TFFSW report *Creating Choices* and its implementation.

Kelly Hannah-Moffat considers some of the limits to feminist engagement with the state in the context of federal women's penal reform. She argues that while there were well-intentioned efforts to restructure and re-conceptualize techniques of punishing women, and while some significant improvements were made in the conditions of confinement of *some women*, attempts to fundamentally alter the technology of imprisonment and the ideals of reformers were conceptually limited.

Stephanie Hayman explores the parallels between the Canadian reform experience and restructuring of Holloway women's prison in London in the 1970s. She examines the widening gap between the ideal and reality, and the risks advocacy groups take when entering into partnerships with governments.

Patricia Monture-Angus is a Mohawk woman who was a member of the TFFSW. She exposes the effects of the colonial legacy of racism and its impact on Aboriginal peoples through the imposition of a White justice system. She reflects on the problems inherent in seeing a prison as a place of healing, the appropriation of Native spirituality and the dangers of focusing on culture but ignoring racism and systemic problems.

Margaret Shaw explores some of the consequences of ignoring violence perpetrated by women and the problems of understanding and preventing violence and disorder in prisons. She considers the importance of seeing such events within a broader context, including not only how women learn to use violence themselves, but also the contribution of the institution, the staff, the administrative decisions, and the complex ways in which violent events are built up and spiral out of control.

Re-Forming the Prison
Rethinking our Ideals
Kelly Hannah-Moffat

After years of documenting and agonizing over the government's neglect of the federal female prisoner, feminist reformers welcomed the opportunity to participate in the unique reform initiative presented by the Task Force on Federally Sentenced Women (TFFSW). Reformers anticipated that their involvement would ensure that proposed government reforms would at long last appropriately respond to the diverse needs and experiences of women prisoners. A well-intentioned process to restructure federal women's prisons that included the participation of Aboriginal women, the Canadian Association of Elizabeth Fry Societies (CAEFS), the government and some federally sentenced women ensued. The result: a landmark document, *Creating Choices*, outlining a new women-centred model of corrections.

The implementation of the ideals embodied in *Creating Choices* and events subsequent to the TFFSW have left some people disillusioned and others wondering if it is possible to significantly reform prisons. This chapter considers some of the limits to feminist engagements with the state in the context of federal women's penal reform. Well-intentioned attempts to restructure and re-conceptualize techniques of punishing women resulted in some significant improvements in the conditions of confinement of *some women*. However, attempts to *fundamentally* alter imprisonment, and the ideals of reformers themselves were limited. On a material level, the new regional facilities have not been able to create the "healing" and "empowering" environment envisioned by the authors of *Creating Choices*. I argue that correctional bureaucracies are resistant to change and the creation of a separate and unique space for women prisoners presents an ongoing struggle. Prisons, by any name or in any form, are limited in their ability to respond to the needs of women offenders or appreciate the context of their offences.

The "Will to Empower"[1]

"Empowerment is like democracy: everyone is for it, but rarely do they mean the same thing by it" (Iris Young 1994:49). *Empowerment* is a common term originally associated with social movements of the 1960s and 1970s that sought radical political changes. More recently, the concept of empowering individuals has become a common tenet of diverse political strategies and policy initiatives. The growing mass of policy and academic literature in a variety of contexts confirms the widespread acceptance of an empowerment ideology (see, for example, Shaw 1999; Snider 1994; Townsend 1998). Yet, few scholars have critically and reflexively evaluated the logic and interpretative politics of empowerment. Strategies such as empowerment can assume multiple meanings depending on how they are used and by whom. I argue that empowerment, at least in a penal context, has lost its radical characteristics, and it is now as easily embraced by the state as by reformers.

The increased reliance on empowerment politics indicates a much wider systemic shift in governing,[2] wherein governments and corporations with little or no interest in granting real power to dispossessed groups have merely adopted discourses of empowerment. In coercive institutions, like the prison, governing is most commonly associated with the external policing and regulation of an individual's behaviour. An emphasis on strategies such as empowerment, however, suggests a greater reliance on self-governing, making links between the aspirations of individual prisoners and those of government, and contributes to the formation of prudent subjects prepared to take responsibility for their actions (Rose 1993). Yet, there are some important limitations and contradictions inherent in the use of a language of empowerment to achieve organizational changes.

A new neo-liberal (empowerment) strategy of penality is different from past welfare models, which see the state as responsible for reforming offenders.[3] A neo-liberal penality

> seeks through the calculus of punishment primarily to press upon the offender (and the potential offender) the model of individual responsibility. Accepting responsibility for one's actions does not imply accepting or obeying any specific set of morals. It implies accepting the *consequences* of one's actions. The individual is free to choose, in a way and to a degree never envisaged by normative disciplinarity—but if those choices lead into criminal offending, they must take the burden of their choice. (O'Malley 1994:15)

This *responsibilizing*[4] quality of an empowerment strategy allows it to combine and co-exist with more coercive, centrally defined goals of Correctional Service of Canada (csc).

The language of empowerment was introduced into discussions on penal reform to propose a radical alternative to the management of incarcerated women. The empowering approach did recognize women's power to make choices, unlike correctional regimes of the past that were maternal/paternalistic (Dobash, Dobash and Gutteridge 1986; Faith 1993a; Hannah-Moffat 1997). However, feminist reformers did not anticipate the redefinition and compromised version of empowerment that emerged as a result of integrating this ideal into the pre-existing penal culture. One of the most significant practical problems with attempts to integrate a selected ideal of empowerment into a penal context is the premise that prisons can be designed to empower prisoners.

The tffsw feminist assumption of common disempowerment among women stressed some of the undeniable similarities of women as a group. Although this condition is magnified for women prisoners, and even more so for those who are Aboriginal, feminist reformers maintained that women should not be treated as powerless victims of their social and personal circumstances. For feminists, empowerment is embraced as a way of transforming the structure of societal power relations that allow women to make choices and regain control of their lives. For example, Young (1994:49) notes that empowerment can mean "the development of individual autonomy, self-control, and confidence" and/ or "the development of a sense of collective influence over social conditions in one's life."

Young's comments capture some of the difficulties associated with the current emphasis placed on empowerment in women's penal regimes. In this context, at least two interpretations of empowerment can be identified. A *women-centred empowerment model* of punishment feminizes the discourse and practices of imprisonment without fundamentally challenging or restructuring the disciplinary relations of power in prisons. Ironically, the Correctional Service of Canada (csc) claims it is committed to empowering women prisoners. However, empowerment for the csc is not about a fundamental restructuring of relations of disciplinary power in the prison, but rather about *adding* a new dimension to existing relations by using empowerment strategies to responsibilize, wherein women's crimes are decontextualized, and they are expected to assume sole responsibility for their reform and offending. This new strategy of *responsibilization* appears to be less intrusive and less regulatory, and as such it is not usually contested by reformers.

Here lies one difficulty in the discourse of empowerment. While the strategy of empowerment coincides with the feminist reform objectives of giving women power to make choices about their lives, it is also compatible with the long-standing goals and objectives of correctional officials. Empowerment is defined by csc (1994:9) as "the process through which women gain insight into their situation, identify their strengths, and are supported and challenged to take positive action to gain control of their lives." While older welfare penal strategies of rehabilitation believe the state is responsible for the offender's reformation, this empowerment strategy makes the offender responsible for her own rehabilitation. In this new correctional framework, she is responsible for her own self-governance and for the minimization and management of her needs and of her risk to the public or herself. The responsibility of the csc is simply to facilitate this process. For example, if a woman is provided with a job-training program and completes the program, she is then seen as capable of obtaining employment upon release and is expected to do so. The current economic environment and rate of unemployment are not constructed as relevant, and in fact a woman's failure to secure employment and her reliance on social services is often interpreted as "irresponsible."

Given this understanding of empowerment by the csc, the provision of "meaningful and responsible choices" in the new women-centred prisons takes on a new meaning. The choices women are empowered to make are limited to those deemed by the administration, and not necessarily the prisoner, as meaningful and responsible. For example, programming choices about treatment, such as whether to attend feminist therapy or Alcoholics Anonymous, are deemed meaningful and responsible choice. To choose whether to escape or riot is not meaningful or responsible, even though this choice may be truly empowering and liberating to the prisoner. Judges, parole boards, correctional officers and therapists, who often invoke a white, middle-class morality, not the prisoner, ultimately determine what is a meaningful and responsible or empowering action. Under a new self-governing regime of empowerment women can be regulated through the decisions they make without resorting to an overt expression of power. These new technologies steer choices rather than deter through punishment.

The correctional program strategy for the new prisons was designed to "ensure that women receive the most effective programs at appropriate points in their sentence" (CSC 1994:4). This CSC document identifies four core programs: Abuse and Trauma, Substance Abuse, Parenting, and Education and Employment Skills. These programs are seen by the government as representative of the primary needs of women in prison. Their existence provides women with the opportunity to make "meaningful and responsible choices" within a "supportive environment," and thus, to be empowered. The substance abuse program, for example, like the others, is based on a "model of self change" rather than on traditional "therapy." The "self-change model" places responsibility for risk minimization and change squarely onto the shoulders of the offender. However, if a known substance abuser chooses not to participate in these programs she is constructed as being in denial or as defiant and uncooperative and as a result, more risky. A woman choosing to participate in such programs—at times simply because she knows that it will improve her chances for parole release—is expected to constantly monitor herself and control her own risk-generating behaviour. When she fails, more coercive forms of discipline are mobilized. For example, a positive urine test for drugs or visible signs of drug or alcohol use can lead to institutional charges, segregation, revocation of privileges, cancelled visits or, in the case of community supervision, return to prison. However, the "new techniques [like empowerment] do not so much replace these traditional measures as embed them in a far more comprehensive web of monitoring and intervention" (Simon 1994:33). In this respect, models of self-help and responsibility ultimately *re-legitimate* the prison and the continued reliance on discipline.[5] In effect, an "empowering-responsibilizing strategy" leaves the prison and the central state generally more powerful than before, with an extended capacity for action and influence (Garland 1996:454).

The CSC, by virtue of their legal role and responsibility in the criminal justice process, seeks to make offenders accountable and responsible for their criminal behaviours, irrespective of structural or situational forces in their lives. Having offenders take responsibility or ownership for their actions is a paramount concern for correctional institutions. A feminist strategy of empowerment, as well, does not imply the displacement of offender accountability. In fact, feminists have fully acknowledged that the negation of personal responsibility often results in the "disempowerment of women by rendering them harmless victims, thus stripping them of self-determination" (Shaw cited in Kendall 1993b:14). However, feminists emphasize that women prisoners' life circumstances and the social context of their offences must be acknowledged. The difference is that the CSC sees empowerment as linked to individual responsibility, not structural relations of power.

Despite the rise of "empowerment discourse," women-centred corrections is about responsibilizing the prisoner and not empowerment as defined by those who wrote *Creating Choices*. This primary emphasis on responsibility de-contextualizes feminist/Aboriginal constructions of women's oppression and it disregards feminist/Aboriginal analyses of the social, economic and political barriers experienced by women, and by marginalized women in particular. The new strategy of empowerment softens but still reinforces traditional methods of punishment that women-centred regimes sought to replace.

Within a prison setting the accomplishment of real empowerment is particularly problematic. Prisons are organized to limit individual expressions of autonomy, control and choice. They are sites of repression, wherein there is an undeniable imbalance in the relations of power between the "keepers" and the "kept." Rarely are the "keepers" able or willing to relinquish their power to facilitate empowerment. Women prisoners have little influence, collective or otherwise, over their lives while incarcerated. Ironically, it can now be argued that women are being sent to prison to be empowered!

The Unempowerable Prisoner

One of the unanticipated outcomes of the new women-centred regime is the advent of a new category of prisoner—the unempowerable. The recent dichotomization of empowerable and unempowerable prisoners, which is essentially a reconfiguration of the categories reformable and unreformable, was not part of the discussions of the TFFSW. The Task Force and its report envisioned that all women would benefit from the new women-centred vision of women's corrections. One pitfall of this report was its failure to respond to or acknowledge the wide range of incarcerated women and their potential resistance to this new benevolent regime of punishment. This oversight has contributed to a tragic situation, wherein women defined by the Correctional Service of Canada as "maximum security" are excluded from the regional facilities and their "empowering regimes."

In attempting to "empower penal government" the CSC currently faces a significant dilemma consisting of prisoners' resistance and the general failure of the new correctional regimes to adequately responsibilize "problem prisoners." Given that the "will to empower" is more often than not imposed on a captive audience of prisoners, even if by a well-intentioned state, resistance is not surprising.

The most significant long-term recommendation of the TFFSW was the closure of the Prison for Women (P4W), and the construction of five small regional facilities and an Aboriginal healing lodge. Four new regional prisons and an Aboriginal healing lodge are now operational. However, P4W also remains open. While the majority of the federally sentenced women were transferred to the new prisons, a few women (approximately twenty) have remained at the infamous P4W and in separate, segregated women's units in men's maximum-security penitentiaries.[6] According to the CSC, these women are high risk/high need and, therefore, not suitable for the new empowering prisons. The incidents at P4W in April 1994, and at the NOVA Institution and the Edmonton Institution for Women (EFIW), two of the new regional prisons (involving self-injury, suicide attempts, escapes, a prisoner's death and assaults on staff), and the government's reaction to these incidents, further show how the contemporary rhetoric of empowerment can disguise and conceal ongoing repressive (and sometimes abusive) penal practices. These highly publicized and scrutinized events led the CSC to develop new managerial techniques and rationales for the "resistant prisoner." These plans for the more "disruptive" prisoners reveal the persistence of disciplinary powers. Contrary to pronouncements on the empowerment of all women prisoners, the CSC now claims that:

> There is a small group of highly disruptive women who have extensive experience in either or both the mental health and the provincial correctional systems. Many of these women are high risk to themselves and others and are also in need of intervention (high need). Their behaviour increases the risk for the internal security of the institution and for their escape from the institution. *It has been determined that the community-type design of the new regional facilities and the accompanying concept of empowerment and personal responsibility envisioned by the Task Force does not adequately meet their needs, either in terms of security or programming,* (Reynolds 1996:7, emphasis added).

In other words, the objective of accommodating and responding to the unique needs and experiences of women prisoners is secondary to the protection of the public from "dangerous criminals."

The CSC's redefinition of some prisoners as, in essence, "unempowerable," requires the deployment of what Garland (1996:46) called "a criminology of the other," which "represents criminals as dangerous members of distinct racial and social groups that bear little resemblance to *us,* trades in images, archetypes, and anxieties, rather than in careful analysis and research findings." Recent correctional policies and narratives of the unempowerable (high risk and high need) offender demonize and pathologize women who resist well-intentioned, empowering correctional interventions. These women (who include many Aboriginal women or those defined as mentally ill) are ultimately portrayed as risky and as a danger to the prison culture, the public and to themselves.

The provocative image of the "risky violent woman" who is not amenable to benevolent, empowering regimes is used by the government to legitimate the continued operation of P4W and to expand security measures. The total number of "enhanced security" cells in the new prisons has doubled from the number in the original design of the regional facilities. All of the new prisons have made changes to accommodate "problem prisoners." None of the new security developments are perceived by the csc to contradict its wider philosophy of empowerment, because *this* group of prisoners is not seen as amenable to those principles. In fact, the csc now claims that one of the "lessons learned" during the operationalization (implementation) of *Creating Choices* is that "one size does not fit all" and that "although most women will very much benefit from the cottage-style housing, with its day-to-day routine ... this is not the answer for some" (Reynolds 1996–8). Subsequently, the "difficult offenders," who are either resistant to or identified as resistant to this kinder, gentler form of punishment, are now subject to a traditional type of punishment.

The Redefinition of Needs as Criminogenic or Risk

Another unanticipated and largely ignored shift away from the idealism of *Creating Choices* is evident in the recent correctional discourse of women prisoners' risks and needs. Increasingly, correctional researchers, using gender neutral research methodologies, are reconceptualizing women's needs as criminogenic or as risk factors. In general, Canadian research on risk assessment and classification, and the development of the Offender Intake Assessment process—a new method of classifying offenders—is driven by the requirements of the larger male population. In many ways, this classification trend, which represents an attempt to standardize correctional practice through the creation of a universal template for prisoner classification, contradicts the main premise of differential treatment embodied in *Creating Choices*.

In the csc's attempts to understand the differences between men and women's risk factors an interesting slippage between the concepts of need and risk has occurred. It seems that where there is an unsatisfied need there is a *potential risk factor.* In some cases, these two categories are indistinguishable. The blending of risk and need creates an interesting paradox. It combines two quite different elements: traditional security concerns, which are generally associated with danger and the prevention of harm to others, and a more recent emphasis on needs, which by contrast implies that a prison is lacking something and entitled to resources.

In *Creating Choices,* women prisoners' needs are influenced by feminist (and therapeutic) analyses of the experiences of criminal women and, more generally, of women. The reformers' emphasis on needs arises out of two assumptions: first, because the woman prisoner is not a risk to society, her correctional management should not stress risk; second, the woman prisoner has a multiplicity of needs which must be addressed holistically during her incarceration (TFFSW 1990:89–90). More recently, the CSC has acknowledged that women offenders have a "different range and types of problems that contribute to their criminal behaviour than do men," that "environmental, situational, political, cultural and social factors experienced by women offenders, as well as physiological and psychological factors, are not the same as those experienced by men," and that "a holistic approach to correctional programming for women should be adopted" (FSWP 1994:5).

While the members of the TFFSW initially supported the concept of "woman-based criteria for classification," they ultimately concluded that "assessments to gain better understanding of a woman's needs and experiences are more appropriate than classification" (TFFSW 1990:92). This conclusion relies on the perception that classification is based on security risks, whereas *needs assessment* "looks at the whole spectrum of women's needs from a holistic perspective, including the needs relating to programming, spirituality, mental and physical health, family, culture and release plans" (TFFSW 1990:92). It is argued that this type of assessment allows staff to respond to "the constellation of needs by appropriate support and intervention strategies, which also consider the protection of society and the reduction of risk" (TFFSW 1990:92).

However, correctional researchers and technicians, who dominate present policy discussions about the "needs" of women prisoners, tend to emphasize the criminogenic characteristics of women's needs. In this instance, "criminogenic" refers to characteristics or factors that are linked to an individual's involvement in criminal activities. According to Blanchette (1997a:40) *criminogenic needs* reflect risk factors of the offender that are changeable and, when modified, reflect changes in the likelihood of recidivism. This principle asserts that "if correctional treatment services are to reduce criminal recidivism, the criminogenic needs of offenders must be targeted" (Andrews 1989:15). This interpretation of needs as criminogenic neatly locates them within a realm of correctional managerialism and justifies normative interventions aimed at reducing the effect of criminogenic needs/risks.

Much of the recent policy literature on the female offender uses the hybrid term "risk/need," and correctional research tends to identify certain offender characteristics as both risk and needs. Some of the characteristics which give rise to criminogenic needs include dependency, low self-esteem, poor educational and vocational achievement, parental death at an early age, foster care placement, constant changes in the location of foster care, residential placement, living on the streets, prostitution, suicide attempts, self-injury, substance abuse, and parental responsibilities (FSWP 1994:5). Besides these characteristics, awareness and acknowledgement of women prisoners' survival of abuse and trauma play a key role. While some policy literature suggests that survival of abuse or trauma does not constitute a criminogenic factor because "there has been no statistical link between surviving violence/abuse/trauma and criminal behaviour" (FSWP 1994:5), correctional researchers are decontextualizing and linking an adult history of abuse to violent recidivism (Bonta, Pang and Wallace-Capretta 1995). Similarly, while feminist researchers (e.g., Heney 1990) have argued that women's self-injury is often a "coping mechanism" and should be treated as a mental-health concern, correctional researchers who correlate self-injury with violent recidivism argue that a history of self-injury is a risk factor (Bonta, Pang and Wallace-Capretta 1995). As well, risk minimization and needs satisfaction are often linked to therapeutic intervention. For example, a 1995 report on the mental health of federally sentenced women that recommended the development of an "Intensive Healing Program" for high-need women notes that some women have "special needs which make them a management problem" (Whitehall 1995). It also argues that "needy (or 'unempowerable') women" require more intensive supervision and that a woman prisoner's resistance to therapeutic intervention is a risk factor.

There is now great distance between certain feminist interpretations of women's needs as they are identified in *Creating Choices* and recent operational interpretations of needs. Unlike the present tendency to speak of risks and needs as if they were indistinguishable, the TFFSW clearly outlined what it perceived to be a set of distinct cultural and gender specific needs shared by most female prisoners. While the TFFSW was critical of past methods of assessing and managing women's needs, and of the traditional models of security classification and risk management used in women's prisons, which were designed for and validated on the male population, this practice persists (Hannah-Moffat and Shaw forthcoming). The TFFSW argued that traditional techniques of classification tend to over-classify female prisoners and fail to contextualize their offences and social circumstances, especially violent offences (Axon 1989b; TFFSW 1990; Shaw and Dubois 1995). Many reformers and researchers continue to argue that the category of "risk" is not highly relevant in the case of female prisoners (TFFSW 1990; Arbour Commission, Public Hearings 1995).

In summary, the emergent "needs-talk" which informs women's correctional management does not rely on feminist interpretations of women's needs or their claims to entitlement; rather, it depends on correctional interpretations of women's needs as potential or modified risk factors that are central to the efficient management of incarcerated women. Again, there is a wide, but subtle discrepancy between the ideals of reformers and correctional practice. An (un)intentional by-product emerging in the correctional logic of the new women's prisons is that the concept of "need" shifts from a vindication of a claim for resources (the feminist view) to a calculation of criminal potential (or risk of recidivism). Thus, correctional strategies and programs now "govern at a distance" by regulating women through their needs. Unlike past feminist narratives on women's needs that stress women's entitlement, the CSC uses a language of needs to facilitate responsibilization. The prisoner is expected to "cure" herself and manage her own risk by acknowledging and managing her criminogenic needs.

Definition, Redefinition, Appropriation of Women's Issues

Feminist analyses of reform concentrate on how women's issues (or any issue for that matter) are institutionalized, and how demands are neutralized, to present the appearance of change without addressing underlying problems. While these efforts have improved women's conditions, the integration of a feminist ideology into criminal justice institutions is problematic. While this integration has many unintended consequences, it has also reinforced and reconstituted some institutional ideologies.

The project of integrating feminist ideals of reforms is systemically limited by the prisons' ability to appropriate, redefine, institutionalize and transform women's issues. Canada's new vision of punishment for women has re-formed and strengthened the prison, rather than challenged its legitimacy and appropriateness.

The history of prisons and their reform reveals that the prison has failed at nearly every stated objective of punishment; yet this institution persists as a primary means of dealing with those who violate the law. Arguably, we should not abandon the project of prison reform, but we should refocus our efforts by concentrating on minimizing the use of incarceration and expediting the release of prisoners. To accomplish these objectives the prison must be disempowered and instead we need to invest in our communities and in alternatives to incarceration. What seems abundantly clear is that recent reforms that sought improvements have inadvertently solidified our reliance on the prison as an appropriate space for women. In essence, we have created an expensive and extensive network of prisons for a relatively low risk population of women, who would be better served through improvements in community resources.

Notes

1. The phrase "will to empower" is taken from B. Cruikshank (1994). This discussion of empowerment is a modified version of longer articles (Hannah-Moffat 1995, 2000).
2. In speaking about a shift in governing I am referring to the debates within the governmentality literature that suggest past welfare-based models of governing are displaced by more neo-liberal forms of self-governance. For a more detailed analysis of this argument see Hannah-Moffat 1999; 2000. More recent analyses of neo-liberal strategies of government draw our attention to how "public authorities seek to employ forms of expertise in order to govern society at a distance, without recourse to any direct forms of repression or intervention" (Barry, Osbourne and Rose 1996:14).
3. For a more extensive discussion of welfare penality, see Garland 1985.
4. The term responsibilization is commonly used by governmentality scholars interested in the reconfiguration of state and non-state patterns of governing. It refers to how the individuals (as opposed to the "state") are increasingly expected to be responsible and accountable for their own risk management and self-governance. For additional information, see O'Malley 1992, 1994; Garland 1996a; Simon 1994.

5. For further elaboration on the idea of the re-legitimating of prisons, see J. Pratt 1997.
6. These facilities include Springhill Institution in Springhill, Nova Scotia, the Regional Reception Centre in Ste-Anne-des-Plaines, Quebec, and Saskatchewan Penitentiary in Prince Albert, Saskatchewan. Maximum-security women in Ontario are housed at the Prison for Women in Kingston. It is anticipated that this institution will close once alternative accommodations for this population are found.

Prison Reform and Incorporation
Lessons from Britain and Canada
Stephanie Hayman

Introduction

Observing the implementation of the Report of the Task Force on Federally Sentenced Women (TFFSW), *Creating Choices,* with the eyes of an outsider it is impossible not to be struck by the similarities with previous developments in other jurisdictions, but more specifically with what happened when the decision was made to rebuild Holloway Prison for Women in England for much the same reasons as those used to advocate the closure of the Prison for Women (P4W) in Kingston. The resonances are profound: the hopes and commitment of all those initially involved; the belief that the new would be infinitely better than the old; the understanding that women needed to be treated differently in order to achieve equity with the immensely larger male prisoner population. But why should it be necessary to think about what happened in a jurisdiction many thousands of miles from Canada? Surely we should be looking ahead and assessing what the "new" has to tell us? In this chapter I will examine the possibility that the past sets lessons that we would be foolish to ignore. Specifically, the parallels I shall examine are: 1) the gap between hope and reality when it comes to reforming women's imprisonment, as a consequence of the time-lapse between planning and implementation; and, 2) the risks advocacy groups take when entering into partnerships with government.[1]

Planning and Implementation

Redeveloping Holloway

I shall start with Holloway Prison because of its historical similarities with P4W. Opened in 1852, a forbidding presence on the skyline of North London, it was not until 1902 that it became solely the preserve of women. It has remained so ever since, apart from a brief period during the Second World War. For years there had been a tacit acceptance by Her Majesty's Prison Service that Holloway should be replaced, because of its outdated radial design, and by the mid-1960s it was more a question of when and where, than why. By then Holloway housed a third of all imprisoned women in England and Wales and, in contrast with P4W, held remands and unsentenced, as well as sentenced, women. (In the United Kingdom there is no federal/provincial divide.) The prison was also a national resource for women with mental-health needs.

During the late sixties a conjunction of circumstances made it possible for a small group of people to set about planning a replacement for Holloway. This was largely because the attention of the Prison Service was almost entirely focused on the needs of the male estate, as exemplified by the huge, inadequate Victorian prisons for men in London. Although these, too, merited replacement various statutes governing their sale made this impossible. Holloway had no such encumbrances. Moreover, it was felt that money spent on Holloway would be beneficial to a large proportion of imprisoned women, whereas the equivalent money spent on men would have a much more limited effect. Women were also an easier target to get past the political lobby, in that their offending did not attract so much public attention; they were seen as a safer option.[2] What needs to be understood at the outset, however, is that those involved in the English project were not working in accordance with a public document such as *Creating Choices*. The Holloway planning committee included no independent voices from the volunteer sector, let alone representatives of minority groups; the venture was purely an in-house Prison Service initiative. The philosophical ethos was that new methods of "treating" female prisoners would only be feasible within a new building, as well there was a clear expectation that by the year 2000 there would be relatively few women imprisoned in England and Wales. In consequence, the design of the new prison was predicated on the assumption that it would eventually be used as a secure hospital for women. The TFFSW was to have similar expectations about the growth of the incarcerated federal women's population:

> The regional facilities will not all be the same size and the number of cottages will vary between facilities and over time; firstly, because the size will reflect the size of the regional population and secondly, because the effective implementation of community strategies should, over time, reduce the need and length of stay in these facilities. (TFFSW 1990:116)

The replacement of Holloway proposed initially by the civil servants was radical for its time, designed "to be slipped unobtrusively into its urban setting, a place to which the local community might come"(Rock 1996:9). The new prison's construction—on the same site and with the women still imprisoned within it—was contingent upon the staged dismantling of the old prison. Yet unanticipated delays caused an extraordinary fifteen years to elapse before the new prison was fully completed. By then the belief in "treatment" for women offenders, so essential to the prison's design, had long since been replaced by that of "positive custody," with the ratchet of security being tightened as the eighties' conservatism took firmer root. It could be said that the original Holloway planners also viewed imprisoned women as being "high needs, low risk,"[3] even though the terminology and methods of providing for them were different. This assumption was challenged in the seventies as women began to receive longer sentences and the rationale for "treating" women began to recede. There was "the impression that women offenders were becoming ... more dangerous, more criminal and more like men in their offending behaviour" (Rock 1996:178). During construction Holloway's security specifications were increased because of the perceived security requirements of an extremely small group of Irish and Palestinian women terrorists and fear of a sustained Irish Republican Army (IRA) bombing campaign. Increased financial constraints forced modifications to the physical structure, with the fatal decision to lower ceiling heights and narrow corridors contributing to a building which induced claustrophobia. The vision of a low-security Holloway, set within a secure perimeter, never actually materialized. The time-span for the rebuilding of the prison meant that many of those associated with the original plans had moved on to other positions and "no significant person or group claimed property in the new Holloway or ardently wished to defend" the initial vision of the prison (Rock 1996:197). The re-developed Holloway was born into a world which no longer accepted the rationale for its existence—treatment—and was sceptical of the need to treat women differently from men.

The Canadian Experience

Within Canada the time line for the construction of the new federal prisons was markedly shorter and they were, of course, much smaller (Holloway holds in excess of 500 women). But even so, the world into which they emerged had changed. The federal institutions, as originally planned, reflected the Canadian ethos of the late eighties that imprisoned women were largely "high needs, low risk." Crucially, however, and unlike the Holloway project, many of the civil servants associated with the initiative remained in place to oversee and champion the vision. However, the lack of independent voices at the implementation table lessened the National Implementation Committee's (NIC) collective credibility when fighting other officials to retain the concept enshrined in *Creating Choices*. The NIC was subject to Treasury demands and could not always resist them. During the construction period there was considerable pressure on the design teams to abide by the budget. For example, at the Okimaw Ohci Healing Lodge (hereafter referred to as the Healing Lodge), the Planning Circle was repeatedly asked to reassess the importance of many components of their plan. In this instance, the gymnasium was deferred, a workroom deleted and administrative space reduced,[4] yet the Correctional Service of Canada (CSC) continued to press for further savings. But money was later found to double the capacity of the enhanced units in each of the other facilities as it became clear that there was an underestimation of the numbers of maximum-security women. The enhanced units were to be used to assess new arrivals and those requiring temporary segregation. However, the enhanced units had much higher levels of security and women could not move unescorted from them to other parts of the institution. It is instructive to note that the TFFSW report does not actually mention enhanced units but refers to "assessment cottages" for women first entering the prison, which are "designated for special use … for those who are especially high risk or high need" (TFFSW 1990:116) and to provide "space, privacy and access to land" (TFFSW 1990:115). It is clear that the vision of *Creating Choices* was modified long before it became a complete physical reality.

By the time the first three prisons (the Healing Lodge, NOVA Institution in Truro and the Edmonton Institution for Women) opened, both the political and penal climate in Canada had been influenced by an increasing emphasis on "law and order," and only the Healing Lodge managed to escape the intense media gaze. All too soon this gaze focused primarily on the Edmonton Institution for Women (EIFW). Although the Edmonton City Council had actively solicited the new facility, the local community was largely hostile and a series of escapes increased public concern about the possible risks posed by federally sentenced women. The almost complete closure of the EIFW on May 1, 1996, followed a period of intense political pressure, particularly from the Reform Party, with the public believing that potentially dangerous women were out "on the lam," (although none committed further offences during their brief absences). On May 12, 1996, it was officially known that the presumed suicide of inmate Denise Fayant in February 1996 at the EIFW was indeed murder, and this discovery has subsequently obscured the fact that the decision to close the EIFW for a period was made before this was known. The public perception of the reason for the closure has become linked to violence. The Institution reopened on August 29, 1996, and gradually readmitted small groups of medium-security women to the prison in the weeks that followed. Meanwhile, in order to upgrade facilities, the CSC spent $289,000 at Saskatchewan Penitentiary and $222,000 at the Regional Psychiatric Centre in Saskatoon, so as to hold the maximum-security women who were now barred from all new institutions rather than just the Healing Lodge. This happened despite the fact that *Creating Choices* envisaged that all federally sentenced women, regardless of their security level, would be housed in the new regional facilities.

As a consequence of the escapes at the EIFW, all the new prisons, with the exception of the Healing Lodge, had their visible security measures increased, signalling that *all* the imprisoned women were potentially dangerous. Every federally sentenced woman paid the price for the misbehaviour of the few. It is simplistic to assume, however, that had the women not escaped from the EIFW then all would have been well, because that overlooks the difficulties involved for women, staff and officials in the opening of any new facility. Making this assumption specifically about EIFW would be to ignore: that the EIFW was unfinished when the first women arrived; that the design of the building did not provide adequately for the large number of maximum-security women who were sent there during those first months; that the cottage-style living demanded very different skills of the women from those developed at P4W; and that the staff were largely new to the CSC, had extremely high expectations, were often confounded and distressed by the unexpected behaviour of the women and were sometimes inconsistent in their responses. Above all, making this assumption would be to ignore that *Creating Choices* failed to grapple with the dilemma of what to do with violent, or "difficult to manage," women, thus allowing, as Shaw (1996:194) demonstrated, a solution prompted by "traditional analyses of violence" to be imposed.

Whatever the underlying reasons for the perceived necessity to close the EIFW for a period, the removal of the maximum-security women from the new facilities and the subsequent erection of the fences ensured that the model proposed by *Creating Choices* was never fully implemented. The same could be said of what was proposed for the rebuilt Holloway. In the British case, security was based on untested assumptions about the dangerousness of (some) women, and the ideas (of the officials) were "actually to prove surprisingly unstable and fickle, liable to sweeping revision, even capsizing, under the blows of apparently minor events" (Rock 1996:63). In Canada, buffeted by the severe assaults of the media and politicians, overseers of the carefully constructed TFFSW plan were neither able to resist the calls for closure nor to mount an internal staff response to the situation. Had there not been this external pressure, it is conceivable that the medium-security women and some of the maximum-security women not involved in the incidents could have remained at the EIFW. Perhaps one lesson of the English experience is the inevitability of significant time lapses between conception and implementation of any new venture. In the Canadian context this meant that the new prisons, faithful to the vision of *Creating Choices*, no longer reflected what the public thought appropriate for imprisoned women by the time they opened. It is also inevitable that there will be unexpected problems, or even some that are eventually foreseen but not fully prepared for, as with the multiple functions of the enhanced units in Canada. New ventures require careful and courageous nurturing if they are ever to be tested fully—and without this testing there is no way of determining where the real flaws as opposed to the perceived flaws lie. In Canada the largest question, as yet unsatisfactorily answered, is how do the authorities know that all the maximum-security women could not have managed in the new facilities?

Advocacy Groups

Fundamental to what happened in Canada was a constellation of people coming together at a time when feminism had impacted at the highest levels of government. Most crucial, in terms of the ability both to finance and influence change, was the Commissioner of Corrections, Ole Ingstrup, who was prepared to listen to the voices of those outside correctional institutions and particularly the voice of the Canadian Association of Elizabeth Fry Societies (CAEFS), whose representatives were to act as co-chairs of the TFFSW. During the remit of TFFSW, the situation at P4W became so grave that to have failed subsequently to act upon the published recommendations would have been seen as a betrayal of all involved, including corrections' officials.

Yet the original decision by CAEFS to participate in the TFFSW involved much soul-searching and protracted negotiations with the CSC. CAEFS had long been pressing for a royal commission on federally sentenced women, as such a commission would have wider powers than a task force. CAEFS had fought hard to achieve its pre-eminent position as an advocate for imprisoned women and its relationship with the CSC was sometimes problematic. However, CAEFS recognized that in the new Commissioner they had someone who was in a position to deliver change, as was made clear by CAEFS' Bonnie Diamond: "Time goes so quickly and I do think that Ole Ingstrup is very open to alternative ideas. The average term for a Commissioner of Corrections is three years and he has already been in the position for six months" (CAEFS 1989:3). Balancing the CAEFS' preference not to be involved in the creation of new prisons against the dangers facing federally sentenced women, CAEFS decided it could not take refuge in principles when women were dying within P4W.

Initially, the involvement of Aboriginal women was not expected to be as large as it finally became. Indeed, it was first suggested that only one Aboriginal woman should be on the TFFSW and that that person should be on the arguably less influential Steering Committee. The Native Women's Association of Canada (NWAC) had other ideas. In an interview, one NWAC member said that the CSC's assumptions were: "totally, flatly unacceptable to us because when you put one Aboriginal woman on a committee like that you're just so alone and so marginalized and you've got no support." The NWAC was initially reluctant to be involved at all, partly because its volunteer membership was so heavily committed to other "grassroots" issues and partly because Aboriginal custom did not differentiate between men and women. Discussions with the Elders convinced the NWAC that it was essential for Aboriginal voices to be heard but, as Patricia Monture wrote in *Creating Choices,* "participation of Aboriginal women in this Task Force must never be viewed as a recognition that the jurisdiction of the federal government of Canada … in the affairs of our Nations is valid" (TFFSW 1990:17). There were eventually five Aboriginal women on the Steering Committee, including two federally sentenced women, while the Working Group had two Aboriginal representatives. (The significant gap in terms of cultural identity lay in the fact that the Working Group had no representative from Quebec.)

The final outcome of the Report's implementation, however, was that Aboriginals remained part of the planning process to an unprecedented degree, whereas CAEFS did not. All of this suggests a cynical use of CAEFS in order to legitimate *Creating Choices* and perhaps a degree of post-colonial wariness about cutting short Aboriginal participation, but I would suggest otherwise. After interviewing so many of the key participants in this project I have no doubt about their commitment to the need for change, which came to mean closure of P4W (even though the Terms of Reference clearly stated that the TFFSW would not be premised on its closure). They knew that P4W was not a place where women could "heal," in much the same way that officials involved in the redevelopment of Holloway believed the old prison impeded progress towards "treating" women. Hindsight makes it possible to say that the CAEFS' withdrawal from the implementation process[5] was almost inevitable because their instincts were so keenly attuned to the abolition rather than the construction of prisons. But CAEFS would also be right to say that they were frozen out:

initially, in the decision solely to have civil servants on the National Implementation Committee; later, in the failure to keep CAEFS informed of developments (CAEFS at times learned of major decisions from the press rather than from the CSC). The central factor was that the CSC was footing the bill and all TFFSW's careful planning was ultimately thwarted by its inability to consign decision-making authority to those outside government.

So why did this not happen to the Aboriginal partners? Or has it, but in a more oblique way? The failure to fully implement *Creating Choices* is nowhere more apparent than at the Healing Lodge because a disproportionate number of Aboriginal women are classified as maximum security and therefore ineligible for transfer to the Healing Lodge. Thus those most in need of the transformative possibilities of Aboriginal justice are confined at P4W or within men's institutions, in conditions far removed from the openness of the Healing Lodge, which is distinguished from the other prisons by the extent of its grounds (160 acres), the lack of overt security such as fences and its extraordinary design, which is focused on the circular Spiritual Lodge.

It was always intended that the Healing Lodge would have at least 60 percent Aboriginal staffing, that the talking circle would be used as a means of addressing issues as they arose and that Aboriginal principles would underpin its day-to-day management. Further, there had been an explicit commitment to the authority of the Ke-kun-wem-kon-a-wuk (the Healing Lodge Circle) regarding the overall management of the Healing Lodge. As the *Healing Lodge Final Operating Plan* (1993) makes clear, the Kikawinaw (which means Director—the term Warden is not acceptable) was to "report and be accountable" to the Ke-kun-wem-kon-a-wuk. By the time of the Healing Lodge's formal opening in August 1995, this position had been reversed and the Ke-kun-wem-kon-a-wuk had been informed that their role was to support the Kikawinaw in her decision making. This role reversal is alarming, especially in the context of the colonial history of residential schools for Aboriginals. It is particularly important that the Healing Lodge be seen as an Aboriginal initiative, even though it is presently financed by the CSC. A start could be made with the restoration of the authority of the Ke-kun-wem-kon-a-wuk.

At the Healing Lodge it is essential that most services come from an Aboriginal perspective—Elders and their wisdom cannot be replaced by the dominant culture's psychologists and psychiatrists, although all may have their role to play in a holistic approach to the healing of Aboriginal federally sentenced women. The unadulterated strength of the Nekaneet Band's spiritual base was partly why the Cypress Hills' location had been chosen. As a member of the Band explained to me: "As you drive around here [the reserve] you won't see any semblance of a church or anything like that. We've never been watered down in that sense.... We're secure with the fact that this is the way our Elders were taught by their Elders ... that's good enough for us." The education and work-skills programs already slotted into the daily routine of the Healing Lodge are essential for survival in a society so influenced by the dominant culture, but they need to be complementary to the larger endeavour of providing Aboriginal healing for women, rather than healing for Aboriginal women.

The goodwill of the Nekaneet Band has been expressed in a most generous and tangible way, both by the provision of a sizable piece of land for the facility and in the Band's wish to be part of the practical philosophy of the Lodge, through its Elders and teachings. By the end of 1998 the Nekaneet's Elders were no longer as actively involved as when the Healing Lodge first opened. Under section 81(1) of the *Corrections and Conditional Release Act* (CCRA), Aboriginal communities may apply to the Minister to provide "correctional services to aboriginal offenders" and in subsection (3) "the Commissioner may transfer an offender to the care and custody of an aboriginal community." As yet, there is little sign of the possibility of this happening with the Healing Lodge. Bearing in mind the power of a prison to continually assert itself as a traditional prison and, in this case, the number of non-Aboriginal Canadians occupying the more senior administrative positions at the Lodge, there is a considerable risk of the expropriation of the Nekaneet's goodwill and their incorporation into a venture whose outcome they had not envisaged. Given the isolation of the Healing Lodge and the lengthy sentences many of the women are serving, it is unlikely that the Lodge will be able to provide a continuously stimulating environment should women reside there until parole eligibility. Planning for this next step needs to start now and, ideally, it should be linked to the relevant CCRA provisions. Then there are those federally sentenced Aboriginal women who will never be permitted either of these options. With the Solicitor-General's September 1999 announcement that maximum-security units will soon be built at the new prisons—but not at the Healing Lodge—the only conclusion, based on demography, is that a disproportionate number of Aboriginal women will again be held at EIFW.

There is also a larger question to be addressed in the context of the Healing Lodge and one I consider to be of great importance. Again, remembering the colonial history of European Canada's engagement with Aboriginal communities and its present manifestation at the Healing Lodge, who, or what, will be blamed should Aboriginal women released into the community from the Healing Lodge then be convicted of a further offence? The CSC? The women themselves? Or Aboriginal culture and spirituality?

The Role of the Voluntary Sector

In Canada the CCRA specifies that appropriate outside organizations should be consulted regarding the provision of programs for prisoners. In the United Kingdom there is no such legislative requirement. A number of volunteer organizations are involved in providing services and advocating for women prisoners, but none have the immediate scale or public profile of CAEFS. The redevelopment of Holloway was located in an era when it would have been highly unusual for officials to consult publicly or join forces with the voluntary sector.

It is fair to assume that the emergence of privately financed prisons during the eighties, allied with a government expectation that the voluntary sector should bear some of the burdens previously thought to be a public responsibility, could have led to increased dialogue with non-governmental organizations. This did not happen, and events at Holloway during the nineties, such as the shackling of a woman during labour and the Chief Inspector of Prisons' highly public walkout from the institution in protest of the dreadful conditions prevailing by the beginning of 1996, were mostly subject to the media's own interpretation of events. This is not to say that the voluntary sector had failed to attempt to publicize what was happening; rather, that their combined voices were not powerful enough to engage the consistent attention of a media generally more interested in "headlines" than in a sustained, knowledgeable role. There was, however, another reason for the voluntary sectors' reluctance to be open about dialogue with the Prison Service and that lay in its wish to be seen as transparently independent, so that any advocacy would not be tainted by the label of incorporation. Even during the darkest days at Holloway in the mid-eighties, when conditions within the psychiatric wing were spiralling to a state of bleak despair, there were no calls for united action across the divide of Prison Service and advocacy groups. There were many public demonstrations protesting about conditions within the prison, mostly fired into action by what was then a newly formed group, Women in Prison, and what Rock (1996:288) called "an informal network" of officials, politicians, journalists and activists. But there was no sense that the Prison Service could be thought of as a possible public ally in attempting to provoke change. Sympathetic officials could not afford to be seen to be involved with such alliances.

Nor was there any means of holding the Prison Service to account for its failings. To this day, there is no official publication along the lines of *Creating Choices,* against which Prison Service officials may be measured, and the most influential of all recent reports into the state of the prisons in England and Wales, published a year after *Creating Choices,* ignored women entirely (Woolf:1991). It has been left to the Prisons' Inspectorate and volunteer sector groups to provide anything that would even come near to the scale of the TFFSW's consultations prior to the writing of the final report.[6]

Incorporation?

So the question of incorporation is another area which might be pondered in relation to what was attempted at Holloway and what has happened in Canada. When the Holloway Project began there was no question of it being anything other than a Prison Service venture and, even had the political landscape altered and a role been offered at a later date, it is doubtful that the advocacy organizations would have wished to be a full partner in any such enterprise. The volunteer sector's preferred method generally continues to be one of influencing policies through private meetings, through specific research projects or by informing the public (with the assistance of the media) and thus indirectly influencing officialdom. Some voluntary organizations might now be represented on Prison Service Working Groups, sharing their expertise in various areas, but they are no nearer to being seen as possible partners than they were in the seventies and eighties. Ownership of the prisons' industry still firmly resides with the Prison Service and for it to be otherwise would make the voluntary sector complicit in something that it largely abhors. But the right decision, for the right reasons, can have unintended consequences and had the Prison Service listened, officially, to the combined wisdom of several campaigning groups it is arguable that the situation in Holloway, as the new building emerged, could have been ameliorated earlier than it was. So should the advocacy organizations have been campaigning for more formalized links precisely because the situation was so desperate in Holloway, or would their independence as advocates for imprisoned women have been too compromised?

This was the dilemma that confronted CAEFS and Aboriginal women: could they stand by when at last given the chance to effect change? They found they could not, so—for the best of reasons—they now find themselves partly responsible for a document, *Creating Choices,* which they have had no part in implementing officially and whose implementation has in some cases caused greater hardship to a group of women most in need of their help. There is a temptation now amongst some working within the new prisons to say that perhaps the TFFSW overestimated the malignant effect of the physical details of P4W and that insufficient attention was paid to the problems federal women carried into the prison with them. (In other words, the women were the problem.) While there is some truth to the latter part of that statement, it would be a travesty of reality to suggest that the design of P4W did not adversely affect the women—and in that, all on the the TFFSW can take some comfort, because they enabled the great majority of federally sentenced women to reside in facilities a world away from the claustrophobia of P4W. Yet while *all* the maximum-security women remain unprovided for, members of TFFSW remain to some extent responsible and that is perhaps the uncomfortable price they must pay for having had the courage to redraw the boundaries in the first place.

Conclusion: The Need for Vigilance

The two parallels on which I have chosen to focus, while seemingly some distance apart, are in fact inextricably linked. In the past century, society has made few advances in our responses to offending, with prisons remaining central to society's concepts of appropriate punishment. In the United Kingdom this is nowhere more graphically illustrated than at Holloway Prison, which remains a facility struggling to fulfill its many mandates within a design concept unsuited to its task. Its planned transformation was derailed by the passage of time, rather than solely by changing perceptions of imprisoned women. The prison lacked consistent champions who could fight for the "vision" and preserve the integrity of the proposed building in the face of budgetary constraints. The vision simply collapsed and there was no document along the lines of *Creating*

Choices around which the next intake of officials could group. Similarly, the lack of a British *Creating Choices* meant that there was nothing to which the voluntary sector could point and demand an official response as to why things had gone so terribly wrong.

Those involved in the Canadian venture need to be vigilant because time will never be on their side. Penal philosophies are as prone to reassessment as any other and, while fashions change, the traditional prison remains a very seductive alternative. There are already signs of this mentality reasserting itself and, in combatting it, the voluntary sector has a vital part to play. These groups are able to point to *Creating Choices* and ask "why?" simply because *Creating Choices* is in the public domain. It is a very powerful weapon for these organizations and I would therefore argue that they were right to be involved in its creation. But the names of these organizations, both Aboriginal and non-Aboriginal, have lent a legitimacy to the project which it would not otherwise have had, so they are equally right to fight publicly, and critically, for its integrity. To allow the csc's perspective to be the sole interpretation of the vision outlined in *Creating Choices* would be a betrayal of the federally sentenced women themselves.

Notes

1. In drawing the analogies I shall largely refer to the Edmonton Institution for Women and the Healing Lodge in the Cypress Hills. This chapter is based on observations made during a four-year period of research which has twice taken me to all of the new institutions and the Prison for Women, as well as to some of the units now holding maximum-security women and the Burnaby Correctional Centre for Women. During my research I have interviewed members of the Task Force, federally sentenced women, prison staff, officials, members of the Nekaneet Band, those working in the voluntary sector and academics.
2. The fullest and most cogent assessment of what happened at Holloway is contained in a book written by Paul Rock (1996).
3. This is a phrase frequently used when summarizing TFFSW's assessment of federally sentenced women.
4. Planning Circle Minutes, February 24, 1993.
5. CAEFS formally withdrew from the partnership on June 18, 1992.
6. For example: HM Chief Inspector of Prisons (1997); N. Seear and E. Player (1986); D. Wedderburn et al. (forthcoming).

Aboriginal Women and Correctional Practice
Reflections on the Task Force on Federally Sentenced Women[1]
Patricia Monture-Angus

> We have often said that the women inside have the understanding to help themselves, that all that is required is the right kind of resources, support and help. The money spent on studies would be much better spent on family visits, on culturally appropriate help, on reducing our powerlessness to heal ourselves. But the reality is that prison conditions grow worse. We cry out for a meaningful healing process that will have real impact on our lives, but the objectives and implementation of this healing process must be premised on our need, the need to heal and walk in balance. (Fran Sugar and Lana Fox, cited in Task Force on Federally Sentenced Women 1990:5)

As we approach the tenth anniversary of the report of the Task Force on Federally Sentenced Women (TFFSW), perhaps it is time to revisit the implementation of this report in the last decade and see how true it has remained to the original vision of the women who were asked to participate in this project. The Aboriginal women who were involved in the TFFSW, at least those of us with long-term commitments to prison work, clearly believed that the solution to the situation (from over-representation to a lack of culturally relevant programs) of Aboriginal women who were (are and remain) federally sentenced lay in our ability to access the traditions of self-determination of First Peoples. These traditions of course include practices and laws regarding matters of justice. The vision articulated in *Creating Choices* required the Correctional Service of Canada (CSC) to find new ways to connect Aboriginal women to their communities and traditions as *the* method of providing correctional services for Aboriginal women.

Both dislocation and disconnection are the result of colonial experiences such as child welfare apprehensions, residential schools and the registration system established under the Indian Act. Dislocation and disconnection remain predominate experiences of those who live within correctional institutions in Canada.

Almost all the healing experiences that the Aboriginal women who have been in prison reported lie outside the conventional prison order. They come through the bonds formed with other women in prison, through the support of people on the outside, and from the activities of the Native Sisterhood. There are occasional reports of positive relationships with caseworkers, but these stand out as exceptions to the prevailing pattern. The refusal of Aboriginal women to trust the "helping" services of the prison becomes one more strike against them. Many of those interviewed share the experience of being seen as uncooperative. They were kept at high security classification and denied passes. Aboriginal women spoke of having their parole applications turned down because they refused treatment or were uncooperative (TFFSW 1990:66).

There is nothing definite since the implementation of *Creating Choices* (and many of us would argue that this vision has not been significantly fully implemented) that clearly establishes that times have fundamentally changed in the last decade. The establishment of the Okimaw Ohci Healing Lodge was the centrepiece in the correctional change envisioned by the Task Force. Little research[2] has been completed on the introduction of these new institutions (several other Lodges have also been built in the prairies), and they are institutions no matter how much Aboriginal culture and tradition inspires their contour, shape and form. This direction is an important context because it demonstrates the degree to which Aboriginal communities have been willing to embrace conventional correctional practice.[3]

The government of the Nekaneet First Nation where the Okimaw Ohci Healing Lodge is located, understood the degree to which the initiative was a part of the legal and bureaucratic structure of the Canadian prison system. In their negotiations, the community addressed this concern by recognizing that the building of the Lodge was only a first step and *not* a final step. Their vision was that as time passed the Lodge would move toward more and more community control and administration. This was also the vision of a significant number of the Aboriginal women who participated in the Task Force. Anecdotal evidence clearly suggests that this is not what has happened. Rather, as time passes the philosophical foundation (that of meaningful choices and an opportunity to "heal") of the Lodge has shifted toward the Canadian correctional mentality (where punishment and risk are the central values). Chief Larry Oakes of the Nekaneet First Nation has had at least one meeting with the Commissioner of Corrections (in the fall of 1998) to discuss the community vision and further community involvement (such as the hiring of more community members or the sharing of resources with the community and from the community). As of November 1999, despite several commitments made by the CSC, there are no negotiations underway based on this community vision[4] and in my view this is fully unacceptable.

On a recent visit[5] to the Lodge in Nekaneet, I did not experience an Aboriginal place or space. I believe there are a number of reasons for this result. Given the fact that I was just visiting as opposed to researching, these comments should be taken as preliminary. However, as bell hooks points out, her experience of the world is often an experience of "white space" (hooks 1995: 46–47). One of the qualities that is well developed in many people who have membership in a "group" (here at least race/culture and gender operate together) is our skill at analyzing the "space" we are in. For some of us, this is a constant and conscious exercise.

I have visited the Lodge several times since the grand opening in 1995. Each time I went, entry to the Lodge was without any measure of security except for the requirement to sign the official visitor's book. But on the last visit, each of us was asked to a private room just off the lobby. No explanation was offered for this calling aside (and for those who cannot do the translating, not offering was an exercise of power). The door was closed by the Lodge staff. The staff member, a woman, searched each and every one of us with a hand held scanner in the isolation of this small room behind a closed door. (Perhaps prison staff consider this privacy.) I have never experienced such a high level of security (and this is precisely how I experienced the procedure) at any men's prison despite the fact that I have visited at the "special handling units"[6] on more than one occasion (there you just walk through the metal detector).[7] If I, a seasoned prison volunteer and visitor, was intimidated by this process, then how would the "average" person visiting a prisoner respond?

Although some may consider this a very small example, it set the tone for the rest of the two-day visit to the Lodge. It was replicated in many other instances and incidents during the two days. After the visit, it was very clear to me that it was security and not any Aboriginal healing philosophy (which requires as a basis fundamental respect for all human beings) that was the visible and the apparent "mentality" at the Lodge. This could also be seen in the clear distinctions drawn between staff and residents—a distinction that I did not detect on any of my earlier visits.

One of the reasons for the discomfort that I felt in the space of the Lodge was the discovery that the local Cree community has been almost fully excluded from the facility. This centrally defies the very reason that the TFFSW believed the Lodge and other correctional initiatives for Aboriginal women needed to be under the control of Aboriginal people themselves. In setting out their plan for the future the TFFSW recommended:

> the establishment of a healing lodge somewhere in the Prairie Provinces which would serve as a choice for incarcerated Aboriginal women. It was clear from the outset however, that this conclusion was only the conclusion of this Task Force. In order to be accepted, this idea must not only be embraced by the Correctional Service of Canada but *must be developed by and connected to Aboriginal communities*. (1990:122, emphasis added)

It is necessary to note that the authors understood that the "connection of the lodge to an Aboriginal community will be essential to its survival" (TFFSW 1990:138). It is illogical to suggest the purpose and meaning of the word "connection" meant merely to locate the facility on Aboriginal land. The "prisonization" of the Healing Lodge, at the same time, defeats the very purpose of locating the Lodge in a First Nations community.

The structure of the "programs"[8] being offered at the Lodge is also a concern for me. As of August of 1999, there are currently at the Lodge, two resident Elders who are women from the Blood nation. Anyone who knows the history of the prairies understands that there is (or at least was) a strained relationship between the Blood and the Cree nations. This is also an issue of respect for both the territory, the community and the visitors to those territories. As a woman who lives outside her own traditional territory, I am acutely aware of the fact that certain "protocols" or Indian law apply when one travels to another nation's territory. Equally, standards of behaviour change when one is a visitor to another's territory. It is my understanding from the son of the two local and recognized community Elders that none of the non-Cree Elders recently employed by the Lodge initiated these protocols before coming into the territory.[9] I understand that these protocols are fairly common knowledge among those Indian people who live their traditional way of life. One of the reasons I was taught to respect territory was the fact that earth is mother and it is she who keeps the songs, ceremonies, and languages for the people. Here, my concern is principally that Lodge staff (and the csc more generally) have not facilitated these arrangements as they are the ones responsible for the invitations. This is seen in the example of hiring Elders and not facilitating and also not ensuring that the proper protocols are followed.

What is clear to me now is the fact that the "choices" philosophy is conditional on taking on responsibility that is not essentially a part of non-Aboriginal understandings of the world. This is further complicated because even Aboriginal people who do acknowledge their own traditions will not understand this meaning of the word responsibility.[10] Equally, correctional structures embrace a sense of taking responsibility that is lopsided from the Aboriginal point of view because it is solely offender based (that is, what the wrong-doer must do to become "right" again).[11] This is a lopsided view of what I mean by responsibility. As I try to understand what has gone wrong with the "healing lodge" experiment, I am convinced that the exclusion of the people who belong on this territory is a key factor in what has happened. The respect for territory (as all law comes from the land, from "Mother Earth") and the sacred protocols of the First Nation that occupies that territory are essential elements in ensuring the vision, and there is a necessity to ensure that these elements are looked after before beginning anything. Respect for the territory and the traditions of the specific First Nation living in that territory (here the Cree) is a responsibility that was owed to the people of Nekaneet (who surrendered land for the building of the Lodge) that has been forgotten.

The women's Healing Lodge has been deemed a medium-security facility by csc. This is very frustrating, given the Task Force recommendation to build the Lodge concluded that "all Aboriginal federally sentenced women will have the opportunity to serve their sentences at the Healing Lodge" (1990: 148).[12] Unfortunately, many of the women that the Lodge was visioned around will never serve their sentences at the Lodge as the institution is now too full, and clearly, selection is based on the borrowed notion of security classification. Therefore, work on developing "better" risk prediction scales undertaken by the CSC has a direct, but generally invisible, impact on the new institutions and the lives of the Aboriginal women who live in them. Unfortunately, this impact has not been expressed in any of the literature that I have seen on the development of risk predictors or on the new Aboriginal institutions. This is symbolic of a larger structural problem in the delivery of correctional services to First Nations. The isolation in which Aboriginal initiatives are developed in this federal bureaucracy has a profoundly negative impact on the amount of Aboriginal visioning that is possible.[13] Granted the work of the Aboriginal Issues section of the CSC within National Headquarters is very important, it is unfortunately often separate and distinct from the rest of the CSC organization which marches on to their own correctional tune.[14] Our dreams are limited by correctional expectations that we will accept certain ideas such as risk management and risk prediction scales. This must be seen for what it is. It is a clear form of systemic discrimination that does nothing to challenge the colonial mentality.

An idea such as risk management is one that is contrary to how I was raised as an Aboriginal person to think about relationships. As I have noted in other writings, relationships are the central construct in "Indian" law as I understand it.[15] People (or any "thing" with spirit) were not intended to be managed but rather respected. The conclusion is that one of the foundational ideas of current correctional philosophy is, in my opinion, incompatible with Aboriginal cultures, law and tradition. This incompatibility is a greater obstacle than simple theories of cultural conflict attribute to it. In fact, the TFFSW believed that "assessment will be conducted at the Healing Lodge with high participation from women and will be tailored to individual needs in a manner that is relevant to Aboriginal women" (1990:149). This standard is currently being breached by the Service in both the development of risk-management scales and in the current practices at the Lodge.[16] This opinion is a substantive criticism that is much larger than questioning the cultural relevance of programming[17] within correctional institutions, which has been a significant preoccupation in the many justice reports that address Aboriginal experiences and concerns.

This discussion, because it has introduced the larger contextual (that is, colonialism) and cultural issues, has now brought me to the place where I can make some comments about the specific idea popular among prison administrators regarding their ability to determine risk.[18] These risk scales are all individualized instruments. This must be seen as a significant and central problem for applying these instruments to Aboriginal people (male or female). This individualizing of risk absolutely fails to take into account the impact of colonial oppression on the lives of Aboriginal men and women. Equally, colonial oppression has not only had a devastating impact on individuals but concurrently on our communities and nations.[19] This impact cannot be artificially pulled apart because the impact on the individual and the impact on the community are interconnected.

For example, the Aboriginal Justice Inquiry of Manitoba (1991:485) noted in their report that Aboriginal "women move to urban centres to escape family or community problems. Men on the other hand, cite employment as the reason for moving." Once in the city, many Aboriginal women face issues that they had not expected, ranging from systemic and overt racism to subtle forms of racism, as well as a lack of opportunities. The Aboriginal Manitoba Justice Inquiry notes that "what they were forced to run to is often as bad as what they had to run from" (1991:485). And often, what they can experience in the city (from shoplifting to prostitution, drug abuse to violence) arising from their experiences of poverty and racism, leads to contact with the criminal justice system. Yet, a criminal court is not interested in hearing about this long trail of individualized and systemic colonialism that originally lead these women to conflict with the law. Courts are only interested in whether you committed a "wrong act" with a "guilty mind." This is a clear example of how the individualized nature of law obscures systemic and structural factors. This is a problem that exists within the court process but also in other justice decision-making practices such as security classification, risk assessment, penitentiary placement, parole, and so on.

Examination of the risk-prediction scales identifies many similar considerations taken into account to predict risk across the different measures. For example, "[t]he Case Needs Identification and Analysis protocol identifies seven need dimensions, including *employment, marital/family, associates, substance abuse, community functioning, personal/emotional and attitude*" (Motiuk 1997, emphasis added). Several of these dimensions are particularly problematic for Aboriginal "offenders." Aboriginal people do not belong to communities that are functional and healthy (and note that colonialism is significantly responsible for this fact). Therefore, constructing a "community functioning" category ensures that Aboriginal people will not have access to scoring well in this category. Again, this is not a factor for which individuals as individuals can or should be held solely accountable. Rather than measuring risk this dimension actually merely affirms that Aboriginal persons have been negatively impacted by colonialism.

In 1989, the Aboriginal Women's Caucus (a group of Aboriginal women who work or volunteer in the area of criminal justice) submitted a brief to the Solicitor General. They concluded:

> All Aboriginal, First Nations citizens are in conflict with the law. We are First Peoples with an inherent right to exercise our own systems of justice and the values these systems represent. The issue of Aboriginal women and the criminal justice system is merely the most blatant example of the oppression of First Nations People under a system of laws to which we have never consented. This position is supported by a number of recognized organizations including the Canadian Bar Association. (cited in TFFSW 1990: 23)

The understanding of the Aboriginal Women's Caucus affirms my position with respect to holding individual Aboriginal women accountable for the negative impacts colonialism has had on their lives and in their communities.

In my opinion, relying on a security classification system that disappears systemic factors leading to criminal behaviour is a violation of the *Charter's* section 15 equality provisions. In a recent Supreme Court of Canada decision which involved the application of section 15 to Aboriginal people resident off reserve, L'Heureux-Dubé J. wrote:

> Thus, in the case of equality rights affecting Aboriginal people and communities, the legislation in question must be evaluated with special attention to the rights of Aboriginal peoples, the protection of the Aboriginal and treaty rights guaranteed in the Constitution, the history of Aboriginal people in Canada, and with respect for and consideration of the cultural attachment and background of all Aboriginal women and men. (*Batchewana Indian Band* v. *Corbiere* 1999: paragraph 67)

This clearly demonstrates that Canadian courts are developing the skill necessary to assess claims of "double" disadvantage. This analysis is encouraging for anyone who wishes to litigate concerns of Aboriginal women who are treated unequally and disadvantaged by virtue of their status as both Aboriginal and women in a correctional system which applies standardized tests and offers standardized programming which are culturally inappropriate and are often largely developed for men by men.

In addition, the security classification of women also strains the common sense interpretation of section 28 of the *Corrections and Conditional Release Act* (CCRA) which provides that persons confined in a penitentiary shall be confined in the least restrictive environment. Obviously, the CSC has a duty to extend the guarantee in section 28 of the CCRA equally to male and females (and/or Aboriginal and non-Aboriginal persons). If risk-prediction scales are not valid for Aboriginal women (and I have not seen convincing documentation that they are) then security decisions based on these scales cannot be reasonably applied to Aboriginal women.

As I have noted elsewhere, I am not a great fan of the *Canadian Charter of Rights and Freedoms*.[20] This is not the source of my conclusion that legal action under section 15 might be a beneficial course of action. In 1990, under the heading of "Charter Challenges Signal the Need for Change" the TFFSW recognized:

Charter challenges, both in the past and currently, under the equality and other provisions of the *Canadian Charter of Rights and Freedoms*, have emphasized the inequalities and injustices experienced by federally sentenced women and have mandated immediate action to reduce these inequities. These cases assert that in certain institutions the rights of federally sentenced women have been breached by the failure of the system to provide equal means for women to serve their sentences within a reasonable distance from their homes; to provide equal parole opportunities; to provide equal programming; and to provide equal quality and standards of facilities both in comparison to men and in comparison to federally sentenced women serving their sentences in another institution (84).

Litigation as a strategy, including actions taken under the provisions of human rights codes, was successful in securing the commitment of the CSC to commission and broadly mandate the TFFSW. Since 1990, the year the Task Force reported, further evidence has accumulated, such as the Arbour Inquiry, which demonstrates that it is certainly possible to conclude that things have gotten worse for all federally sentenced women including Aboriginal women. This makes the case in 1999 all that much stronger. In 1989 and 1990 when I participated in the TFFSW, I hoped that the goodwill extended by Aboriginal people, would lead to significant changes in federal corrections. As the tenth anniversary approaches, it is clear to me that the trust placed in the CSC by Aboriginal people has not fully realized the cooperative change I once thought was possible.

Notes

1. An earlier version of this paper was prepared for the Inter-disciplinary Workshop on Risk Assessment, Risk Management and Classification organized by professors Kelly Hannah-Moffat (University of Toronto) and Margaret Shaw (Concordia University) held in Toronto, Ontario, on May 21 to 23, 1999. The support of Status of Women Canada is gratefully acknowledged.

2. The most significant research was completed by Connie Braun (Cree) in her M.A. thesis. In this work she documents the experiences of Aboriginal men at the Hobemma facility against their experiences of conventional prisons. Please see *Colonization, Destruction, and Renewal: Stories From Aboriginal Men at the Pe'Sakastew Centre*. Master's Thesis, Saskatoon: University of Saskatchewan, 1998.

3. I recognize that there is a large power imbalance between correctional bureaucracies and any of the First Nations, which operates in such a way that First Nations do not have a real choice about the amount of correctional philosophy and practice they must embrace in these negotiations. This has a further consequence of blocking the degree to which Aboriginal communities and the citizens in those communities have deconstructed the level of imposition in many of these new initiatives.

4. Conversation with Chief Larry Oakes, April 27, 1999. Chief Oakes also kindly gave me his permission to write about this issue in this paper.

5. I visited the Lodge on August 3 and 4, 1999, with Kim Pate (Executive Director, Canadian Association of Elizabeth Fry Societies), Dawn McBride (President, Canadian Association of Elizabeth Fry Societies) and Denise McConney (Professor, ITEP, University of Saskatchewan).

6. These are "super-maximum" security units often described as "prisons within prisons."

7. I imagine that one of the justifications that the CSC will offer for this practice is the cost of the permanent walk-through metal detector. I do not for one minute believe the solution to the increased security measures at the Lodge (and their intrusiveness) is to purchase one of these larger machines. Rather, I think the practice itself in a medium-security women's facility needs to be reconsidered.

8. I am not convinced that ceremony and spiritual commitments can be respectfully described as programs.

9. Interview with Chief Larry Oakes, August 3, 1999.

10. In the past, the people the CSC hired as Elders (because at times the individuals hired have not earned the Elder title in their own communities) has been a serious issue.

11. I am not suggesting that one system is better than the other. Rather, I am asserting that only one system, the Aboriginal system of law as responsibility, makes sense to me. This is a natural consequence as I believe in the Aboriginal system.

12. Please see Chapter 2 of the Task Force Report, *Creating Choices,* for a discussion of the hesitations the Aboriginal women had with regard to participating in the TFFSW. I do understand that the degree to which I feel violated in this process arises out of my Aboriginal values and teachings about respect. It is, therefore, a little incongruous that the CSC should be held to such a standard.

13. As many First Nations communities do not have access to the professionalization of justice relationships, I worry that these consequences are by their very nature not necessarily always visible.

14. This reminds me of the advice I gave to the Working Group members of the TFFSW when queried whether Aboriginal women should have their own chapter or be integrated into the report. I think my response surprised some members as I said: "Both!" Sometimes, as Aboriginal women, we need our own space. Other times, the issues are similar enough that we can share space. The choice should not be forced as either/or. As Aboriginal women (First Peoples) we have the right to belong and the right to stand aside.

15. Please see the chapter titled "Roles and Responsibilities" in Patricia Monture-Angus 1995b.

16. While at the Lodge, several women indicated to me that their participation in ceremonies was counted by the Elders and staff and this number was used to rank their commitment to Aboriginal ways. This suggestion and practice is not only outrageous but incredibly disrespectful of the culture and ways as I understand them.

17. During my trip to the Lodge, one of the individuals I visited expressed a concern that there was not a significant enough Aboriginal *component* to the programming. The idea that all we could expect at a Healing Lodge was a *component* of the programming was offensive to me. At an institution such as the Lodge, it is my view that programming should be fully Aboriginal and not just a mere component. A review of the summary of programs offered by the Lodge, prepared by the institution's staff, clearly demonstrates that the vast majority of the programming being offered is the standard programming being offered to all federally sentenced women irrespective of their race and culture. This was not (and is not) how I understood the Lodge would operate.

18. I do understand that the popularity of risk management indices is tied to public demands around safety.

19. For a fuller discussion on the relationship between colonialism and institutions of criminal justice in Canada, please see Patricia Monture-Angus, "Lessons in Decolonization: Aboriginal Over-Representation in Canadian Criminal Justice" in David Long and Ovide Dickason, *Visions of the Heart* (Toronto: Harcourt Brace 1996 (second edition forthcoming).

20. Please see the discussion in *Thunder* in the chapters titled: "Aboriginal Women and the Application of the Charter" and "Seeking my Reflection: Law and Constitutional Change."

Women, Violence and Disorder in Prisons

Margaret Shaw

As this book stresses, penal regimes do not seem to learn much from the past. They are heavily influenced both by the internal culture of (men's) institutions and by political pressures and public demands. Much of their day-to-day practice avoids the public eye except when there are major disturbances. When events do demand public scrutiny, the standard response is to appoint a commission of inquiry and apply a legal analysis of "what went wrong" and "who did what to whom." The Arbour Inquiry (1996) is a case in point: the investigation of "certain events at the Prison for Women, Kingston," employed a legal framework for assessing what had occurred, and the extent to which regulations and policies were contravened by staff as well as inmates.

There are limitations to such a legal analysis which can only investigate the immediate events. However, at the centre of the issues addressed by the Arbour Inquiry was violence in prison: when and how it arises, and how it might be prevented. Using literature on men's and women's prisons, this chapter explores some of these issues in terms of how we can explain institutional events. It considers the need to take account of the historical context of events. This includes not just a violent incident and its immediate outcomes, but its genesis, the role of front-line staff and administrators as well as inmates and the culture of a specific institution. It argues that violence and disorder in prisons must be seen not as the result of individual pathology but as social and situational events. Beyond this, however, is the need to recognize that violence is gendered, and that violence perpetrated by women differs in many ways from men's violence. This is of particular significance in the light of the events of April 1994, and the failure of the TFFSW to confront the issue that women can be violent.[1]

The Failure to Confront Violence by Women

Until recently, feminism gave little attention to women as *perpetrators* rather than victims of violence or violent crime (e.g., Simpson 1991; Morris and Wilczynski 1993; Campbell 1993). In part, this reflects the fact that men have been, and still are, responsible for most violence. There has been a legitimate focus on violence against women and a need to sensitize society to its extent and seriousness, and women's violence has been framed largely as a response to abusive situations or past abusive relationships. Most of the work which has considered women's violence has centred around the *least* frequent but most sensational event, homicide (Shaw 1995; Shaw and Dubois 1995). This research has shown that murder or manslaughter by women usually involves a family member, often an abusive male partner (Johnson and Rodgers 1993). But women also use violence in other situations (and less fatally), which cannot always be directly related to abusive relationships, such as that against other women, children, acquaintances and, very occasionally, strangers.

By avoiding women's violence, explanation has been left open to traditional pathologizing interpretations, which deny women any agency, encourage a "backlash" effect in which some writers try to prove that women are just as violent as men (e.g., Pearson 1997), and feed the media fiction that women who use violence are somehow extraordinary freaks. One prison activist reports a journalist's chilling comment that "a woman putting out another woman's eye was news, a woman putting out her own, was not" (Tchaikovsky 1998:35).[2] Such accounts reinforce the dominant value system, providing deviant images of unruly, violent and disturbed women "against which the standard of normality can be set" (Faith 1993b:271). For the media, violence by women doubles the fascination.

The silence around women's use of violence was evident in *Creating Choices* (TFFSW 1990). Overall, the report portrayed women as victims of violence and abuse, more likely to injure themselves than others as a result of those experiences. When the fight between staff and prisoners at the Prison for Women in Kingston (P4W) occurred in April 1994, the only responses or explanations available to the Correctional Service of Canada (CSC) were those used in men's penitentiaries. The six women involved in the fight were placed in segregation. When they continued to protest, these women (and three others who had not been involved in the incident) were strip-searched by the male emergency response team, an act that created further isolation and punishment. The appointed internal Board of Investigation (CSC 1995b) explained the event as a violent, planned attack on staff, perpetrated by a group of violent women who were attempting to escape. Fifteen pages of the report were given to profiles of the six women and the three others who were strip-searched, emphasizing their violent histories and institutional records. The report deleted any reference to (the inappropriate) strip-searching of women prisoners by men or the video record of the strip-searching, and justified the handling of the whole "event" as an entirely appropriate response to the situation. As Madam Justice Arbour noted, the CSC had resorted "to the view that women's prisons are, or should be, just like any other prison." (Arbour 1996:178). Violent events were caused by violent individuals, and by implication women's use of violence was just like men's.

Differences Between Men and Women in the Use of Violence: Gender Blindness and Individual Explanations

Defining and studying violence is not easy. The official categories used to classify violent events—assault, murder, robbery—mask a wide range of diverse acts of varying degrees of seriousness. Secondly, they ignore the context in which the behaviour takes place. That context gives it significance and meaning; it includes the history of the event itself, as well as more immediate situational factors. It is important to recognize that a violent event is *never* simple, nor simply reducible to the violent propensities of given individuals. Many academic disciplines make this mistake by seeing violence in terms of the characteristics of individuals. Similarly, in the courts and in institutions using a "clinical model," an individualistic approach has dominated much of the discussion.

In terms of gender, while we need to keep in perspective the much smaller contribution of women to violent offending, there are major differences between men and women in their use of violence (Shaw and Dubois 1995). Most studies in Canada and other countries show that women convicted of violent offences differ considerably from men in terms of the types of violence involved, the reasons for their offence, their relationship to their victims, their offence histories, their level of risk to the public, their likelihood of committing further violence and their own experience of violence in childhood and as adults (Immarigeon and Chesney-Lind 1992; Reiss and Roth 1993; Maden, Swinton and Gunn 1994). Women's violence is qualitatively and quantitatively different from men's.

There are also major difficulties in studying *women's* violence. Much of the research on violence has been conducted on men, or is gender blind in failing to take account of women's experiences. For example, most assessments of risk or violence potential and most studies of violence in prison are based on male populations. Alternatively, explanations for women's use of violence emphasize the pathological or biological, assuming mental instability or hormonal imbalances when women act in such "unfeminine" ways (Allen 1987a). When comparisons between women and men are attempted, the results are usually confounded by differences in the way the genders are *treated* by the criminal justice system, and the populations studied are so unbalanced in size and characteristics that few definitive conclusions can be reached.[3]

Many disciplines and studies indicate a *blindness* to the effects of gender. It is assumed that men and women similarly experience, use and react to violence. Such studies have systematically ignored the gendered differences in child-rearing patterns, in their learning patterns, in how they are differentially taught or expected to use aggression or violence in society, in the social controls exercised over them, and in their differential access to power in daily relationships or in their own victimization as children and adults. Yet as Anne Campbell (1993) has argued, while the outward expression or result of violence by men and women may be apparently similar, the meaning of that anger is different. For men, aggression is "a means of exerting control over other people when they feel the need to reclaim power or self-esteem," but for women it is "a temporary loss of control caused by overwhelming pressure and resulting in guilt" (Campbell 1993:viii). For women, use of violence is a *failure* of self-control, for men, a means of *imposing* control. Women are, on the whole, not taught to use anger or aggression but to suppress these emotions or behaviours. Accounts of men's experience of aggression show that it is more likely to be in a public setting, to be within a group, to act as a reinforcement of their masculinity and self-worth, and to be justified and glorified "as an adult extension of the routine physical encounters of boyhood" (Campbell 1993:66).

A further problem is that there is very little research exploring the way violence is racialized. Aboriginal women and men and other minorities are more likely to be charged and imprisoned for violent offences than the majority population. Such groups are seen as more likely to use violence than others, so any individual's violent act is interpreted as a characteristic of race. The act is rarely placed in the context of the individual's greater social and economic disadvantage or their experience of systemic and individual racial discrimination outside or in prison. Reading the story of Yvonne Johnson's stolen life (Wiebe and Johnson 1998) is one of the most powerful ways of appreciating not only the complexity of violent events, but the impact of racism and poverty on the lives of Aboriginal women and men.

The problems of trying to study violence, particularly violence involving women and women in minority groups, are enormous. Explanations of disorder in the prison similarly focus on the characteristics of individuals, and assume that change must be sought within those individuals, not their environment. For men, this has resulted in a willingness to see violent behaviour as largely the product of individual violent men without account of the contribution of the institution to violent incidents. But for women in prison, there are *additional* problems because of the greater willingness to see aggressive or violent behaviour by women as "unfeminine" and (almost) by definition pathological. Thus it is important to consider both the systemic problems of violence in the institution—how it affects both men's and women's prisons—as well as the way it is gendered and racialized.

Disruption in Men's and Women's Institutions

What information do we have about violence and disruptive behaviour in women's prisons? In some countries rates of disciplinary charges may be similar among men and women, in others they are considerably higher for women. Nevertheless, there is considerable evidence that women in prison are charged for more trivial behaviour and much less serious violence than men (Hattem 1984; Nesbitt and Argento 1984; Pollock-Byrne 1990). Women are also more likely to act alone than in a group. A comparison between institutions for young offenders in Australia and Germany, for example, showed major differences in the extent and type of violent and aggressive behaviour for which males and females were penalized (Kersten 1990). Girls were more likely to self-injure or attempt suicide and less likely to fight than boys. Much male aggression was seen as normal masculine behaviour, while fights between girls were seen as "unfeminine" and expressly penalized. Other studies show that younger women, those with a history of offending as juveniles, single women without children and those serving shorter sentences are more likely to be charged with disciplinary offences than others (Lindquist 1980; Mandaraka-Sheppard 1986).

Explaining Disorder in Prisons: Situational Factors and the Role of the Institution

Institutions such as schools or psychiatric hospitals have always recognized the crucial role of organizational and management practices in the generation and prevention of disorder (Hargreaves et al. 1967; Mandaraka-Sheppard 1986; Rice et al. 1989; Cooke 1991; Liebling 1992). In prisons, however, while there has been some acknowledgment of management practices and routines as ways of improving the "handling" of events, the major focus is still on the identification of the characteristics of the individual most likely to be disruptive. Higher levels of violence and disorder in high-security prisons are attributed to the characteristics of their inmate populations. Yet on a day-to-day basis it is very evident that prison routines and practices contribute to the frustrations felt by prisoners. Discipline charges in prison, for example, are often arbitrary and trivial and many prison regulations vague. Quinn (1995:357) notes examples of offences "against good order and discipline" such as "pricking holes in toilet paper," "singing carols on Christmas Day" or "making cat-like noises in the presence of a prison dog."

Many similar examples have been found in Canadian prisons, such as beading in a cell at P4W at two a.m. (Shaw et al. 1991). Thus, to understand violence in prisons we need to consider the context in which violence takes place, and this includes both immediate events or triggers and historical patterns of events. We should study the characteristics of *prison regimes*, particularly staff-inmate relationships, staff training, staff experience and staff morale. Cooke (1989) for example, in his study of a special unit in Scotland for violent male prisoners, has demonstrated the central role of prison regimes themselves in generating or *minimizing* violence. Once transferred to that unit, which emphasized good staff-inmate relationships, a high degree of autonomy for inmates and good group communication and decision-making, levels of violence dropped dramatically. Studies of American prisons have similarly shown that management styles have a major effect on how safe inmates feel and on actual rates of disturbance (Stevens 1994; King 1991; Boin and Van Duin 1995).

Some attempts have been made to integrate situational factors into risk assessments. Clarke, Fisher and McDougall, for example, combine information on the "behaviours, characteristics and situational aspects which contributed to the original offence with institutional measures" (1993: 439) but do not indicate what those "situational aspects" are other than immediate situations such as "refusal to obey an order." Such accounts cannot "get at" the history of relationships and events preceding an event nor at the role which the institution itself plays, because the institution is portrayed as a place where only the inmates "act."

A comparative study of women's prisons found the women saw fights and arguments as caused by such things as boredom, provocation, unreasonable or unfair treatment by staff, denial of rights, favouritism and constant security checks (Mandaraka-Sheppard 1986). This study also found that severe methods of punishment, lack of incentives to good behaviour, variation in the quality of staff and inmate relations, a perceived lack of autonomy, and staff age and experience were related to levels of discipline charges. Such organizational practices and institutional characteristics in fact *overrode* the effects of individual characteristics. When such individual differences as age, marital status, sentence length and level of security were controlled, the prison and its organizational characteristics were independently related to minor and serious misbehaviour. In other words, young and single women with a history of "disruption" in *some* high-security prisons were not charged with aggressive behaviour in similar prisons elsewhere. Differences in the way the prisons were run were more important. As Mandaraka-Sheppard concludes: "we can more successfully predict *situations* in which violence will occur than predict those *persons* who will act violently" (1986:104, emphasis added). Moreover, she stresses that labelling women as manipulative, violent or dangerous set up staff expectations about their likely behaviour, encouraged hostile interpretation of their actions and induced resistance from those women. "Physical violence was more likely to be the result of harsh institutional practices, which induced defiant responses on the part of inmates, which in turn shaped the form of overt behaviour resulting in more punishment" (1986:203).

Disorder and the Pains of Imprisonment

How important are the stresses of being in prison? Looking at events other than violence in the prison is helpful. On the basis of her extensive study of prison suicides, Alison Liebling (1992, 1994, 1995) points to the links between apparently disparate behaviours—absconding, disorder, suicide and self-injury—associated with imprisonment. For example, incidents of disruption, or self-injury and suicide tend to occur early in a prison sentence, at weekends, at night or after significant events such as parole refusal or following a visit. She found suicidal behaviour in prison to be *primarily* situational and environmental.

Moreover, she suggests the "pains of imprisonment" are different and have a more specific impact on women than men. Women are especially affected by children and family responsibilities, and tended to talk and feel anxieties about visits and family issues far more than men. They are also more likely to have a history of psychiatric treatment, previous suicide attempts, substance abuse, social and economic dispossession and physical and sexual abuse than men. For these reasons, she argues that women's reactions to being in prison must be taken much more seriously. As with prison violence, she notes that most studies of suicide have sought a "profile" which identifies certain characteristics associated with its occurrence, but provide no explanation for their connection to suicide.[4] More subjective qualitative aspects of the effects of imprisonment are rarely investigated, yet "one of the most significant changes in our understanding of prison suicide ... has come about as a result of a change in emphasis in research from statistics and recorded information alone to an ethic of listening and trusting accounts of feelings and circumstances from those who are closest to the problem being studied." Thus she concludes that "prisoners talk, when given the opportunity, of frustration, loneliness, boredom, anger.... Some of these feelings originate from the tragedy of their lives. Others arise from the tragically underestimated pains of imprisonment" (Liebling 1994:8).

Rod Morgan's (1994) extensive analysis of prison disturbances parallels this view. He draws a parallel between the prevention of suicide and the prevention of disorder, seeing both as acts of desperation. There is a *spiral of disorder* in which an event, and the response to it, help to create tension among staff and inmates, and increase the grievances of the inmates, leading to further disorder. For Morgan three lessons can be drawn from research on disorder and suicide: i) that the removal or isolation of a disruptive or suicidal individual seldom prevents the "trouble" staff are keen to avoid, and that those so labelled often go on to live up to that label, and that the situation in which their disorderly behaviour was identified often generates further disorder; ii) that it is better to focus attention on the overall regime and the factors contributing to problems than on segregated populations; and iii) that the quality of relationships between basic grade officers and inmates is crucial.

Staff and the Institution

Thus a final problem with the focus on individuals as the source of disorder in prisons is that the stresses on staff or the role of management have often been ignored (Pollock-Byrne 1990; McMahon 1999a). Prison staff are often faced with contradictory, unrealistic and conflicting demands from administrators and the public. Prison administrators in an American study felt frustrated by the growing focus on the rights of inmates, and regarded the media and special interest groups ("do gooders") as "unaware of the realities of correctional administration" (Stojkovic 1995:69). Staff at different levels, such as wardens, unit managers and correctional officers, had differing goals and approaches to problem solving based on their everyday experiences. This led to uncertainty and frustration, and disjunctions between official policies and actual practice, indicating a need to examine routine practices, communication and relationships between staff at different levels within the institution. In women's prisons, Pollock-Byrne (1990) shows that female correctional staff have different kinds of stresses from those affecting male staff, reflecting both their upbringing and their family responsibilities as women. Women's prisons are very clearly influenced by the different management style of the women officers, resulting in greater informality but also in a more confining place which treats inmates as children.

Legitimacy, Fairness and Justice

All of this leads to a broader question—that of the legitimacy of treatment in prisons. In April 1990, there was a full-scale riot in a men's prison in England, which spread to twenty other institutions. It lasted several weeks, with prisoners destroying cells, setting fires, holding staff and prisoners hostage and sitting in public view on the roof. In his inquiry Lord Justice Woolf focused on the importance of fairness and justice in the way prisoners were treated: "A recurring theme in the evidence from prisoners ... was that their actions were a response to the manner in which they were treated by the prison system" (Woolf, cited in Sparks 1994b:20). The riots resulted from a "genuinely shared sense of injustice" not from the actions of a few "uncontrollable" individuals (Sparks 1994b:20). Overcrowding, poor sanitary standards, lack of access to families, among other factors, were the immediate *catalysts* resulting in the riots. Sparks, however, stresses that the problem of creating legitimate treatment toward prisoners is more deep-rooted than just adding new prison buildings or facilities. Inmates themselves must *feel* that they are being treated with fairness and justice in order for the power exercised over them by the prison to be seen as legitimate, and not power which is divisive, oppressive or exploitative. He argues that such a moral basis for the prison is essential.

Elsewhere, Sparks and Bottoms (1995) argue that a sense of legitimacy is crucial and helps to explain why disorder can occur in a brand new prison with good resources and no overcrowding, or why men (*sic*) seen as disruptive in one prison, are not seen as disruptive in another. As they conclude: "every instance of brutality in prisons, every casual racist joke and demeaning remark, every ignored petition, every unwarranted bureaucratic delay, every inedible meal, every arbitrary decision to segregate or transfer without giving clear and well founded reasons, every futile and inactive period of time—is delegitimating" (Sparks and Bottoms 1995:60). This places a particular "onus on prison authorities to attend to the legitimacy of their actions" and suggests that prisoners' criticisms of prison regimes should not be ignored or dismissed, but listened to, taken note of, and have the "chance of being responded to" (1995:59–60). The implications of this issue of legitimacy for women prisoners and for Aboriginal and other minorities are possibly even more important. Given their particular experiences of violence and abuse, of racism and poverty, as well as their links to family and children, they are likely to experience prison in very different ways than men.

What Are the Lessons?

A spiral of disorder is evident in the history of the events leading up to the incident at P4W in April 1994. For a period of eighteen months, staff had withdrawn privileges and increased controls on the women in B Range, where the initial fight took place (Pate 1995). There was anxiety among the staff at the impending closure of the prison, cuts in staffing and programs, and a high rate of staff turnover. After the fight the women were placed in segregation where the staff policy was to maintain "a highly confrontational approach" and to escalate the deprivation when the prisoners failed to keep quiet (Arbour 1996:55). That the TFFSW had not acknowledged women's violence was problematic, but the events at P4W and subsequent difficulties in the new prisons had a history which included institutional policies and staff actions. In both cases staff resorted to traditional punitive ways of handling events, increasing controls in all institutions, and segregating and labelling women as difficult and risky, a process which has had a disproportionate impact on Aboriginal women.

What are the implications of all this for those in prison? It suggests that there are many ways in which the prison has an impact on its inhabitants, both prisoners and staff, whether they are men or women. But it also shows that the experience of imprisonment is both gendered and racialized, and that explanations are complex not simplistic. Women's experiences are different from those of men, and finding a way in which that can be recognized without creating closer controls is the greatest challenge. Better communication between staff and prisoners and the use of alternative responses to rule breaking such as mediation and conflict resolution are ways in which this could be helped. This may mean changing or reducing the rules too. Enabling women prisoners themselves to offer support—peer group counselling—is another important way of responding to the difficulties women experience in prison. Problems need to be identified before they spiral out of control. There needs to be a continued process of support and training for staff, in recognition of their crucial importance, of the stresses involved in working in a prison, of how it can affect their behaviour and reactions, and of the skills needed. What is required includes not only an understanding of how women end up in prison and the significance of racialized experiences, but also the skills required to avoid over-controlling and infantilizing women. We cannot assume that new facilities and conditions will of themselves reduce the effects of penality.

Notes

1. A more detailed discussion of the issues discussed in this chapter can be found in the literature review on violence by women (Shaw and Dubois 1995) and a paper presented at the Arbour Inquiry on violent incidents in prison and how they might be prevented (Public Proceedings (Phase II) November 25, 1995).

2. She notes too that media inquiries usually ask for comments about the rise in female crime and violence, or girls' gangs.

3. In their study of coping skills among the Canadian federal prison population, Zamble and Porporino excluded women on the grounds that "there are major differences between the ways that men and women are treated in prison and probably in their ways of adaptation as well" (1988:32). While their findings are of

interest, they cannot be assumed to apply to women, nor did their study include many First Nations inmates (only 6.5 percent).

4. For example, suicide is higher among remand prisoners, early in the sentence, among those diagnosed as psychiatrically ill, those convicted for homicide, substance abusers, those with prior self-injury, those in special locations (isolated) and for women with a history of arson or violence, major alcohol problems and multiple previous self-injuries (Liebling 1994).

Section II
Therapeutic Concerns

Introduction

This section of the book looks at how the categorization and treatment of women is gendered, as well as racialized, and considers some of the consequences of attempting feminist treatment.

Shoshana Pollock argues that the dependency discourse both in *Creating Choices* and in psychological writing, constructs women's lawbreaking as an individual personality characteristic. It obscures the social and material realities of women's lawbreaking. Her interviews with Black women prisoners expose how this dependency is enforced by their social and material circumstances and how they often make choices to resist and avoid such dependency.

Kathy Kendall examines the role of the psychological sciences in constructing knowledge about, and disciplining, women prisoners. She focuses, in particular, on those deemed "unruly" and "mentally unfit." Her discussion of contemporary developments is placed in a wider historical analysis of scientific interpretations of women's behaviour.

Gillian Balfour examines the practices of feminist therapists working inside and outside P4W and their attempts to contextualize the offences of women in terms of their experiences of victimization. She argues that women's "narratives of survival," which can be seen as challenges to oppression or acts of resistance, are redefined by feminist therapists using conventional clinical models as "needs discourses," wherein the therapist becomes complicit with the correctional system and its concern with the diagnosis of individual problems and the calculation of risk.

Dependency Discourse as Social Control

Shoshana Pollack

In their essay detailing the genealogy of dependency discourse, Nancy Fraser and Linda Gordon (1997) argue that the word "dependency" is an ideological term that contains gendered, racialized and classed assumptions. They examine the way that dependency is used in four arenas or "registers" of public discourse (the economic, social, political and psychological), all of which have their own cluster of connotations, resonances and meanings. In all registers of public discourse, however, definitions of dependency "tend to enshrine certain interpretations of social life as authoritative and to delegitimate or obscure others, generally to the advantage of dominant groups in society and to the disadvantage of subordinate ones" (1997:123).

Drawing upon Fraser and Gordon's analytical/historical paper, the first part of this essay argues that the dependency discourse in *Creating Choices* (TFFSW 1990) operates ideologically to obscure the social and material causes of women's lawbreaking. The TFFSW adopts liberal notions of dependency which, through the use of a psychological discourse, constructs women's lawbreaking as a result of individual personality characteristics that render them "dependent." Dependency is thereby constructed as a form of female pathology. This construction of women's lawbreaking leads to approaches to program and policy development, such as self-esteem programming, that are individualistic and leave the social and material realities of women's lives unexamined. The second part of this essay presents interviews with Black women in a Canadian federal prison. Results from these interviews pose a challenge to *Creating Choices* by indicating a disjuncture between an individualized conception of dependency and women's lived experience, exposing the social and material forces that operate to *enforce* dependency. Furthermore, these interviews show that women's choices are often motivated by a desire to *avoid and resist* various forms of dependency.

Liberal Constructions of Dependency: Dependency as Individual

> The dependence on men, alcohol or drugs, and/or state financial assistance which is part of the lives of many federally sentenced women, has robbed them of the opportunity and ability to make choices. To break out of this dependent cycle, these women need to experience the success associated with making sound, responsible decisions. (TFFSW 1990:56)

In these two sentences *Creating Choices* lays bare one of its over-riding assumptions: that women's crime results in large part from their dependence, on men, drugs, alcohol and government financial assistance. Moreover, this dependence causes women to be unable to make appropriate decisions to govern their own lives; they are infantilized (Shaw 1992:448) and denied any sense of agency (Kendall 1994a:5). In addition, this type of dependency discourse *individualizes* structural inequities such as those based on race, class and gender, rendering the social causes of dependency invisible. Notions of dependence and choice in *Creating Choices* reflect liberal assumptions about individual autonomy; generally, that "good" choices are equally available to all people. This perspective "masks how historically organized and tightly constrained individual choices are" (Razack 1998:24). Therefore, the individual who is unsuccessful in living independently, "has simply chosen badly" (Razack 1998:24).

Liberal constructions of dependency rely on its opposite construct, independence. The level of dependency of all others is measured against this highly specific norm and constructs those who do not live up to this model as deviant and suspect. In socio-economic discourses, this model of independence contains classed, racialized and gendered assumptions, specifically that an independent person "has access to a job paying a decent wage and is not also a primary parent" (Fraser and Gordon 1997:135), while the paradigmatic model of the independent person is, typically, a white, middle-class, employed male.

Liberal constructions of dependency also obscure the way that the independence of dominant groups relies significantly upon the dependence of subordinates. Historically, white, middle-class men were able to achieve economic independence in the public sphere by relying upon women to care for and maintain the home and family. They were in fact "dependent" upon their wives to keep the family unit functioning. More recently white, middle-class women have gained "independence" by relying on other women to care for their families. Thus, as Sherene Razack points out, it is "poorly paid women of colour who support the freedom of mostly white, middle-class men and women to participate in the paid labour force" (Razack 1998:30). Independence is therefore largely an illusory concept because of the necessary reliance upon the work of others to achieve such a state. The liberal discourse about independence and dependence masks these relationships of privilege and subordination.

Dependency is thus a result of *social relations* that are classed, gendered and racialized and that are often shaped by state discourse, policies and practices. For example, during the industrial era, white working men's assertion of their entitlement to economic independence relied upon the ability to contrast their condition with those men who were categorized as dependent; those who were on government relief, slaves and Native peoples. Thus, notions about economic independence in the labour force "were deeply inflected by gender, race and class" (Fraser and Gordon 1997:130).

Dependency as Pathology

Liberal notions of (in)dependence were also commonly used to describe the condition of slaves and Native peoples in a way that depoliticized their relationship to colonial forces. Early uses of dependency referred to the political relationship between an imperial power and an indigenous population, but during the industrial era dependency came to mean a personality or character trait. As a result, "[in] this new conception, it was the intrinsic, essential dependency of natives and slaves that justified their colonization and enslavement" (Fraser and Gordon 1997:29). This shift in meaning slid very easily into an analysis that locates the cause of dependency within the moral and psychological failings of those who are colonized, abused and/or poor.

Creating Choices combined imagery associated with economic, sociological and psychological meanings of dependency when discussing the needs of Aboriginal women. They write that "dependency is a particularly relevant issue for Aboriginal women who have been historically streamed into dependence on non-Aboriginal institutions. Research indicates that culturally relevant programs are essential to help Aboriginal women to work through their dependency" (TFFSW 1990:56, emphasis added). In stating that Aboriginal women can "work through" their dependency on non-Aboriginal institutions, the TFFSW adopts a therapeutic/psychological discourse that divests dependency of its social and economic origins. Instead, dependency is constructed as a character trait that can be addressed through therapy and programming. Thus, the dependency of Aboriginal women is constructed as a culturally specific pathology.

The psychologized dependency discourse reflected in Creating Choices also carries with it gendered connotations. In the post-industrial era of the 1950s medical constructions of dependency gained prominence and associated dependency with traditionally feminine characteristics such as irresponsibility, immaturity and an inability to make decisions (Fraser and Gordon 1997:136–37). One of the most poignant illustrations of how women's social positioning became obscured through medical discourse was the emergence of a new psychiatric label. The 1987 edition of the Diagnostic and Statistical Manual of Mental Disorders codified these characteristics into an official psychiatric illness called Dependent Personality Disorder (DPD). DPD was most commonly diagnosed in women (Fraser and Gordon 1997:137). The same qualities that are deemed to be symptomatic of women's mental instability been historically been associated with other "dependent" groups, such as slaves, Native peoples and people receiving welfare, as well as used as a justification for their subordination. What is common among all these images is that "social relations of dependency ... [are] absorbed into personality" (Fraser and Gordon 1997:143).

Caribbean–Canadian Women in Prison

My interviews with Caribbean–Canadian women in prison indicate the inadequacy of liberal notions of dependency in understanding these women's experiences. The concepts of dependency and independence that emerged in these interviews pose a challenge to individualized/pathologized notions of dependence in *Creating Choices*. Instead, the women I spoke with indicated that their lawbreaking is often an attempt to *avoid* dependency and to provide for the various family members who are in fact *dependent upon them*. Specifically, these women's experiences reflect efforts to remain self-sufficient and responsible for themselves and their children in a social and economic climate that is not responsive to such efforts. Their experiences illustrate women's active *resistance* to relationships and practices that enforce Black women's dependency.

The following discussion is based on individual and group interviews with Caribbean–Canadian women federally incarcerated in Ontario. Out of a much larger interview project, I will be discussing themes of dependency and independence that emerged from individual interviews with five Black Caribbean–Canadian women and one Black women's focus group of four participants (three of whom also participated in individual interviews). These women had been imprisoned for shoplifting, drug importation/trafficking and/or fraud. As a result, their prison sentences were comparably short, with sentence lengths ranging from just over two years to four years. Four of the six women had at least some college education. Four women also had children for whom they were sole providers. The women ranged in age from twenty-four to forty-four years old.

The Black women in this study all identified themselves as Caribbean–Canadians. All but one was born in either Jamaica or Barbados and immigrated to Canada sometime during their childhood. According to the Correctional Service of Canada (CSC) in 1996, 10.1 percent of federally sentenced women are Black (Solicitor General Canada 1997). In addition, the *Report of the Commission on Systemic Racism in the Ontario Criminal Justice System* (1995) states that Black women are disproportionately represented in Ontario prisons, being sentenced to prison at "almost seven times that of white women."

Socially Enforced Dependency

Black women that I interviewed bear little resemblance to the "dependent" women portrayed in *Creating Choices*.[1] They were neither reliant upon men nor the state for financial support and, although some women were convicted on drug importation charges, none themselves were drug users. Therefore, as Puss stated,[2] Black women do not represent the dominant image of a federally sentenced woman:

> We don't fit the stereotype of the "normal" inmate that's in here.... I don't know what is a "sugar daddy."... I had to take care of myself.

Moreover, most women spoke of their dreams, desires, and goals in terms congruent with socially sanctioned values. For example, they placed a high premium on self-sufficiency, education, planning for the future, providing for their children, and heterosexual unions. The conceptual theme underlying these issues was that of independence. Independence was a term which women used to describe both their own personalities and a mode or means of structuring their lives. Independence meant "fending for myself," not asking for help from others ("I'm not a beggar. I hate that.") and minimizing the control that others have over their lives. Sandra's comment typifies their perspectives on independence:

> I am a *very* independent, resourceful person. I will do anything and everything to provide the best for my family. There are certain things I won't do, because that's not me. I'd rather go out and steal a turkey before I'd ask a man to buy me a turkey. Because I'm independent and that's the way I saw my mother. She would rather sacrifice and do it herself, than ask anybody to help her. So, I am set in my ways, kind of, because this is the way I seen it. And I've been watching it from generation to generation, right back down onto me.

Despite aims of self-sufficiency, Black women found that their independence was being undermined by inadequate job wages, government and social services, gender inequities and systemic racism. These factors all intersected in various ways to produce conditions in which their options for survival and independence were extremely limited.

Women in the focus group said that their motivation for breaking the law was "financial gain." They distinguished their own lawbreaking from that of other women, whose crimes are often seen as connected to addictions and abuse. R.J. said:

> So all the Black women I know are in this institution, they're here for financial gain. None of us are suffering from the norm of being a drug addict or being sexually molested by our father…. We're in here purely for financial gain. We don't fit the stereotype of the "normal" inmate that's in here. We're here for *financial gain*.

These women seemed acutely aware that the way that "a normal inmate" is constructed has little to do with their own experiences. When discussing the circumstances of their conviction, their stories reverberated against the dominant narrative about women in prison: that they are victims of abuse and that their lawbreaking stems from this victimization. Sandra stated:

> You can't say it's because of the abuse. I've never been abused so I can't say that I done it because of that…. The reason I did it was because of money. I wasn't abused. It was because of money.

Although some of the Black women in this study were victims of childhood and/or adult male violence, in all cases the primary motivation for breaking the law was the need for money. The refusal to accept the dominant psychological/ abuse script is captured in the repeated comment that they broke the law for "financial gain" and "because of money." In asserting the primacy of lack of money and opportunities in their lives, Black women emphasized the political roots of their struggles that the psychological/abuse script minimizes.

These women spoke persistently about the *social and economic* causes of their need for money. Some of the women in this study had had previous paid employment in low-level jobs in financial institutions, corporations and medical care facilities. A few participants were working at these jobs at the time of their arrest. They were also either sole providers for their children or supporting themselves through part-time work while continuing their education at college or university. However, most women found that the wage they received was not sufficient for providing for their families, even with subsidized child care, and sometimes turned to illegal means to supplement their income. As Puss explained, after her divorce her ex-husband did not help cover the costs of taking care of the family:

> That job that I had at that time didn't make me cover the mortgage payments, didn't make me pay the car, didn't make me afford to pay the daycare so I could go to work. Couldn't give my kids a proper meal three nights out of the week. So I resorted to what I say "through my work," which led me to my life of crime.

Similarly, Goldtooth explained the difficulties of re-establishing her life on parole while working at a low-wage job:

> I went to work nine to five. I couldn't even afford my babysitter by the end of the week. And I was only fending for one child.... So you go out there and say let's try working. I go every day. It just wasn't working! My three hundred and forty dollar pay cheque. Expenses for the week. I live in a halfway house. I have to eat everyday. My child has to eat.

The women's main concern was finding a way to remain independent from both the state and other people. Although a few of the respondents in this group of women had received government financial assistance at various times in their lives, most spoke of the choices they made around economic survival as attempts to *avoid* state dependence. Government financial assistance was seen as undesirable for two reasons: the amount of assistance was inadequate for supporting their family, and reliance upon the state impeded their ability to function independently.

There was a common perception that receiving welfare meant accepting living in poverty. Most women were struggling to avoid "going under," which referred to staying above the poverty line; "If I wanted to stay on welfare I could ... but my kids would be under the starving margin. And there'd be like serious poverty and what's the sense?" (Jovinka).

Women spoke not only of the inadequacy of welfare, but of the degradation and mistrust they experienced from the professionals charged with dispensing welfare cheques: "Sometimes they make you feel like you're degraded" and "they just think you are milking the system." In addition, professionals associated with the state were not regarded as helpers or allies, but rather as extensions of state control and surveillance:

> And when you reach the age of sixteen where you can make decisions for yourself, you don't want nobody making decisions for you.... But they just nose into your life, everything, everything you do, you've gotta think, where are they? What are they thinking? What's gonna happen next? (Puss)

Jovinka agreed, "Sometimes you don't want the system in your life anyway. They control it."

Government assistance in the form of subsidized housing was also viewed as impinging on their independence. Puss saw subsidized housing perpetuating and enforcing Black people's ghettoization and marginalization:

> And then when you do get into [subsidized housing] they want to stick you in a predominantly *Black* area where all the *Black* people are, where they think you want to be. So, you start a chain that can't be broken.

Many women were therefore aware of the serious consequences of accepting subsidized housing. Thus, in order to resist this method of marginalization some women avoided subsidized housing, opting instead for living in mixed neighbourhoods. This often further aggravated their need for financial resources to cover the cost of providing for themselves, their education and/or their family.

Illegal Work: Resistance to Enforced Dependency

Illegal work often functioned as a means of shifting class and race relations by moving Black women "inside" mainstream Canadian culture and making them feel more independent. Shoplifting, fraud and drug importation were a means of releasing Black women from the poverty and racist practices that reinforced their marginalization. Relying upon or supplementing their income through illegal jobs, women were able to adequately support themselves and their family. Having their own money gave them a feeling of security and well-being, knowing that they could provide for themselves. As Goldtooth explained:

> It made me feel independent. Really independent. I don't have to ask you for nothing. At least I could always stand on my feet. No problem. No problem.

Illegal work provided Black women with financial resources and feelings of independence and self-sufficiency. In addition to the relative "freedom" they had, to define the terms of their employment and to make enough money to stay above the poverty line, women's social status also increased in various ways. For example, illegal work often allowed women into mainstream society in a way that was previously inaccessible to them. As they started to accrue more material belongings and other symbols of "success," Their social worth also increased. Puss stated that after her marriage broke up she initially broke the law to be able to make the mortgage payments, the monthly bills and to give her children things they needed for school. However, she discovered that as she acquired more material items her social status had changed.

> With acceptance came respect, came people liking me more. You're more socially accepted kind of thing.... I felt I was happy. I felt good. I felt like I was "it" you know, nice car, nice house, you know, I was wearing the most up-to-date clothes. I felt good at the time.

Money also helped shift balances of power between professionals and clients. For example, Alex found a willing and receptive consumer base within the middle-class professionals in relation to whom she was usually the "client." She stated that these professionals often provided a market for her shoplifted items. A consequence of this arrangement was that "they're making me feel like I'm accepted ... like I'm special, too." Alex distinguished this class of people who were able to pay up front from her own peers who "take three payments when they get their family allowance." Illegal jobs in the underground economy allowed Black women to play an active part in consumer culture and increased their social status. They were able to move from an exclusive position of "client" of services to a more equal position involved in market exchange. In this way, marginality was a site for "carving out spaces in which to manoeuvre and resist" (Evans 1995:503). Alex's experience also illustrates the role of the middle class in sustaining and perpetuating Black women's illegal work, with little risk to themselves. It is, after all, she who is doing time for shoplifting and who was tried and convicted by professionals similar to those who bought her merchandise.

"Dependency" as a Social Relation

In an article about the power of the law to exclude and marginalize African–Americans, Monica Evans (1995) discusses the various ways that Black women have historically constructed spaces of resistance. One example she gives illustrates how resistance to state-enforced dependency and marginalization can become criminalized. She describes a woman who while receiving welfare also worked a part-time job to pay for her college education. Evans (1995:505) writes that this is an example of a young woman who "stole away" from state-created dependency and from legal rules that could only hurt her. Saving money for college in violation of welfare rules and in violation of the rules preventing access to knowledge is the "insubordination" of an outlaw, kicking against the legal system that perpetuates her subordination.

Understanding dependency as a social relation of subordination, rather than as a personality disorder, exposes the state's role in enforcing and perpetuating marginalization based on gender, race and class. Within this context some lawbreaking behaviour, such as the above example, is very often a conscious act of resisting enforced dependency.

This analysis challenges the individualistic perspective of *Creating Choices,* which views dependency as an issue to "work through," and points to the contradictions of addressing dependency within a prison, which the women are clearly dependent on. Although individual women may benefit from some forms of therapy and individualistic programming, these approaches do little towards alleviating the social factors that contribute to many women's lawbreaking. In fact, it can be argued that imprisonment further marginalizes women from access to material resources and further exacerbates the social causes of their lawbreaking.

Conversely, understanding the social causes of dependency points to very different directions in program and policy. Policy and program implications that flow from this analysis are more community oriented as the potential for social issues to be addressed within an institutional setting are minimal. These policy and program implications include improved social assistance, the creation of adequate job opportunities, affordable quality daycare, and access to education and material resources, so that resistance to state dependency is no longer criminalized.

It is important that the experiences of Black women be integrated into correctional policy and programming. Although *Creating Choices* contains an emphasis upon the role of racism in Aboriginal women's lives, the voices of Black women and other women of colour are absent from this document. This omission may be related to the document's over emphasis on gender as the primary axis of oppression in federally incarcerated women's lives. An alternative analysis, such as the one offered here, illustrates the convergence of racist and classist practices that enforce Black women's dependency. As has been argued, there is a relationship between resisting dependency, Black women's social positioning "outside" mainstream white society and Black women's lawbreaking. Black women's lawbreaking was economically motivated and thus cannot be understood on the basis of gender oppression alone. A more complex analysis of the multiple ways oppression shapes various women's experiences and how that challenges liberal notions of independence/dependence may better explain the role that social positioning plays in shaping women's choices.

Notes

1. I am not suggesting that some Caribbean–Canadian women *do* resemble the federally sentenced woman depicted in *Creating Choices*. However, the Caribbean–Canadian woman I interviewed did not resemble this document's construction of the dependent woman.
2. All names used are fictitious.

Psy-ence Fiction
Inventing the Mentally-Disordered Female Prisoner
Kathleen Kendall

Introduction

This chapter took root about seven years ago, while I was working for the Correctional Service of Canada (CSC) in two separate capacities. First, between May 1992 and March 1993, I undertook a program evaluation of therapeutic services at the Prison for Women.[1] Second, between April and October 1993, I worked as a Special Advisor on Female Offenders at CSC National Headquarters. In the latter post, I was helping with program design for the new federally sentenced women's regional facilities.

In both instances, I felt a growing unease. Underlying my gradual trepidation was a sense that, despite good intentions, my work ultimately contributed toward an oppressive penal regime. I came to see that any positive radical potential within my projects was likely to be either stripped away or compromised beyond recognition. Worse, my efforts were used to legitimate and reinforce conditions completely contrary to my aims. Specifically, my attempts to acknowledge structural problems such as racism, sexism, classism and violence were ultimately transformed into pathologies lying within individual women prisoners. This occurred as social and political analyses became replaced with psychological ones. For example, my program evaluation had shown that prisoners identified the pains of imprisonment to be not only contrary to therapy and rehabilitation but also the greatest contributing factor to their emotional distress. However, others applying a psychological model used these findings as evidence of the women's lack of ability to adjust to and cope with the prison environment. In shifting responsibility onto the women, not only were moral judgements being made about them, but the research was also de-politicized. In the end, rather than confront the incongruity or consider alternatives to incarceration, the solution was to develop programs aimed at helping the women adapt to the prison and to heighten security measures.

My experience demonstrated not only the power of psychology but also the limitations imposed by the cultural sensibilities, mentalities and material structures of corrections. Prisons are ultimately about discipline, security and punishment. Unequal relations of power are the very bedrock upon which prisons are constructed (Hannah-Moffat 1997:189). While I would argue that the motives of most people working within corrections are honourable, these intentions become displaced and distorted by the contradictions and demands of the institution as well as by legal accountability and public pressures.

The psychological sciences are a powerful tool enabling correctional workers to negotiate, uphold and obscure the paradoxes and dominant power relations within the prison. By the psychological sciences (psy-sciences), I mean psychology, psychiatry and the other disciplines which designate themselves with the prefix "psy" (Rose 1988:179). I am not implying that people within corrections employ these psy-sciences in a conscious way. Rather, they use them because it "makes sense" to, in three very important ways. First, the psy-sciences promise solutions to a variety of social problems. Second, it is believed that these answers and the work informing them are objective and neutral. As such, the psy-sciences are conferred high status and given legitimacy. Finally, they are consistent with the individualism underlying the philosophy of liberal democracy in Western nations.

This chapter overviews the historical relationship between the psy-sciences and Canadian female prisoners. Focusing mainly on federally sentenced women, I will argue that this association has intensified, leading to the current concern over mentally-disordered female prisoners. I conclude that this recent preoccupation is rooted in a social and political process rather than a scientific truth.

The Historical Legacy of the Psy-Sciences

Scholars have argued that nineteenth-century social changes including urbanization, industrialization and immigration created unrest and anxiety among the populations of both Europe and North America. To stave off social decay and restore order, reformers employed scientific methods of observation, calculation, classification and rationalization. Informed by the Enlightenment, reformers postulated that general laws underpinned the social world. Scientific methods were employed to discover such laws. It was believed that, once these laws were known, social life could be predicted, contained and controlled. Social order would then be re-established in an economic and efficient manner (Douglas 1992; Foucault 1977; Rose 1988, 1999).

One of the first applications of the scientific method to social problems was the division of deviant populations into different categories and institutions. This involved the removal of lunatics, paupers and criminals from the gaols containing them all together, into separate institutions: asylums, almshouses and penitentiaries.

In Canada, this occurred with the creation of two key institutions: the Kingston Penitentiary in 1835 and Toronto's temporary Lunatic Asylum in 1841. A permanent asylum, the Provincial Lunatic Asylum, was established in 1851 (Oliver 1998; Moran 1998; Carrigan 1991).

Administrators and reformers soon demanded further categorization and division within individual institutions as a means to achieve increased capital, efficiency, order and control. Thus, institutional populations were closely monitored and classified into ever more precise categories of difference. The psy-sciences emerged, in part, from such procedures.

Similar techniques were carried out on other populations in establishments such as schools, workplaces and hospitals. Information gathered from these studies was then used to establish averages, or norms, for populations. Once such norms were created, individuals were compared to them and encouraged to embrace them. As people internalized these, they sought out expert advice (from psy-professionals) to help them achieve "normality" and ultimately exercised power over themselves. Through this process of normalization, individuals voluntarily complied with their own regulation in everyday practices. Foucault (1977) calls this covert method of social control disciplinary power and argues that it increasingly came to replace sovereign power in which control was established through physical, overt and repressive means.

Numerous writers suggest that far from being neutral and objective, scientific knowledge reflects power relations within society (see, for example, Habermas 1987; Harding 1986; Kuhn 1996). The norms established by the nascent psy-sciences thus reflected the values of the dominant social, political and cultural group: white, Western, middle-class males. The further away individuals are from the dominant norm, the greater is their perceived difference and deviance. People's "otherness" is then used against them to legitimate their own oppression and maintain social inequalities.

The institutionalization of asylum and prison populations suggests that these groups failed to be normalized while in the community. Penitentiary and asylum populations have historically comprised the most marginalized groups within society. When measured against white, middle-class, male standards, they can, in fact, never be normal. However, the psy-sciences work to obscure the economic, social and political contexts within which the actions and behaviours of these groups occur and through which judgements of them are made. By debasing people's differences or "otherness," social problems are regarded as individual failures and weaknesses.

The Invention of Criminal Lunacy

Efforts to refine the classification of institutional populations led to the construction of the mentally-disordered prisoner. This category was first officially recognized by alienists, or nineteenth-century psychiatrists, as criminal lunacy or criminal insanity. Criminal lunatics were identified as containing elements of both madness and badness—a determination that could only be made through expert examination. By claiming specialized knowledge about this group, alienists were able to extend their power into the legal domain (Foucault 1978; Menzies 1991; Menzies, Chunn and Webster 1992).

However professionally advantageous to alienists, criminal lunatics were considered a nuisance by both the asylum and penitentiary administration. Within the penitentiary they disrupted the silence and discipline underpinning management philosophy. Inside the asylum, it was believed that their criminality would contaminate and harm "innocent" patients. Furthermore, there was a lack of space within both institutions in which to isolate them. Consequently, criminal lunatics were kept in temporary and make-shift, even dangerous, quarters. They were also frequently transferred back and forth between the two establishments.[2]

The new category proved philosophically problematic since criminality implied responsibility for one's actions while lunacy suggested a loss of reason and therefore an absence of responsibility. Female criminal lunatics were even more of an enigma because the sexual ideology of the time maintained that women were inherently virtuous and innocent. This belief meant that women who transgressed social boundaries were generally more likely to be regarded as insane than criminal. A number of writers have documented the ways in which scientific discourse pathologized women in the nineteenth century (see, for example, Mitchinson 1991; McGovern 1986; Warsh 1989). Specifically, physicians claimed that women's biology made them sick, and that this sickness contributed to their greater propensity toward madness (Chesler 1972; Penfold and Walker 1983; Showalter 1985). Since insanity implied that a person was not accountable for their actions, women so labelled could violate social norms yet retain their moral purity and goodness.

However, a duality surrounded the very small minority of women who were labelled as criminals. They were treated either as victims of circumstance and environment or as more morally degenerate and harmful than their male counterparts (Boritch 1997:175). Consequently, ambiguity surrounded female prisoners and they were dealt with neglectfully, paternalistically and cruelly (Cooper 1993:33–49).

As Menzies and Chunn (forthcoming) note, the idea that women could be both mad and bad was almost incomprehensible. The tiny percentage of women who came to be labelled as insane criminals therefore provoked a great deal of curiosity, bewilderment and scorn. At the same time, however, they were either disregarded as anomalies of little importance or rationalized as extreme variations of women's greater predilection to madness. As with the male criminal lunatics, they were considered an annoyance to both the asylum and the prison. However, like women prisoners, female criminal lunatics were treated with particular negligence and hostility.

The blending of femininity, criminality and madness appeared incongruous and therefore unfathomable. In refusing to be normalized and by breaching classificatory divides, female criminal lunatics revealed the limitations of science. Consequently, they threatened to expose the immanent failing of the broader scientific program that promised to establish social order and control (Kendall 1999a, 1999b; Menzies and Chunn forthcoming, Chunn and Menzies 1998). Having helped to create such a threat, the psy-sciences must continually work toward neutralizing it.

The Growth of the Psy-sciences in Canadian Prisons

Despite the constant threat of demise, the psy-sciences have come to hold an ever increasing role in the governance of Canadian populations, both inside and outside institutions. As previously argued, the psy-sciences are central to the disciplinary power regulating the everyday practices of people. Numerous writers have demonstrated how women and girls have been historically control-led through the family, education, peer groups and the media (Valverde 1991; Strange 1995; Gleason 1997, 1999).

While the psy-sciences help to inform everyday techniques of regulation, their role within Canadian prisons has been considerable but variable. In the early years the psy-scientists mainly worked on classifying inmates. Additionally, they appear to have been less involved in institutions for women than in ones for men (Hannah-Moffat 1997). This last suggestion contradicts the findings of other, especially British, researchers who maintain that the psy-sciences held a central and disproportionately larger role in the early governance of female prisoners (see, for example, Sim 1990; Dobash, Dobash, and Gutteridge 1986). However, as Hannah-Moffat (1997) argues, these writers tend to neglect the everyday types of regulation imposed by matrons, volunteers and ministers. This latter kind of non-expert control emphasized domesticity and sexual morality. While fundamental to the governance of female prisoners, such control was informed by and existed alongside the expertise of social workers, psychologists and psychiatrists. Together, both forms of governance reinforced gendered and racialized norms in Canadian women's prisons (Sangster 1999; Ruemper 1994; Strange 1983, 1985). It is important to recognize that the lesser involvement of the psy-sciences was also a reflection of the disregard and negligence which typified the treatment of female prisoners more generally.

Throughout the twentieth century, the psy-sciences gradually became more important in the regulation of Canadian prison populations. Key to this develop-ment was the report of the Royal Commission to Investigate the Penal System in Canada (the Archambault report) published in 1938. In recommending a reha-bilitation philosophy, this report ushered in a greater role for scientific experts. Prisoners were to become law-abiding citizens through refined classification and appropriate treatment delivered by psychiatrists, psychologists, physicians and other specialists. While the start of World War II prevented the immediate expansion of these professional services, they eventually greatly proliferated within prisons. For example, classification soon became contingent upon the history taking and psychological testing of inmates. A central psychiatric facil-ity, consisting of nine cells, was established within the Kingston Penitentiary in 1948, and in 1949, electroconvulsive therapy was officially approved for use within penitentiaries. Soon thereafter, a Deputy Commissioner was appointed the task of supervising and developing medical and psychiatric services, as well as examining correctional treatment. The first full-time psychologist was offi-cially appointed within the Correctional Service in 1951 and the first full-time psychiatrist was employed in 1959 (Watkins 1992, Jolliffe 1984; Chalke Report 1972).

The formal establishment of the medical model within Canadian prisons during the 1960s provided the psy-experts with even greater opportunity for involvement within corrections. The model developed out of the treatment orientation recommended by the Commission Appointed to Enquire into the

Principles and Procedures followed in the Remission Service of the Department of Justice (Fauteaux Commission 1956). The medical paradigm presumes that criminal behaviour is a symptom of offenders' physical and/or mental illnesses. Therefore treatments were designed to cure the ailments of individual prisoners.

The psy-experts employed a variety of interventions, including plastic surgery, drug therapy, psychotherapy, aversion therapy, group counselling, and individual counselling. It was claimed that these methods were humanitarian and benevolent because they were for prisoners' "own good" (Ekstedt and Griffiths 1984; Goff 1999; Joliffe 1984).

The Psy-sciences in Women's Prisons

The bulk of reports and publications regarding mental illness and techniques to cure them were concerned with male prisoners. However, the odd description of psy-practices with female prisoners incarcerated in Ontario facilities did surface (see, for example, Flint 1960, 1964; Haslam 1964; Benson 1968; Canadian Corrections Association 1969; Lambert and Madden 1974; Ross and McKay 1976, 1978, 1979). From these it would appear that female prisoners were exposed to a variety of treatments rooted in psychology and psychiatry. However, as Hannah-Moffat (1997) writes, such interventions continued to exist alongside non-expert methods of governance such as hairdressing and domestic science. Furthermore, it is difficult to ascertain the degree to which the psy-sciences were absorbed into women's prisons because records have been lost. Nonetheless, the available accounts cast doubt on the therapeutic efficacy of the psy-treatments received by women prisoners.

For example, in the early 1960s, LSD was administered to at least twenty-three women on an experimental basis. Some inmates received the drug a number of times, and others while in dissociation or segregation. The experiment was reported in the *Canadian Journal of Corrections* in 1964 by one of the researchers (Eveson 1964). Despite this publication, silence surrounded these experiments. Only recently, after a complaint was made by one of the subjects, have the experiments come to public attention and an investigation been undertaken by CSC (1998a; Proctor and Rosen 1994).

A second, independent review argues that the one conducted by CSC representatives was inadequate (Gilmore and Somerville 1998). This review raises concerns regarding the ethics of LSD experiments. In particular, it suggests that there was a strong indication that the experiments were undertaken for the purposes of behaviour modification in order to control unruly prisoners within the institution. The investigators also state that it was unclear whether the women had given informed consent, and raised the question of whether it is even possible to give informed consent within a coercive environment. Finally, they note that experiments using electro-convulsive treatments were also conducted with the population at the Prison for Women which may have similarly been undertaken for behavioural and managerial rather than therapeutic purposes.

Although lacking in detail, Eveson (1964) reports on other P4W studies involving drug addiction and pain tolerance. He furthermore records that during his employment at P4W there was a part-time psychiatrist, as well as a psychologist and social worker.[3] Joliffe (1984) reports that psychiatric interviews and EEG testing were conducted within the prison to examine psychopathology and neuropathology. Hannah-Moffat (1997) also notes that the P4W population received cosmetic surgery and aversion therapy along with other psychology programs. In at least one instance, a hysterectomy was performed to rid a prisoner of her premenstrual tension, which "allegedly exacerbated her violent tendencies" (Kershaw and Lasovich 1991:78).

The P4W population also had access to the Narcotic Addiction Treatment Centre in Matsqui, British Columbia, which opened in 1962. Additionally, prisoners who were considered to have mental illnesses which were unmanageable within P4W were sent to the Regional Treatment Centre's Female Behavioural Unit within the walls of the Kingston Penitentiary for Men. Others, whose problems were considered more severe, were taken to St. Thomas psychiatric hospital. Both of these facilities were, however, often hesitant to accept P4W women. It is also doubtful how helpful temporary placements within these facilities were given that available descriptions paint a very bleak picture of both their conditions and methods (see, for example, Kershaw and Lasovich 1991).

Although female prisoners were increasingly subjected to psy-treatments throughout the 1960s and 1970s, they remained marginalized by corrections and ignored by wider society. As with women's experience in the general population, prisoners' special circumstances and needs, including their mental health, remained largely unconsidered. Thus, while female imprisonment had not yet become a social issue, the mentally-disordered female offender was not recognized as a serious social problem.

While the psy-sciences were gaining in dominance, ethical concerns were being raised about the intrusive nature of their treatments and questions were beginning to be asked about their perceived lack of success in rehabilitating offenders. This contributed to another change in penal philosophy—the adoption of the opportunities model. This paradigm is still operant and is based on the assumption that since rehabilitation cannot be imposed, the role of the prison authorities should be to provide opportunities for reformation. The onus is with the prisoners, who can choose to take advantage of the opportunities provided for them or not. Programs emphasize education and job training. Despite shifting the responsibility for change onto prisoners, corrections has not necessarily provided the opportunities that prisoners are supposed to take advantage of. Additionally, inmates are penalized if they fail to embrace the opportunities offered (Ekstedt and Griffiths 1984).

The introduction of the new model did not signal a complete break from the previous paradigm. Rather, elements of both the opportunities and medical model co-exist. While the opportunities model stresses classification and risk management techniques, the medical model continues to emphasize mental illness and psychological disorder. Specifically, techniques are used to identify the criminogenic needs of prisoners—those factors said to contribute toward a person's risk of criminal behaviour. Many of these are considered to be mental-health or psychological needs. Once the needs are identified, it is maintained that prisoners can then be provided with appropriate opportunities to address them through programming.

In Canada, this hybrid framework has been largely supported by psychologists and criminologists working with and for the CSC.[4] While it is doubtful that this new approach has provided any real opportunities for inmates, it has provided the psy-sciences with great opportunities for expansion. Indeed, a whole industry has developed around the invention of various tools and techniques used to measure risk and need, as well as the deisgn and implementation of programs to address them.

The Mentally-Disordered Female Prisoner

While the adoption of the medical/opportunities model coincided with increased concern about the mental health of prisoners, men received much greater attention in this regard until very recently. For example, the Chalke Report (1972) was the master plan for the development of psychiatric services in federal correctional facilities. It provided an overview of the current situation and made a series of recommendations, including the construction of the regional psychiatric centres. Nowhere does it mention female prisoners except to suggest that the women's Narcotic Addiction Treatment Centre in Matsqui be used instead as a psychiatric centre for men—it eventually was (Chalke Report 1972). Similarly, a report published in 1980 by the Steering Committee on Mentally and Behaviourally Disordered Inmates (CSC 1980) makes no specific mention of gender. As such, it is impossible to ascertain if women are included or excluded in the issues raised and data provided. Women are included in a 1985 study examining the mental-health needs of inmates (Hogan and Guglielmo 1985). Here, a survey of 105 women at the Prison for Women found that 73 were "mentally disturbed," the great majority of whom were identified as substance abusers. However, subsequent discussion makes no special note of the women. A 1988 report entitled *A Survey of Case Management Officers' Perceptions Concerning the Prevalence of Mental Disorders* reports that 8.9 percent of the population surveyed had mental or behavioural disorders other than substance abuse. While women prisoners were considered, no gender differences were found (CSC 1988).

Thus, despite the existence of psy-interventions and infrequent reports of the emotional and mental disturbances of female prisoners, as mentioned earlier, there appears to have been very little serious concern over the mental health of women prisoners. This may be largely due to the general neglect of female offenders at the time. It could also be accounted for, in part, by the apparent incongruence and therefore incomprehension of femininity, madness and criminality discussed earlier.

Serious anxieties about women's mental health begin to appear with the release of two 1990 government reports: *Creating Choices* (TFFSW 1990) and the *Task Force on Mental Health, Special Needs of Female Offenders* (Deurloo and Haythornthwaite 1990). Each of these documents emphasizes that female offenders have special mental-health needs. While *Creating Choices* highlights the link between mental health and past experiences of victimization, the *Task Force on Mental Health* stresses that women prisoners are substantially more mentally disturbed than men. Indeed, this study states that only 5 percent of women prisoners show no evidence of serious disorder. Coinciding with these reports was a series of self injuries, suicides and disturbances at P4W. Furthermore, there was growing public pressure to address the needs of female prisoners. More generally, the feminist movement drew attention to women's inequality and victimization in Canada and spearheaded policies and actions to redress these wrongs.

In response to all of this, the number of psychologists and counsellors was gradually increased at P4W. As Balfour notes in the next chapter, most of these workers adopted a feminist-therapy model. While the employment of these new experts helped to contain immediate crises and address public pressure, they did not eradicate the problems and became regarded by the government as extremely expensive to maintain. Additionally, suspicion surrounded the blatant feminist approach.

In May 1992, these concerns were dealt with in part by contracting me to carry out a program evaluation of therapeutic services at P4W. The level of psysciences at the time was very intensive; for example, ten therapists, two staff psychologists and a student social work intern provided individual counselling alone. Sixty-seven percent of the total prison population was seeing a counsellor individually. As Balfour suggests, the therapy offered was problematic because it essentialized and individualized the prisoners. Yet, I also found that the great majority of women supported the services provided by the counsellors.[5] Perhaps this is unsurprising, given the pains of imprisonment and other hardships experienced by the population as well as the advocacy role many of the counsellors adopted.

At the outset of this chapter, I noted that in my study, prisoners identified the prison environment to be the greatest cause of their emotional distress. The counselling offered many women a means of coping with the immediacy of their confinement. However, the women also stressed that the prison environment posed severe limitations on all programming, particularly those aimed at improving their mental health. Unfortunately, this contradiction between therapy and prison has been largely ignored while the use of therapy as an adaptive mechanism to incarceration has become central to current and future mental-health services for federally sentenced women.

The Mental Health Strategy for Women Offenders (Laishes 1997) is the framework for all future mental-health services provided for federally sentenced women. It ultimately individualizes and pathologizes prisoners while de-politicizing their actions. For example, it claims that women suffer significantly higher incidents of mental disorder than men—with 74 percent of federally sentenced women having a personality disorder. There is no mention of the limitations the prison environment imposes upon mental-health programs other than to state that certain women need greater security.

Furthermore, the mental-health (and other) needs of women are determined by a Case Needs Identification and Analysis Protocol (CNIAP). The areas this classification tool identifies women to be lacking in are those for which they are determined to have needs. Unfortunately, the CNIAP is rife with moral judgements. For example, some of the indicators include: unemployment, "family is unable to get along as a unit," resides in a criminogenic area, has no credit, has used social assistance, takes risks inappropriately, and has difficulty performing sexually (Motiuk and Blanchette 1998).

The CSC found it difficult to manage some of the women in the new regional facilities and therefore developed a special strategy for them—the *National Strategy for High Need Women Offenders in Correctional Institutions* (CSC 1999a). This model is founded upon the notion that unmanageable women have severe mental disorders.[6] In essence, it calls for increased security at the regional facilities, heightened supervision and intensive therapy aimed at "transforming the thoughts and behaviours that are the source of the women's problems" (Laishes 1997:10). This approach is consistent with the cognitive, social-learning framework adopted more generally by the CSC as an overarching guide to treatment (Canada 1998b:7). It assumes that prisoners have deficient thinking patterns. Treatment therefore aims to replace faulty cognitions with socially acceptable ones (Fabiano, Porporino and Robinson 1990). This is a moralistic framework, resting on the assumption that individuals have free will and are autonomous and entirely responsible for their actions.[7]

The *National Strategy for High Need Women Offenders in Correctional Institutions* (CSC 1999b) was informed by a wealth of mostly psychological research undertaken specifically to address these "difficult to manage" prisoners[8] (McDonagh 1999; Morin 1999; Warner 1998; Rivera 1996; Whitehall 1995).

Conclusion

The mentally-disordered prisoner is a nineteenth-century construction that evolved from the classification of institutional populations. Female prisoners labelled as mentally disordered have been largely ignored until recently. Although regarded as management problems and subjected to contemporary treatments, they were not seen as a serious social problem. However, recent attempts to address the needs of female prisoners have focused on mental health. This has resulted in the pathologization of all federally sentenced women and the creation of the severely mentally-disordered female prisoner. In this way, the mentally-disordered female offender has become a serious social problem. This is not to deny the emotional distress experienced by female prisoners. Rather, it is to emphasize that how this distress is defined and understood is not the result of a scientific discovery of the "truth." It is instead a social and political process.

The psy-sciences have served an important role in this process. Through it, they have helped to regulate female prisoners, assisted the csc in managing the contradictions of imprisonment, and expanded their own power. Such instrumentality will likely ensure the further expansion of the psy-sciences within women's prisons. The spate of recent psychological research is a potent warning of this (see, for example, Blanchette 1997a, 1997b; Blanchette and Motiuk 1996, 1997; Dowden and Blanchette 1999; Bonta, Pang and Wallace-Capretta 1995; Loucks and Zamble 1999). As McMahon (1999b) suggests, this work is worrying not only because it pathologizes women prisoners, but also because it dehumanizes them and obscures its own complicity through claims of scientific authority and neutrality. Yet, in failing to achieve the promise of establishing social order, the psy-sciences may someday be the victim of their own creation.

Notes

1. See Kendall 1993a, 1993b, 1993c, 1994a.
2. A criminal lunatic asylum was finally erected within the walls of the Kingston Penitentiary in 1855. However, after much debate, women prisoners were disallowed and became the initial occupants of the first custom-built construction, the Criminal Lunatic Asylum at Rockwood, Ontario. Unfortunately, as the building was not yet complete, the women were kept in converted horse stables. That Asylum stopped taking criminal lunatics in 1877 and returned them to the Kingston Penitentiary. In 1915 the insane ward at Kingston Penitentiary closed, and criminally insane prisoners were transferred to provincial custody in the reformatory at Guelph and elsewhere. See Kendall 1999a, 1999b; Friedland 1986; Sims 1981. For an account of criminal lunatic women held in British Columbia's psychiatric system between 1888 and 1950, see Menzies and Chunn forthcoming and Chunn and Menzies 1998.
3. See, also, Scott 1982. George Scott worked as a psychiatrist at P4W during the 1950s–1960s. He betrays his own sexism through very sexualized accounts of his encounters with female prisoners. For example: "Around my desk she came, breathing violence and anger. I met her straight on and wrapped my arms around her waist. She was unable to strike me or scratch me, but went on biting me. My right arm around her waist moved automatically to grasp her long black hair. With a tug I flipped her off balance and with a noisy thud she struck the floor like a sack of potatoes. There I was, standing astride her. She was motionless. She looked at me with a meaningless stare then closed her eyes" (Scott 1982:152). The abusive nature of this interaction is apparent.
4. See, for example, Andrews 1996; Andrews, Bonta and Hoge 1990; Andrews, Zinger, Hoge, Bonta, Gendreau and Cullen 1990; Coulson and Nutbrown 1992; Gendreau 1981; Gendreau and Andrews 1990; Gendreau and Goggin 1996.
5. Shaw (1990) and Rivera (1996) also found prisoners to be extremely supportive of the counselling they received at P4W.
6. This population is, in fact, said to have a constellation of needs, making different categories of women incompatible and thus requiring distinctive program approaches. Three discrete groups are identified as follows: "those with anti-social and behaviour and criminal attitudes; those with special needs resulting from serious emotional and mental-health issues; and those with special needs resulting from cognitive limitations and basic skills deficits" (McDonagh 1999: ii). Most women are said to fit into the first two categories.

7. The social-learning approach is also consistent with Dialectical Behavioral Therapy (DBT). DBT is a key component of the *National Strategy for High Need Women Offenders in Correctional Institutions* (CSC 1999a, 1999b) and a favoured model by the CSC for use with female prisoners. DBT was developed by Marsha Linehan in the U.S.A. for working with "borderline personality disordered" patients. Essentially, DBT applies a variety of cognitive and behaviour therapy strategies and attempts to integrate the dialectics of Zen with Western psychology (Linehan 1993a, 1993b). As with similar psychological frameworks, it essentially individualizes and pathologizes people. I find the dialectical aspect particularly dangerous, because its embrace of contradictions (while potentially liberating) is, in fact, profoundly confusing. The CSC brought over "coaches" from Linehan's organization, the Behavioral Technology Transfer Group, to train some of their workers in DBT. Soon the CSC will be offering its own training (Tillson 1999).

8. These "difficult to manage" women are among the most socially, economically and racially marginalized in Canada. A number of them were involved in various "institutional disturbances." However, investigations into these incidents demonstrate that the women's actions were not spontaneous or pathological, but were associated with problems in institutional practices and policies (Arbour Commission 1995; CSC 1997a, 1997b, 1997c, n.d.p.). Despite the various official rulings, the CSC continues to hold the women responsible for the incidents.

Feminist Therapy with Women in Prison
Working Under the Hegemony of Correctionalism
Gillian Balfour

Introduction

Creating Choices (TFFSW 1990) has become symbolic in Canada of feminist engagement with the state. What remains unclear at this point is whether this has been a successful venture, or one bound to repeat a history of co-opting feminist principles (see section I of this book). The recommendations of *Creating Choices* focus on the importance of "women-centered" custodial and mental-health practices for federally sentenced women. The aim is to allow for greater diversity in vocational and therapeutic programs that are to be holistic and respectful of women's experiences of racism, poverty and violence. Feminist therapy is to play a key role in this new correctional model. However, as a part of a feminist strategy for prison reform, feminist therapy has been seriously undermined by the paramilitary imperatives of a prison bureaucracy. Consequently, feminist therapists have assumed the position of experts rather than advocates, and prisoners face more intensive therapeutic controls under this "women-centered" model. The social rights of women in prison for dignity, respect, empowerment and choices (as set out in *Creating Choices*) have been removed from their socio-political context of gender inequality.

In 1992, I conducted ten open-ended interviews with self-identified feminist therapists working with women in conflict with the law. The women interviewed were volunteers with community-based organizations, such as shelters for battered women and rape crisis centres, as well as working inside a women's prison. Each of the women I interviewed was trained in clinical psychology or social work. The following is an analysis of the paradigms and strategies of five feminist therapists working with women in prison.[1] What becomes clear is that feminists working within the prison/justice bureaucracy must reconcile their principles with the conditions of the institutions in which they find themselves.

"I Guess My Feminism is a Problem"

Feminist counselling grew out of work in women's shelters and crisis centres for victims of physical and sexual violence. Volunteers, often survivors of violence themselves, offered lay-counselling—support and practical assistance by non-credentialed service providers. The principles of feminist counselling include: a recognition that women are experts of their own lives and a commitment to equality within a therapeutic relationship, to bring society into therapy so as to explore women's experiences of sexual inequality and to politicize women's experiences through advocacy (Brody 1987; Greenspan 1983). In short, feminist counselling is concerned with the impact of power and inequality on women's lives. Substance abuse, attempted suicide and eating disorders are understood not as illnesses but as signs of protest or resistance to conditions of powerlessness (McGrath 1992). Consciousness-raising groups are used to encourage women to build cohesive social networks that provide practical and emotional support (Butler and Wintram 1992). "It is vital that women develop a strong consciousness of the roots of female pain" (Greenspan 1983:243). The goal of consciousness-raising is to see how one's own power is inextricably linked to the collective power of women (Burstow 1992). Feminist therapy has been described, in fact, as a philosophy more than a treatment approach (Kendall 1993b). It is important to consider the implications of feminist therapy under a correctional regime wherein the conditions undermine the therapy's potential.

Counsellors I spoke with expressed frustration with the lack of legitimacy granted to feminist therapists working in the prison. During the short period of time the Task Force on Federally Sentenced Women was in existence, several Aboriginal women prisoners committed or attempted suicide. Counsellors working with these women and those profoundly affected by these events, were accused by other prison staff of causing or condoning the suicides. Ironically, as Karen told me, when there were no problems with prisoners, management and security did not acknowledge the work of the counsellors as crucial to the "good order of the institution." She noted:

> When there is a crisis, everyone has to run around trying to point the finger. Looking for an explanation from somewhere else for the outbreaks of suicide. But when things are quiet, no one talks about the outbreak of mental health. It's like housework. You only notice it when it's not done. If everyone is just sailing along, they don't realize that we are working our butts off to keep it there. But if something happens, it's "how come you did not do enough?" Certainly I have spent a lot of time being called a con lover. In some way I suppose if I was traditional, I would blend in more. So I guess my feminism is a problem.

Feminists working inside a prison experience isolation and lack of acceptance. They are offered little legitimate support or recognition by prison administration and/or guards. Counsellors find themselves overwhelmed by not only the sadness of the prisoner's lives but also by the lack of support they encounter from prison administrators. As Kim put it:

> It is such hard and deeply difficult work, that is why it felt like such a slap in the face to be also attacked by CSC [Correctional Service of Canada]. There was actually an article printed in the local newspaper in which the warden made clear statements about too much therapy in

the prison and it was causing emotional upheaval and suicides. That was devastating for us. Walking into the prison one day after a suicide a staff saying to us, "so you've done it again—lost another one." They have no idea what we do.

Solidarity amongst the counsellors in the prison is especially important when administrators challenge their methods of intervention. Unfortunately, prison administrators' lack of understanding of feminist counselling and women's mental-health needs in general makes the counsellors' work difficult. Feminist counsellors are perceived as unconditionally supportive and naive. For example, a counsellor was confronted by the warden after being witnessed hugging a prisoner who had seriously self-injured herself. When asked to appear before the administration to discuss what was perceived as her "rewarding inappropriate behaviour," other counsellors appeared collectively in her support. She said:

> What keeps us sane and what keeps us here is each other. Sometimes we feel like a house of cards, that if someone quits we are all going to collapse because we cannot take it. I think part of (staff attitudes towards the counsellors) is ignorance, part of it is that we are radical. When things are going well and they are not in the press, they will tolerate us. I suppose that as radicals and when things don't seem to be going well, we are very easily identified.

Prison protocol is another important dimension of the work of feminist counsellors who are often forced to work with women in segregation cells so the prisoners' behaviour can be monitored. If counsellors insist a woman in crisis be removed from segregation and brought to their office, the prisoner must remain in handcuffs. One counsellor noted:

> We need crisis beds that are not in segregation and we have been fighting for that. We should have somewhere that is not segregated and is a healing place, so that they can go there and be safe without being treated like they are being punished.
> You are always weighing the damage that you are going to do by putting her in Seg against keeping her alive. To me those are decisions we should not have to make.

Feminist counsellors working inside believe that prisoners must have access to community programs. Such access will diversify the options for support and help to develop social networks in the community—an important consideration for release planning and parole eligibility. Community-based counselling would also overcome the problems of confidentiality that cast a shadow over prison programs, where therapists' records are accessible to prison security and administration. As one counsellor noted:

> There is so little privacy for women. There are severe repercussions
> if the wrong information gets out or in a context that it gets taken in-
> correctly. For instance if it goes to the parole board and the members
> aren't particularly sensitized or educated about these things, it can have
> serious repercussions on the woman [e.g., disclosure may influence
> parole decisions].

Counsellors try to work proactively with the issue of confidentiality. Prisoners must sign contracts agreeing to speak only within the group about things
that are discussed, and are free to discuss only what they feel they are willing
to have known by the group. The counsellors do not pressure the inmates to
make disclosure a condition of the therapeutic relationship, recognizing that
only prisoners can assess their personal safety. As Leslie told me,

> We do not make ourselves the keepers of privacy—we cannot. You know
> these women and if you can trust them, or not—you need to decide if
> you can say anything in this group.
>
> We say "you are the ultimate decision maker in terms of confi-
> dentiality, and what you are willing to risk. You know what being in
> a group in here is all about, I do not. If you do not want to disclose
> anything, that is fine." We accept all levels of participation. We do not
> push participation. They are the ultimate judges as to what risk they
> want to take.

The principles of feminist counselling (empowerment, consciousness raising and politicization) are rooted in the experiences women—not the expert
knowledges of psychology and psychiatry that have ignored the socio-political
context of women's lives: poverty, racism, isolation, and violence. However, the
application of these principles is limited within a prison bureaucracy, not because
of the inherently oppressive nature of therapeutic discourses (see Kendall in this
book), but rather because of conditions (structural and ideological) that underpin
a prison bureaucracy.

Feminist Therapists as Experts—Women as Victims

As a method of addressing the isolation and alienation experienced working inside the prison, feminist therapists have positioned themselves as experts to gain
respect and credibility. Part of this expertise is the result of the clearly different
needs of women in prison as distinct from those of women in the community.
Women prisoners present dilemmas and challenges not seen by therapists in a
community-based agency or shelter. The life experiences of many inmates encompass extreme sexual and physical violence, long-standing chronic substance
abuse problems, past psychiatric hospitalization and their own use of violence.
These conditions make building a therapeutic relationship difficult. As a result,
there is a need for specialized skills and strategies when working with women

in prison. As Kim put it:

> Sitting around sharing the warm fuzzies for six weeks is grossly inadequate compared to what women's needs really are. We must be more aware of how much more work we have to do as therapists.

Counsellors I spoke with make a clear distinction between community-level support agencies for women, such as emergency shelters and crisis lines, and the type of intensive long-term counselling that women in prison require. Women's experiences create a complex set of practical as well as emotional needs. According to counsellors like Karen, the analyses of and responses to women's behaviour must move beyond unconditional validation:

> From having worked at a rape crisis centre I think that the work of para-professional counsellors, like volunteers on a crisis line who provide support, validation and information is important. That is their role. But I think that is unfortunately what has been seen to a large extent as feminist counselling. For me that type of counselling (para-professional or volunteer) is very important and valuable, but it is different from long-term counselling.

Feminist therapy inside a woman's prison, therefore, is a compromise of feminist and clinical principles. The strategies for working with prisoners, as expressed by the therapists I spoke with, are constrained by an analytical framework that locates women's behaviours and needs in the context of victimization. I found that counsellors pursued agendas within the counselling sessions that sought to reconnect the problems of incarceration with past experiences of abuse. As such, "memory work" often took priority over other issues raised in the counselling sessions. For example, in discussing the agenda setting process, Leslie commented:

> I sometimes will contract [make an agreement] with women if I feel the session is going out of control. I will talk about prison issues, providing there is time to work on therapeutic stuff. So the first half hour is the prison, the last half hour is the emotional work, which often tends to be memory work. Also, if I believe that prison stuff is being used to avoid doing the [memory] work because it is so hard to think back on the abuse, I will push or encourage women to find out why these daily hassles are becoming so overwhelming. So I contract that I'll listen to them problem solve and bitch. We only do the therapeutic work thirty to forty percent of the time and the rest of it is institutional shit.

The result of this transformation has been the emergence of a not-so-new analytical framework about women in trouble, or what Karlene Faith describes as the "victimization-criminalization continuum" (Faith 1993a). Feminist criminologists and prison reform advocates have focused on the vulnerability of women to sexual exploitation and victimization as a means of establishing a gender-specific theory of crime (Adelberg and Currie 1987, 1993; Gelsthorpe and Morris 1990). A vulnerability focus in theorizing women's law breaking can easily become just another face of the social control of "unruly women" that has always obscured the race and class dimensions of women's lives (Faith 1993a). Beth Richie's (1996) study of criminalized Black women is critical of this analytical framework as an explanation of Black women's criminalization. She challenges the manner in which feminist theory has constructed victimization as an experience unaffected by race. Her study shows that Black women have much higher self-reported rates of victimization than white women, and Black women are more zealously criminalized than white women.

From the perspective of feminist counsellors, women's actions of violence, addiction, fraud and self-injury are justified and rationalized *only* in the context of victimization. Karen, Leslie and Anne testified to this link:

> My analysis may lead me to understand how [violent offenders] got to the point where they are buying into the male model of power over someone ... physical power which is perhaps reminiscent of what their abusers did to them.
>
> For women in prison who have survived long-term physical and sexual abuse, certain prison conditions such as lock-downs, strip searches or confinement within segregation cells can lead to self-injurious behaviour to cope with the anxiety and tensions of imprisonment or to control episodes of dissociation or numbness.
>
> I have a few clients that I see individually in prison who are very dissociative and who are multiples. That seems to be presumably from being a victim of child sexual abuse.
>
> With the women that I see in the prison, first of all they are heavy drug users, and very chronic users. Usually their problems start back at a very early age. Most of the women are survivors of some kind of multiple victimizations around sexual and physical abuse.

The severity of the impact of abuse experiences should not be minimized. However, this perspective obscures the conditions of imprisonment as a form of abuse itself and the structural realities of poverty and racism that determine also women's life chances. Margaret Shaw (1992:13) stresses that the impact of gendered realities such as childcare responsibilities, economic dependency, isolation and limited access to work experience or education upon women's vulnerability to victimization must be brought into view. Elizabeth Comack's study of provincially sentenced women in Manitoba illustrates the importance of recognizing that the way "abuse is played out in a woman's life will be very much conditioned and contoured by other factors related to her structural location in society" (Comack 1996:121). These analytical frameworks allow us to contextualize women's victimization as part of the racism and poverty that also make women vulnerable to coming into conflict with the law.

Nancy Fraser's (1989) analysis of "needs" as a political discourse is helpful here in making sense of how women prisoners' experiences of abuse have been redefined away from the socio-political reality of gender inequality and into an expert discourse. Feminist strategy for working within state institutions has been to make political claims out of women's needs for greater resources and opportunities. One danger in this strategy is that women's needs can be reinterpreted rather than satisfied. The subversive potential of feminist political claims can be dismantled; a de-politicization of women's needs and experiences can take place. This de-politicization, thus, repositions women as clients in need of expert assistance.

An example of the redefining of women's "needs" away from the context of racism, poverty and sexism is a recent study of women who have broken the law, *Voices From Within* (Sommers 1995). In her book, Evelyn Sommers dismisses the linkage between social inequality and women's lawbreaking. Instead she argues that very few women suffer from the absolute deprivation that would evoke criminal behaviour (Sommers 1995:42). For her, women's lawbreaking is rooted in needs of a different sort: the expressive need to nurture others and to compensate for the lack of nurturing relationships in their own childhood. In this way, Sommers' analytical framework depoliticizes the conditions of women's lives by dismissing the role of race, class and gender inequality. Rather, women require assistance in overcoming the damaging effects of the lack of nurturing they experienced as children. She states:

> When women are empowered through mutually empathic relationships they are able to interact with the larger world.... The women [I] interviewed understood at some level, that the vehicle to their empowerment lay in their relationships. In their struggles to empower themselves and to experience themselves as effective in the world, they attempted to retain, sustain, or protect the relationships that were exploitive, abusive, unstable.... The women were deprived of the mutual empathy needed for empowerment (Sommers 1995:120–21).

Women's accounts of abuse are in fact "subversive stories" (Ewick and Silbey 1995).They are "narratives of resistance that recount particular experiences that are rooted in and part of an encompassing cultural, material and political world" (1995:219). In a sense, by engaging with the state, women's accounts of abuse have been stripped of their "historical, institutional, and interactional setting; women have lost their subversive voice" (Ewick and Silbey 1995:211). In order to reconnect women's accounts to their subversive potential, feminist therapists need to locate these accounts in their larger socio-political context. Women in prison need resources and supports that reflect the scope and complexity of their life experiences.

Although the structural conditions of women's imprisonment in Canada have improved with the opening of the new "campus-like" facilities, the development and delivery of mental-health programs for inmates remains a difficult task. Correctional agendas of public protection, reintegration and deterrence influence the direction of therapeutic programs. Consequently, discourses of risk assessment and management have replaced the physical oppressions of the Prison for Women (see Hannah-Moffat in this book). I am concerned that selective representations of women as victims of sexual and physical violence which obscure the context of racism and poverty in women's lives have come to dominate the discourses of women in trouble. In this way, we also obscure our understanding of what causes women at risk to re-offend: the constellation of racism, poverty, violence, and isolation (see Shaw et al. 1990; Shaw et al. 1992; Sugar and Fox 1990). My concern is that the only lens through which women are being seen is that of individual victim.

The counsellors I interviewed are made complicit in this process as they negotiate a position of power within prison/justice bureaucracy. This is evident in the standards and skills of feminist therapists that have begun to reflect institutional standards of clinical training. Therefore, the inattention by the feminist counsellors to the socio-political context of race, class and gender flows from both their clinical training as psychologists and the prison setting. For example, when speaking about the needs of Aboriginal women, Leslie said:

> Aboriginal women want an elder to do the emotional work [with them], as opposed to anyone else, but it is really hard to find an elder trained in psychology or social work, or a woman. And then there is the problem of having her validated in the eyes of CSC.

Validation in the eyes of the CSC is in stark contrast to what Aboriginal women themselves have stated as important in their recovery from the traumas of abuse, poverty and addiction (e.g., healing through traditional ceremonies and support from Aboriginal people). Frank Sugar and Lana Fox's (1990) interviews with Aboriginal women under sentence highlight the detrimental impact of therapeutic programming that stigmatizes Aboriginal women as being in need of treatment. The unique experiences of Aboriginal prisoners, such as being kept at higher security classifications than non-Aboriginal women, being denied passes, and being turned down for parole applications because they have refused treatment is related to the systemic racism of the criminal justice system that has over-incarcerated Aboriginal people. These are not needs that can be remedied therapeutically. It is important to recognize therefore that the needs of Aboriginal women cannot be understood in the same context as non-Aboriginal women.

Feminist counsellors clearly present themselves as experts constructing a discourse of women's offending flowing from the impact of childhood sexual abuse. Feminist therapy in prison combines the tools and legitimacy of a clinical model with the analysis of feminist theory. However, as a consequence of working under the hegemony of correctionalism, the analytical approaches and intervention strategies of feminist therapy have shifted away from the politicized feminist principles and practices towards a more conventional clinical model.

Conclusion

Feminist therapists working with women in prison have successfully advocated that prison programming be sensitive to the impact of sexual violence on the lives of women inmates. Yet, the experiences of isolation and lack of acceptance that have characterized the work of feminist therapists working inside a prison have had a meaningful impact on how feminists are able to meet the needs of women prisoners. In dealing with their institutional constraints, feminist therapists have forged a causal link between women's victimization and both the offences women commit and their potential to re-offend. This focus of feminist therapists on the prevalence and impact of male violence in women prisoners' lives is a powerful context through which to articulate the needs of women prisoners. In my view, however, prisoner narratives of survival have become complicit in the constructing and sustaining of oppression of women. Recounting women's experiences of male violence is no longer a means of resistance and challenge to patriarchal claims to the truth of women's powerlessness, passivity and dependency. Instead, women's "subversive stories" have been redefined as a "needs" discourse that conform to the hegemony of correctionalism.

Note

1.   The names of those I interviewed have been change to ensure confidentiality and anonymity. The interviews with counsellors discussed here are taken from Balfour (1994).

Section III
Experiencing Imprisonment

Introduction

In this section the voices of women prisoners, women who have experienced imprisonment and women advocates illustrate the impact of imprisonment on women's lives, and underline the extraordinary resilience of punitive penal systems in spite of pressures to reform.

Gayle Horii uses her own experience of imprisonment in both provincial and federal Canadian prisons to challenge and question what punishment is really for and to illustrate her own resistance. She argues that the refinement of language and buildings does not improve the conditions under which women are punished. Instead, she argues that greater emphasis should be placed on education, community resources, public awareness and on limiting and minimizing the use of incarceration.

Elizabeth Comack uses the voices of women in a provincial prison, many of them Aboriginal, to explore and situate not just the extent and nature of victimization in their lives, but how it has affected and influenced them. She exposes how prisoning, or the process of becoming a sentenced prisoner, impacts on these women and, in particular, the dis-abling effects it has on their ability to overcome "their troubles."

Joane Martel examines the practice of segregation and challenges its unquestioned use as part of a wider structure of penal institutions. Based on interviews with a group of women who have experienced incarceration in isolation cells in provincial and federal prisons in Canada, she explores its impact on their lives and self-concepts, as well as the kinds of conditions under which they have had to live.

Finally, Karlene Faith and Kim Pate, two women who have played a major role in advocacy in women's prisons in Canada and elsewhere, discuss their personal reactions to their work, and how they—and their families—became involved in attempts to change and abolish prisons. While their piece does not outline the role of advocacy in a theoretical or "formal" academic way, it provides a vivid account of what being an advocate means, as well as some of the ways they have learned to be effective.

Processing Humans
Gayle K. Horii

> *Melior est justitia vere praeveniens quam severe puniens*
> "Better is justice which truly prevents than justice which severely
> punishes." (Peers 1996)

My experiences of imprisonment may be uncommon, but not the statutory
minimum term of life imprisonment[1] that I was sentenced to when I pled guilty
to second-degree murder for killing my stepmother. The differences within
the prisons and the conditions under which I survived my sentence provided
the uniqueness and also informed my criticism of imprisonment. Reading
the thoughts of Aristotle on *Equity* helped to make sense of my existence. He
said, "to ask not what a [wo]man is now but what [s]he has always or usually
been" (cited in Greenland 1987). I realized that probably less than five minutes of my life dictated my punishment, but it need not wipe out the woman
I was for forty-two years previous to my particular madness, nor dictate how
I live the remainder of my life. Because of the crime I committed, it may be
difficult to accept my assertions that I should be granted human rights and
that I could still maintain decent values. It is a most abstract conundrum, to
wrap one's mind around the fact that a killer and/or prisoner could also be a
good person. These are definitively contrary pictures—that the "self" and the
"not-self" coexist.[2] The prisoner, however, at least presents a complete picture
of herself—an open window—in stark contrast to the duplicitous organizations of B.C. Corrections (BCC) and the Correctional Service of Canada (CSC).

For seven years I stumbled over the confusing mandates of various penitentiaries. I served my first thirty-three months from April 1986 until February
1989 under maximum-security custody, including six months in a women's
prison under B.C. provincial jurisdiction. I served twenty-seven months at
the women's penitentiary, the Prison for Women (P4W), and was the lone
woman incarcerated in a men's low–medium-security penitentiary for two
months and for fifty months in a men's high–medium-security penitentiary.[3] I
also completed three years on day parole in a men's halfway house, all under
Canadian federal jurisdiction. On February 29, 1996, I was granted full parole
and returned to live in the community.

In the first few months of my incarceration, a forensic psychiatrist asked
me whether I understood just how mammoth the system was. I did not understand that his question was actually a suggestion that I not "fight the system,"
as it was a fruitless aim. Accused of being self-centred or proprietary in my
actions—at the first red herring hurled to dissuade me from protesting, I pulled
back, drawn into the accusers' scheme of distraction. However, I grasped a
stronger and better-informed sense of what is right and eventually returned

to pursue the argument. I realized that though there may not be a satisfactory outcome, I needed to see things through since the alternative of doing nothing was highly defeating and often self-deprecating. This sense of what is right was my real world dynamic and this is what I was committed to in the unreal world of prisons.

During the long ordeal of imprisonment I earned the label "political" because my interpretations of various rules and regulations were often contradictory to those espoused by guards and administrators. For example, I did not agree that the policy of segregating a woman who had slashed herself was compatible with the grounds they used: "for the maintenance of good order and discipline in the institution, or in the best interests of an inmate" Commissioner's Directives [CD] 40.1.(a)(b) 1987).[4] How could more punishment be the righteous response to a bleeding woman?

Had I been serving a shorter sentence, I may not have been quite as "political," but when serving life one is assured of only one thing: no definite release date. As a lifer, when each issue of depravity raised its ugly head, I concluded the only choices I had were to struggle now or to struggle later. Paulo Freire (1982:33–34) captured my dilemma:

> The central problem is this: How can the oppressed, as divided, inauthentic beings, participate in developing the pedagogy of their liberation? ... As long as they live in the duality in which "to be" is "to be like," and "to be like" is "to be like the oppressor," this contribution is impossible.... The solution cannot be achieved in idealistic terms. In order for the oppressed to be able to wage the struggle for their liberation, they must perceive the reality of oppression not as a closed world from which there is no exit, but as a limiting situation which they can transform.

Prisoners are automatically oppressed by the generic, absolute imbalance of power structured into prison systems. With no power, few uncoerced choices are available and that includes the choice to say, "No," which is the most terrifying consequence of being a prisoner. As my friend, Karlene Faith (1991) said, "The power to act is precisely what freedom is about, and that includes the act of refusal." Knowing the hows, whens and whys of saying "No" is an exercise in embracing the authority within oneself. One must hold tightly to the rightness, embrace the inherent rights of one's position in the human family. Only with this constant reference as the basis can any efforts towards the elimination of cruelties imposed upon prisoners by the prison authorities be challenged and potentially eliminated. "In the law, rights are islands of empowerment" (Williams 1991:233). However, in practical terms it is only through claims under the *Canadian Charter of Rights and Freedoms* that there is any possible recourse.

Prisons are administered under acts passed by parliament. The *Corrections and Conditional Release Act* (CCRA 1992) provides the regulations; however, these are interpreted by the CSC on their terms, using their methods, with impunity. The basic tools of the authorities, which are the Commissioner's Directives (CDS), the Regional Instructions (RIS) and the Standing Orders (SOS), should be mastered first by those intending to enter the fray. If Claire Culhane,[5] (founder of the Prisoners' Rights Group in Vancouver, B.C. 1975) were still with us, it would be she who could best conduct this effort. Claire understood the "language of oppression" within these tools of authority. Under law (CCRA section 98.1.2), prisoners in each penitentiary are entitled access to the CDS (Canada-wide regulations), yet they have no access to the more specific RIS or to the most pertinent interpretations, the SOS, which are penned by their own warden for the control of the prison in which they are incarcerated. Prisoners may grieve their treatment with reference to specific CDS; however, grievances are easily discounted. The final level of grievance (no further appeals) is outlined in Part III of the CCRA where sections 57–198 are devoted to the description, functions and duties of the Office of the Correctional Investigator (CI), yet the Act itself gives the CI office no clout. Neither the Commissioner nor the Chairperson of the National Parole Board is bound to act on any finding or recommendation made under this section (Part III 179.3).

Even the CI can be refused a hearing by the CSC who will simply *deny* any wrongdoing and paralyze any criticisms with tactical language designed to permanently block any requested solution. For example, in a letter to the CI, the Commissioner of Corrections pointed out:

> the significant difference between our two perspectives, a difference I am increasingly realizing explains just how difficult it is for our two agencies to agree on what needs to be done in respect of the issues you report each year. As you finalize the report, we would want to know what changes are made to any comment that is critical of CSC or any of its employees.... I do hope that these comments will have an impact on the tone and civility of your final report (cited in Stewart 1995a:113–14).

When the "final report" was issued, the Commissioner of Corrections commented: "The Correctional Service cannot accept the general negativism of the Correctional Investigator's observations" (cited in Stewart 1995a:116).

You can see why even the appointment of a woman CI to examine complaints by women prisoners cannot stop the many levels of violations against women inside penitentiaries. The CSC's appointment of Nancy Stableforth as Deputy Commissioner for Women (DCW) added another deceptive layer to the bureaucracy. Since the DCW has no line authority and no warden in any of the regional prisons for women must be accountable to her, this "rank equivalent to that of a Regional Deputy Commissioner" (CSC 1997f:1) carries no power. The wardens only "keep her fully informed" (CSC 1997f:2). Her presence is simply another screen with which the CSC may block truth-seeking inquiries—visualize the metaphor: the plexiglass partition designed by the CSC specifically to slide in front of Marlene Moore's[6] cage so that she could not throw her blood out of the cell as she slashed herself unmercifully. This also underscores the unlikelihood that any task force, document (like *Creating Choices*) or Commission of Inquiry (such as Arbour 1996) could be expected to alter the course of cruelty inside the walls. No matter how well meaning and astute the investigators are or how well-researched, witnessed and documented the incidents of cruelty are, a prison is a prison is a prison. The structure of authority that produces the oppressed and the oppressor alike[7] is the *key* to understanding the problem. Contained within this structure is the authoritative power to agendize language, which is simply another control mechanism. "To name is to know; to know is to control" (Paglia 1991:5).

The language of the oppressor, those reams of rhetoric and countless nicenellyisms that effectively mask the barbarity of imprisonment hidden behind policies fronted by cardboard people and programs are tools of this structure which must be disabled. Overlooking the covert power of euphemisms becomes blind acceptance.

The CSC applies the term "treatment" without definitional challenge. "Treatment" can include the "involuntary transfer" of women to men's maximum-security prisons where they suffer the gamut of isolationism, like the kind that provoked three women to hang themselves[8] at P4W. Meanwhile, the Task Force members met and consulted, the CSC digested *Creating Choices*, and two more women[9] enjoyed "treatment" before they eventually "strung up." Though the Daubney Committee recommended in August 1988 "that the Solicitor General convene a Task Force on Federal Female Offenders" (Recommendation 96), it took the aftermath of Marlene Moore's December 1988 suicide to finally prompt the CSC to convene the TFFSW in the spring of 1989.

There is, of course, a duality of discourse inherent in the ubiquitous structure of the CSC, which is "typically a disparity between the public transcript deployed in the open exercise of power and the hidden transcript expressed safely only offstage" (Scott 1991:73). Both transcripts must be laid open to multi-layered examination. It is through language that the process of dehumanization is enabled just as "the process of humanization is not founded in the conscious production of the necessities of life (Marx) or in the use of tools (Rousseau), but rather in the use of language" (Horster 1991:63). When the CSC uses labels like "violent," without knowing and accepting the prisoner's challenge of the contextual framework in which the so-called violence was enacted, and uses euphemisms for "programs" like "special needs units," which are really modern torture chambers, they ensure the consequences of divorced understanding accompanied by ongoing confusion and tragedy. As Williams (1991:109) states:

an accurate understanding of critical theory requires recognition of the way in which the concept of indeterminacy questions the authority of definitional cages; it is not "nihilism" but a challenge to contextualize, because it empowers community standards and the democratization of interpretation.

Most people remember the Canadian government's use of euphemisms to sanitize the killing of unarmed men, women and children during the 1991 Gulf War, calling it "collateral damage." Euphemisms used by the CSC are less understood. It is punishment, not "treatment," that is administered within fortified sensory-deprivation cells, not in "enhanced security and/or special needs units." Segregation or solitary confinement is clearly *not* a "program."

"Corrections" is plainly a misnomer since reformatories, lockups, jails, prisons and penitentiaries correct nothing, rather they err. The "correct" description for the "business" of the CSC is the Penal Services Among Canada (PSAC). Since many of the "front-line" (those who are in the front, facing the "enemy" first) workers are Public Service Alliance of Canada members, the general public would be reminded of the clear link between "jails and jobs." Should the "War Against Crime" enable the "war against prisoners"? The "management" that a "Correctional Manager, Unit Manager, or Case Manager" normally does is their own job management, not helping prisoners. The titles used in prisons should describe the function of the worker—warden, keeper/gaoler, record keeper.

Prisoner is the only correct term to describes a person locked into a cage or cell within a facility not of one's choice and whose quality of existence therein depends upon the keeper(s). A prisoner does not "live" in one's "house, home or room"—one always has the key to one's house and has the freedom to enter and leave at will, as well as the right to refuse entry to anyone. An "inmate" is an inpatient of a mental hospital, some of whom have voluntarily entered the "institution." A "client" is a person who has purchased the services of a chosen deliverer, is a patron of the one hired and/or is an outpatient—someone who chooses to be a client. The term "residents" is also an obvious corruption. "Institution" attempts to "civilize" the penitentiary since it brings to mind other familiar institutions like hospitals, the family, marriage, etc. All of these euphemisms are used to normalize and sanitize the experience of imprisonment, clearly not "normal" at all. Tragically, many prisoners internalize this fake normalcy and become totally "manageable" (institutionalized). After years inside, many are completely "programmed" (debilitated), are unable to apply critical thinking and have no understanding of "real world" inter-relationships between work, family and community. When released, many "good inmates" fail at "reintegration," returning to prison (their "normal" "homes") over and over and over again. Prison "treatment and programs" produce good "recidivists," not good citizens.

The continual use of the term "offender" justifies everything done to "an inmate in the name of the law." Yet "offender" describes a person who commits an offence—a current transgression, one that is occurring at a specific time. Charged with an offence, the person is tried and if convicted becomes a prisoner. The offence has already happened. It is in the past. The prisoner in prison is not offending. S/he has already offended. S/he may have "offended" once and may never "offend" again, but utilizing the label, "offender" permits an ongoing and static reference justifying brutalization and degradation (euphemistically referred to as "treatment of the offender").

Conduct considered outrageous in society is often rewarded in prisons. In 1991, in Saskatchewan Penitentiary, two prisoners on their knees from the effects of tear gas, died from bullets fired into their backs. The CSC called it "legal intervention." Claire Culhane called it killing. On December 31, 1987, I was suddenly woken at four in the morning by guards surrounding my bed. I was handcuffed and shackled in my pyjamas and carried to a prison van. At the Abbotsford Airport, two waiting P4W guards tossed me into a Lear Jet to fly me back to Kingston, Ontario.[10] They call this the "involuntary transfer" of an "inmate." I call this assault and violation of my prisoner's rights.

In 1994, when the Emergency Response Team (ERT), simply a gang of hooded, armed guards (often "recreational officers"), trained to inflict pain and fear, stomped into the segregation unit at P4W to carry out "cell extractions" (the enforced removal of prisoners from their cells), they easily justified their terrifying assaults on unarmed and naked women. I remember similar incidents. The last one I witnessed was on December 31, 1988. About twelve women had refused to lock into their cells on "A" range just before midnight, the customary lockup time on New Year's Eve at P4W. We normally remained just outside of our cells so that we could personally wish each other a happy new year. At about 10:45 p.m., the warden announced over the intercom that since we had been rude that day the usual 11 p.m. lockup would be enforced. Fifteen minutes before midnight, with shields and batons raised and accompanied by two Dobermans, the ERT from the Kingston Penitentiary for Men[11] stormed onto the range. The women ran into any cell they could lock into before being battered and/or bitten. Then—in the darkness and one-by-one—each woman was "cell extracted." The dull thuds of heads banging on gloved concrete, shrieks of terror and whimpers of subjection, the clanging of cell doors opening and crashing closed and the loud, hoarse-voiced commands competed with simultaneous cries of outrage from those of us already locked. We knew well the macing, stripping and degradation protocol that would follow later in segregation. The next day, all that was left of the struggle was the odd tangle of long hair entwined in bars, the reverberations of boots, batons and shields, and the disturbing memory of excited glints in the eyes behind the helmets. "A" range was locked down for the next four days while five of us went to segregation in protest.

It is a grave error to think that any commission or any other such reactive formation will stop what is termed "certain events" from occurring again at the Prison for Women (or at any other prison for that matter). One must focus less on "events" and hold fast to the criticism of the *process* that produced those events.

Consider the end results of the process of classification, one that justifies a CSC action. The Regional Facilities were initially classified as "Reception Centres" since all federally sentenced women (FSW) were to be transferred to these penitentiaries at sentence. After reneging on their 1990 promise to close P4W, the 1991 separation of mainly Aboriginal women to a "special unit," the subsequent ERT (goon squad) "interventions," hunger strikes by Aboriginal women, many lock-downs and the publicly televised ERT tapes of "certain events at P4W in 1994," women were still being held in segregation. When the courts stopped the "involuntarily transfers" of these women to isolation in the Kingston Penitentiary for Men, the CSC continued to operate P4W as a SHU-like facility.[12] On September 12, 1996, an Interim CD[13] was issued stating that "no federally sentenced woman who is designated as a maximum-security inmate will be accommodated at any of the new regional facilities for women" (CSC 1996a). This ensured that maximum-security women could not benefit from CSC's former agreement with the TFFSW to "allow female inmates to live closer to their families and friends" (*Vancouver Sun* September 26, 1990), which also meant that more women must be classified maximum security to be transferred to P4W in order to justify the employment costs of keeping P4W open.[14] This necessitated the reclassification of the regional prisons which now: "are not reception centres as provided for in paragraph 4 of CD 500." Added to this Interim CD as casually as a footnote was: "notwithstanding ... the placement or subsequent transfer of female inmates may be made to an institution *other than a women's institution.*" (CSC 1996a).

These "involuntary transfers" to men's maximum-security penitentiaries underly the alternate strategy of the CSC—if they can't classify enough women as maximum security to justify the expense of keeping P4W open, the CSC will add another label to these women to warrant their move to another men's penitentiary. However, because women, "having significant mental-health issues," may not always be classified maximum security, on September 19, 1996, a further Interim CD was issued: "Effective immediately and until further notice, the portion of Springhill Institution[15] accommodating federally sentenced women is classified as multi-level." Multi-level is the catch-all classification of any prison which permits a prisoner of any security level to be incarcerated there. An additional caveat is that a multi-level prison is required to maintain the security level of the highest classified-security prisoner held in that location. Therefore, even if a woman is considered a minimum-security risk, if she is labelled as "having a significant mental-health issue," she will be punished as if she is a maximum-security problem![16]

The above process illustrates how easily even harsher controls over women have emerged after both *Creating Choices* and the Arbour Inquiry. The imposition of the most heinous of punishments—sensory deprivation—is applied to the least powerful women who have little education and/or resources and/or few friends and/or family members powerful or astute enough to build the legal and public support required to stop this intentional barbarity. Any person or group willing to expose these immense travesties of justice committed by the csc against women could study the lives of Joey, Diane or Sandy.[17] Heaped upon their short (outside prison) life histories disfigured with abuse, are their lengthy (inside prison) histories scarred with more violations. It is beyond comprehension how these women have survived their ongoing ordeals. After years—yes—*years punished in isolation*, they are now *emotionally paralyzed*. Joey and Diane have already served more than double their minimum sentences of seven years before eligibility for day parole. Each has been incarcerated in P4W for over eighteen years on sentences of their minimum ten years to serve before eligibility for full parole! There is ample evidence to believe that Sandy was wrongfully charged and convicted of murder. The csc now considers her one of the "worst mental-health problems in the system."[18] Yet when I spoke to her just last month she sounded perfectly rational. When in P4W she was an amiable young woman whose passion was fresh-air exercise. I will never forget how her brilliant smile lit up the gym when she danced at Pow-Wows. As a child she had already endured "I think the worst history of abuse I have ever heard."[19] These three women have served the majority of their years inside under various forms of isolation. Why are they all still in maximum security held under segregated conditions?

There are also women serving life in segregation in the Burnaby Correctional Centre for Women (BCCW). Before BCCW was built I applied to BCC seven times for return from P4W but was denied. However, when BCCW opened in 1991 and its federal funding was based on the number of beds occupied by federally sentenced women (FSW), I became a sought-after commodity. My lawyer (John Conroy Q.C.) successfully obtained an injunction[20] to stop my "involuntary transfer" to this modernized gaol because the medium-security conditions I existed under at Matsqui Penitentiary were vastly superior to what I would face at BCCW, where they boast 114 surveillance cameras which observe 114 maximum-security prisoners separated into tiny units, each commanded by a plexiglass-surrounded guard station. This constant watch is aggravated by the lack of communal dining and movement resulting in the ultimate frustration and lack of resources for FSW, and the ultimate control for staff. Nearly 70 percent of the women held in this "ultra-max" prison are serving provincial sentences of less than two years, many of them serving a few months which may not be as harmful as the deprivation of those serving years in this harsh environment. Juvenile boys,[21] prisoners on remand and serving weekends, environmental protesters and now "illegal Chinese immigrants" all compete for their meagre shares of space and "resources."

Even though the planned fortress, BCCW, was still only a conceptual drawing when the TFFSW was established, FSW in B.C. were excluded from the TFFSW. The B.C. Federal Exchange of Services Agreement (BCESA), which eliminates federal standards of treatment for FSW, was not signed until March 29, 1990. *Creating Choices* was published a few days later. In 1988, while incarcerated in P4W, I was told that B.C. is simply too far away from Ottawa for the CSC to be "concerned about"—out-of-sight, out-of-mind. Nothing has changed. FSW in B.C. still have no power and absolutely no choices. BCCW however, retains the right to "involuntarily transfer" FSW to P4W and/or to a men's federal penitentiary as they did in July 1999.[22]

Certainly *Creating Choices* stands as a classic document, but its power is limited to that of any document produced by any group with no authority under law to enforce their recommendations. Open to the discretion of the CSC, the bastardizations of the recommendations were slickly accomplished. Perhaps if the TFFSW had referred to the authority of the Daubney Committee's suggestions in *Taking Responsibility* (1988), the Task Force might have enlisted the potency of a parliamentary committee. Instead, the CSC used *Creating Choices* to conveniently and effectively usurp the authority of the Daubney Committee's recommendations, in particular the focus on community placements for FSW. The CSC noted:

> The 1988 report of the Standing Committee on Justice and Solicitor General ... takes a rare view of the situation facing federally-sentenced women ... [and] 17 of its 97 recommendations to improvements [related to them. One recommendation was that] ... no further prison construction take place without establishing halfway houses for women at the same time [and another was for the] closure of the Prison for Women in the next five years.... [The CSC added that] it is not clear at this point whether the government will formally respond to the Daubney report. (Solicitor General Canada 1989:8–9)

At the time of this writing there are no halfway-house beds specifically for any FSW west of Ontario, a fact that is explained by the lack of funding for this type of arrangement. There is funding for inside contracts, which many professionals continue to spar for. To those of us inside who are designated "subjects for research," we find that "The scholar appears as an authoritative (and often well paid) voyeur bound in hierarchical relations to her relatively impoverished subject" (cited in Duggan 1992:27).

The priority prison axiom, "for the good order of the institution" belies the real mission (the private discourse) of the "correctional" authorities—growth of their "industry," job security and safety, and concealment. Those employed by and under contract for the CSC must promise that "nondisclosure of wrongs," termed "confidentiality," is an acceptable condition for employment. This enables the continuity of some of the worst crimes to be committed, in the name of the state.

Never underestimate the gluttony of "correctional" enterprises. The CSC has ready access to funding and is only accountable (audited) every five years.

They need not wait for approval from anyone before acting. Witness the rapid April 1995 completion in P4W of "a new, higher-security segregation unit … of 10 cells with steel doors … at a cost of $750,000" (*Kingston Whig Standard* April 20, 1995) *before* the Arbour Inquiry was announced. Along with the existing 22 segregation cells and the 25 "separated" cells on "B" range, there are now 57 segregation cells, more than 42 percent of the 135 single-bed capacity of P4W! Are we expected to agree that women are ten times more "dangerous" than men incarcerated in the maximum-security Archambault Penitentiary which has 16 segregation cells (less than 4 percent) out of its 425 single bed capacity? Or could it be that the examples of unarmed women with obviously indefatigable courage (enough to protest their violations in the face of the overwhelming odds of impending physical assault) must be obliterated?

The military-control model (which need only be adjusted and amended to computerized requirements) was designed by and for the patriarchal, male-dominated culture and is as appropriate for attending to the "needs" of women in prison as is circumcision. Attack the processes to illustrate that Band-Aids do not stop the jugular flow. Open doors to the solutions available within true spiritual endeavours and feminist intellectual analyses. Declare that language and behavioural euphemisms strategized to disarm advocates for justice will be obliterated.

Understand that the "correctional" bastions will only use inquiries, commissions, task forces, etc. as smoke screens to increase their numbers and their budgets. Stop the construction of more maximum-security units, the addition of more security devices, of more barriers in the bureaucratic maze, of more levels of "authority." Understand that reform of any corrupt enterprise will only result in reformed corruption. Enlist the weapons of critical education, dissent and protest to decriminalize and to decarcerate wherever possible.

Community resources, education, legal and policy initiatives and public awareness could begin an end to the incarceration of the majority now imprisoned and perhaps put an end to incarceration as a business. Keep constant reference to the proceedings from the International Conferences on Penal Abolition (ICOPA).[23] No battle with the military can be won without a plan of logistics or nothing will change for prisoners except, "now they are modern, now they wear polyester" (Horii 1993).

Put your faith and your trust in the world circles of humanitarians, scholars, creative and strong feminists, Constitutional experts, socio-political activists and penal abolitionists. Their analyses could best ensure both humane treatment within the walls while formulating a practical strategy to end the use of imprisonment as the first reaction to "criminal behaviour." A few of the experts come quickly to mind because I know them and their work well: the indomitable Des Turner[24] and Wayne Northey,[25] Karlene Faith and Liz Elliott,[26] Kim Pate and Patricia Monture-Angus, John Conroy[27] and Sasha Pawliuk,[28] and June Callwood.[29] They continue to serve as role models for me as I[30] continue to serve my life sentence reporting to a CSC parole officer.

Notes

1. *Criminal Code of Canada,* section 235—with ten years served before eligibility for full parole.

2. The idea that the self and the not-self coexist was adapted from the chapter heading by Clifford Geerz (1988) "Us/Not Us: Benedict's Travels." See pages (on self) 1–11, 14–16, 87, 92, 95–98, and pages 45, 46–48, 69–71, 106–13, 116–23, 131–35, 143 and 147 (on other and otherness).

   In many respects I write like an anthropologist attempting to describe "another" from an ethnographer's viewpoint. However, in the same instance, one understands that one is imposing one's own experience on the analysis, either unwittingly or purposefully. Of course, in my case, I am both subject and reviewer. It is this paradox (actually in reverse) that describes my attempts to expose the realities of imprisonment to an audience that has never been imprisoned while also attempting to appear unbiased so that the arguments may be more readily accepted as, at least, logical.

3. With the exception of Mary B. and Mary A., who were fasting in protest of their incarceration in the Spring of 1990 in Matsqui Penitentiary for Men, Abbotsford, B.C.

4. 1987-05-01 *Administrative Consolidation Penitentiary Service Regulations (PSR)* In 1992, this PSR was replaced by *CCRA. 31.(3)(a-c)* adding "and the institutional head is satisfied that there is no reasonable alternative to administrative segregation."

5. Claire Culhane, September 2, 1918–April 28, 1996. Her work was honoured with the following: Marlene Moore Award (1995), "for leadership in the field of community-based programs in Canada, or for furthering the goals of deinstitutionalization, or for outstanding service within a community-based program which has had significant impact on the lives of the individuals who have been helped" (Ontario Board of Parole); Canada Volunteer Award Medal & Certificate of Honour (1995); and Member of the Order of Canada (1995). We miss her so. See her several books: *Why is Canada in Vietnam* (1972), *Barred From Prison* (1979), *Still Barred From Prison* (1985), *No Longer Barred From Prison* (1991). Also see Lowe (1992).

   Claire suffered a heart attack on January 2, 1995, and though under strict orders to cease her activities, she continued her work and while working on a crucial project—to close down all segregation units—she suffered a stroke and died on Sunday, April 28, 1996.

6. Witnessed by myself November 24, 1988, in segregation at P4W. Nine days later, on December 3, 1988, Marlene choked herself to death in the prison hospital. See Kershaw and Lasovitch (1991).

7. Zimbardo's 1971 experiment at Stanford University Scheduled for two weeks using student participants to role-play prisoners and prison guards, the experiment was halted in six days over fears that the violence which developed would escalate to cause serious and lasting injury, both physically and mentally.

8. Pat Bear, March 1989; Sandy Sayer, October 1989; Marie Ledoux, February 1990.

9. Careen Daignault, September 1990; Johnie Neudorf, November 1990.

10. From Mission Medium-Security Penitentiary for Men, Mission, B.C.

11. The Kingston Penitentiary for Men is located across the street from P4W, which enables quick access to the ERT (guards eager for stimulation from their usual

boredom).

12. Special Handling Unit—super-maximum security for men.

13. The information on the Interim CD was obtained from a dated memo and does not have a CD number reference.

14. As of November 1999, there were twelve women incarcerated in P4W and about fifty staff members.

15. Men's maximum-security penitentiary, Nova Scotia. Federally sentenced women are also isolated in the men's Regional Psychiatric Centre, Saskatoon, Sask., Saskatchewan Penitentiary, Sask. and St.-Anne-des-Plaines Institution, Ste-Anne-des-Plaines, PQ.

16. Kim Pate, Executive Director of CAEFS, has ably and inclusively addressed these dysfunctional processes and continues to do so. In particular see: CAEFS 1995, 1998.

17. Further information may be obtained by your request in writing, accompanied by letter of introduction, upon receipt of which I will contact the women for their consent to be contacted.

18. As expressed to me by a CSC employee during a break from proceedings at the National Stakeholder's Meeting, April, 1998, Montreal.

19. As expressed to me in confidence.

20. As of December 1, 1999, my *Charter* writ claiming discriminatory treatment by the CSC is still active and we await our date in court. I have two outstanding Canadian Human Rights complaints (filed in 1988 at P4W and 1992 at Matsqui Penitentiary). Decisions are pending subject to the outcome of my trial.

21. The boys were transferred out of BCCW in 1998 but that doesn't mean that they won't be returned at some point in the future.

22. As the injunction to stop this "involuntary transfer" to Saskatchewan Penitentiary for men was being prepared, the woman signed a waiver on July 22, 1999, in exchange for a guarantee from the warden that she would be returned to BCCW in three months. That guarantee is now disclaimed.

23. ICOPA I, Toronto 1983. See: Margaret Wilson 1931. *The Crime of Punishment* (as suggested by scholar, Brian D. MacLean in *We Who Would Take no Prisoners* (1993). ICOPA IX was held in 1999 in Toronto. Contact Rittenhouse: ritten@interlog.com.

24. Social activist par excellence who continues to rally support from Archbishop Michael Peers, Primate of the Anglican Church of Canada, "Des" would be a valuable contributor to any national community committee in liaison with many organizations such as the Mennonite Central Committee, the Quaker Committee on Jails and Justice and the Church Council on Justice & Corrections.

25. Former editor of "*The Accord*," Mennonite Central Committee, social activist and penal abolitionist.

26. Ph.D., Criminology, SFU. Early work with John Howard and E. Fry Societies, Editor of the Prisoners' Journal on Prisons. Board member of the West Coast Prison Justice Society, Abbotsford, B.C. Watch for her publications.

27. John W. Conroy, Q.C., Chair, Canadian Bar Association, Conroy and Co. Barristers & Solicitors, Abbotsford, B.C. Among many landmark cases in prison law, see most recent *Landry* v. *Regina; Winters* v. *Regina* and series of submissions by the Committee on Imprisonment and Release of the National Criminal Justice Section of the Canadian Bar Association.

28. LLB., formerly with Prisoners' Legal Services, Abbotsford, B.C. Board member,

West Coast Prison Justice Society, c/o Conroy and Co., 2459 Pauline St. Abbotsford, B.C. V2S 3S1. See her most recent Charter challenge: *Alcorn et al.* v. *The Commissioner of Corrections et al.* (10 March 1999).

29. Former *Globe and Mail* columnist, VISION TV host of "Callwood's National Treasures," humanitarian, author of many books, friend of Marlene Moore, and founder of the Casey House, first hospice in Canada for AIDS patients.

30. Gayle K Horii, c/o The Coordinator, Strength In SISterhood (SIS) Society, 6038-189th St. Surrey, B.C. V3S 8A2.

The Prisoning of Women
Meeting Women's Needs
Elizabeth Comack

Feminist criminologists have enjoined us to counter the invisibility of women in prison. We need to hear their stories. Who are these women? What have their lives been like? In the fall of 1992, I interviewed twenty-four women who were incarcerated at the provincial prison for women in Manitoba. My previous research had uncovered that the majority (78 percent) of women admitted to this prison had histories of physical and sexual abuse. I was interested in exploring this issue further in terms of the (inter)connections between the women's abuse experiences and their law violations. These interviews—and the lessons I learned from the women—formed the basis of a book entitled *Women in Trouble* (Comack 1996).

Listening to the women's stories allowed me to appreciate some of the structural constraints and limited choices which the women confront in their lives. In addition to their abuse experiences, many of the women were struggling with the work of raising their children, more often than not under conditions of extreme economic hardship. Most had little educational or vocational training, so job prospects were either limited or non-existent. Many of the women were Aboriginal, and came from communities where colonization had left deep scars. In the face of such obstacles, the ability of a woman to resolve her troubles seemed formidable. It led me to question whether incarcerating these women served any *benefit*—to the women themselves, to their families, to their communities or to the larger society.

Most research in criminology has focused on the "act" of imprisonment and questioned whether it is fulfilling goals like denunciation (making lawbreakers "pay" for their crimes) or rehabilitation (changing the persona of the lawbreaker so that crime is reduced). This approach is one which assumes that prison is the "right" response to people in trouble with the law, and so focuses on how well a particular prison regime is meeting its stated objectives. In contrast, I am interested in what I call the *prisoning* of women, a term I use to get at the process of incarceration and women's experiences of confinement. This approach does not assume that prison is the "right" response to women in trouble. Rather, it questions whether the needs of these women are being met by incarcerating them. This involves adopting the standpoint of the women prisoners and asking: does prisoning enable women to resolve their troubles? Or does it represent a deepening of their troubles?

During my meetings with the women back in 1992, we spoke about their prisoning experiences. In what follows, I will share some of that discussion, as well as some of the insights which emerged from it. This will be my main purpose. But I also want to bring the discussion into the present. Since doing the work for *Women in Trouble*, a number of developments have occurred that raise serious concerns about the prisoning of women in my province.

Life Within the Walls

The women I met with were brought to prison for a range of different actions: writing bad cheques, getting into fights in a bar, killing a rapist, driving while suspended or impaired, stealing makeup, setting fire to a house to escape from abusive parents, shoplifting to buy drugs, robbing a gas station, fighting with family members, defaulting on a fine payment, assaulting an abusive partner … and the list goes on. While the factors and conditions which prompted those actions may be very different from one woman to the next, all of the women shared in common their experience of confinement within the prison walls.

The prison where the women were incarcerated was built in 1893 for male prisoners. It is currently the only facility in the province for women prisoners, and has a capacity of forty-four women. The fact that this is a prison does not escape anyone who visits there. It is a large, imposing structure with limestone walls and barred windows. "Gaol" is carved into the stone above the main entrance. Once you enter the front door, there are a series of barred doors and gates. Another series of key-operated gates and doors inside the main entrance lead to the cells and dormitories. The kitchen and dining facilities are located in the basement. Three rooms on the second floor serve as classrooms, meeting rooms and the recreation area. An interview room is located on the main floor inside the doors that lead to the cells. The visiting area is just inside the front entrance. The only outdoor space consists of a small yard surrounded by a high chain-link fence (most of the women are allowed outside for thirty minutes a day).

Although the prison underwent extensive remodelling and fire upgrading during 1979 and 1980, the deteriorating condition of the building was not lost on many of the women. Margret's response was to find humour in the situation:[1]

> The big joke with Sandy, the girl who sleeps beside me (laugh)—the pipes for the toilet upstairs are directly over her bed, okay? And every night when we lay down—like last night I said to her: "So I wonder how you'd look with raw sewage all over your head?" (laugh) I mean, that's the only way to think of it, eh? Cause even now these are old pipes with—I think paint is holding them together (laugh)—Sandy's going: "Yeah. If they go now I don't know where I'm going to move my bed." (laugh) There's nowhere to move it!

The women were most likely to raise the issue of prison conditions in relation to "the hole"—segregation cells located in the basement. There are no windows and the cells are lit with bright fluorescent fixtures which makes it difficult to maintain a sense of time: "sometimes it would be seven o'clock thinking it was midnight." Women could be sent to the hole for a number of different infractions: violating the conditions of a Temporary Absence, fighting or conflicts with other women prisoners or being found in possession of contraband (drugs). Margret's description of her experience in segregation sounds much like a scene from a Hollywood B movie:

> I got thrown in the hole for fifteen days a week after I got here. And I—it was just totally—I just couldn't believe what they were doing to me. I was—you know, an ice cream pail? I was given an ice cream pail of water and I had to wash. It was like, okay, I had to wash and that was also my drinking water, twenty-four hours worth of it. You only get water every twenty-four hours. There's a camera that watches you. You go to the bathroom, everything, in front of this camera. And they slide food under the door, they slide you this plate.

For most of the women, the age and condition of the prison was not as significant as the experience of being in prison. Agnes described her feelings:

> (How do you find being in here?)
> You have different feelings about it. It's mostly, like—I was just thinking about that today, and yesterday—last night? Mostly had some feelings.
> (What kind of feelings?)
> Like there's, like uh, you're confused, and some women here are so closed, if they feel lonely or really lonesome. Like, I don't know, it's a—awful feeling.
> (Feeling alone?)
> Yeah.

Alyson spoke about the confinement:

> (What's the worst thing about being here?)
> Being locked up. So then you can't go out whenever you want to. That's one thing I hate. 'Cause I always, like, I'm always outdoors when I'm at home, after I'm finished cleaning up inside or cooking. I always go out, be outside, you know, and do something.

The experience of being incarcerated had caused anxiety attacks for Jessica:

> (Do you have any health problems?)
> Well, I have a (pause) I don't know, I get this, like a, they say it's a, like, when I was talking to one of the girls, they said I have anxiety attacks. You know, my heart beats real fast, you wanna panic and you panic it's even worse. You come into a sweat. And I told the

nurse downstairs. She says it's only stress. You know this, it's been happening to me all the time, eh. It started when I was, first when I was in the Remand Centre.

The women also commented on the meanings attached to their incarceration. Like several other women, Margret drew the distinction between having her body locked up and maintaining control over her mind:

They can lock me up. They can lock up my body. They can take away all my freedom. What's inside of me—no, what's inside my head—is mine. They can't take that. They can't lock it.

Margret also expressed concern about the long-term effects of prisoning on women:

I don't think women should be incarcerated. Seriously. I see too much destruction. I see these women losing their children permanently. I see homes falling apart. I see women go to pieces. I see so many things happening.

Judith saw prison as a game:

(How do you find things in here?)
Things in here. Now that's a tough one. (laughing) Things in here are, no, it's, it's short and sweet this place. This place is a game. One game. You don't go by the game, you lose.
(What are the rules of the game?)
Go along with everything.

The women's comments reflect their awareness of the punitive nature of the prison regime. This is, after all, a jail. It should come as no surprise that the women experience it as such. Yet, it is within this same context that attempts are made to meet the women's needs.

Meeting the Women's Needs

The women enter the prison with, as one of the women put it, "miles of problems." They bring with them their problems with drugs and alcohol use, their histories of violence and abuse, their lack of education and job skills and their struggles to provide and care for their children. As well, the majority of the women who pass through the prison gates are Aboriginal. In 1992, there were a number of programs and resources made available to the women, many of which were being provided by outside individuals, groups or organizations.[2] In light of these different programs and resources, women like Donna saw prison as offering the potential for change: "Jail is a time out. To think what you've done, to try to work at yourself, try to make yourself better, you know?" Yet, others commented on the difficulties encountered in trying to change their lives while in prison. As Susan said: "I try to, um, get all my problems solved in here. But it seems like every time I do, it's just another problem after another problem. It's pretty hard." Some of the women found the different programs to be helpful. Yet, for the most part, the women were critical of the programs. Barbara saw little point in even attending programs:

> I don't really get into much of the programs here cause I'm not into that stuff. I know my counsellor keeps telling me to go to programs and I tell her "What's the use?" I don't want to sound lazy but, programs don't seem to be helping me. I just come—I go in as the same person, I leave as the same person.

Others, like Kelly, were more critical of the programs themselves:

> All they really do here is teach you how to be in jail. They don't teach you how to survive on the outside once you get out.

While the programs were the subject of the women's critiques, the problems encountered in trying to meet the women's needs run much deeper. Many of the staff were seen as earnest and sincere in their efforts to support the women, but at the same time the women were cognizant of the enormity of that project. Eileen commented:

> People like [the program co-ordinator], [the Abuse Hurts casework-er], a couple of the other counsellors—they care, and they do try really hard but they're, they're so limited in what they can do. And they have so many people that need help. It's very hard.

Part of the difficulty stems from the fact that the women's troubles have their source and basis *outside* the prison walls. Confined within the prison, the women do not have the power or autonomy to attend to those troubles. With regard to drug dependency, for instance, Ruth commented:

> I don't think a drug program works in here.... I don't find it helps. Like, I took the drug program and it was all right and everything but, nothing, you know, of course, you're in here, you're not going to be able to touch anything. It's out there, you know, when you get out. There's a difference.

As well, confinement in prison means separation from the women's potential sources of support. Sally, who was in prison on remand, remarked:

> I am afraid, I'm afraid of, (pause) of the judge turning around and looking at me and telling me that I have to spend the rest of my life in jail, or, you know, anything for that matter, any time, any length of time.... And I'm (pause) I have a lot of support on the outside, like there's um, my family, and my husband's family is all behind me, my friends and their families, they're all behind me, and I'm afraid that if I end up doing time, that I'm gonna lose all that support, or that I'm gonna lose my husband and my family or something, you know?

One of the most significant barriers to meeting the women's needs is the prevailing atmosphere of distrust. Because the staff themselves work within the regulated framework of power and control, many of the women felt that they could not trust the staff. Sally explains:

> You have to have somebody to talk to that you can trust that isn't gonna say anything at all. At no point and time. Unless it is to your own benefit, or to your own well-being. But otherwise, you know, some staff—there are a few staff that are real nosey. And they want to know what's going on. You know, it's just, I don't even talk to my own counsellor—I don't talk to my case manager because I don't know what she's gonna say to who. Yeah, so I don't, I don't bother.

This atmosphere of distrust can easily spill over to the women's relationships with each other. Although women serving long sentences commonly form trusting relationships, when women are doing short time, they often extend their distrust to include the women with whom they are incarcerated. Louise and Judith both commented on this issue:

> You can't trust friends here. (pause) And even—even if you have a close friend, they even stab you in the back. That's why I try not to get close to anybody here, or I don't want to get into arguments or fights. Just come here and do your time.

> (Is there a big problem with gossip?)
> In here? *Oh yeah*, it's *wicked* in here. Oh yeah.
> (I wonder why. Is it something to do, do you think?)
> Oh yeah, it's something to do, something to pass time, you know?

Under the conditions imposed by confinement, gossip and talk among the women become a way of stealing power from one another. In this sense, the gossip and the lack of trust it generates confront the women as yet another form of abuse. Silence is their way of coping with it.

The "miles of problems" which the women bring with them to the prison, coupled with the loneliness, the anxiety and the climate of distrust they encounter when they get there, leaves one wondering: how is it possible for women to resolve their troubles within the confines of the prison walls? For too many of the women, the experience of prisoning becomes just one more thing they have to contend with in the process of overcoming the different problems, conflicts and dilemmas they have previously encountered in their lives. Yet, it would be a mistake to conclude that the experience of confinement has offered *no* benefits to the women. And here lies the irony: for too many of the women, it was only after they were caught up in the criminal justice system that they were given access to the resources they needed to begin to resolve their troubles.

Sometimes this meant access to economic resources. Under a community-work program, prisoners could gain employment at local businesses. At harvest time, for example, local market gardens paid the women piece work for picking vegetables and fruit. This not only took the women out of the prison setting for extended periods, it also provided them with a source of income. Beth, for example, spoke of being able to meet her children at a local shopping centre on a temporary pass so that she could buy them clothing with her earnings.

Sometimes this meant putting Aboriginal women in contact with their indigenous culture. Marilyn told me:

> I'm getting back into my Indian culture. There's stuff I missed. There's sweats almost every week so that helps. I went to two of them already. They've helped. It's just like going, and being in that sweat is just like being in church, like, our church. You pray for anything you want in there. And there's one round that you pray for your soul.

Sometimes this meant providing counselling for problems with alcohol use. For example, when I asked Tina if such resources were available on her reserve, she responded:

> Well, they have a worker there but she doesn't do much—just sits around—waiting for a *miracle* to happen. (laughs) Sorry! (laughing)

And sometimes—in spite of the climate of distrust that prevails—this meant finding someone they could talk to and share their troubles with. One of the most significant revelations to emerge in the women's accounts is that so many of them only began dealing actively with their abuse histories after they came in contact with the criminal justice system. For Eileen, it was a question posed by a probation officer:

> The probation officer I had was really good. I could talk to her and she uh, in fact, I was lucky to get her because I probably wouldn't have started talking about this at all if I hadn't gotten her, you know?

> That was just one of the questions she asked: "Were you abused as a child?" And that just opened up a whole doorway for me because nobody had ever asked me that before. (laughs) So, and she made me talk about it, you know? I went to see her, usually you go maybe twice for a pre-sentence report. I went to see her ten times. And she helped me a lot.

For other women, imprisonment has put them in contact with the workers from the local women's shelter, a resource which is inaccessible to women from many rural and northern communities.

By far, one of the greatest ironies to emerge from the women's accounts is that, for some women, prison has become a safe place, a temporary refuge from their violence-filled lives. When I asked Tina (whose troubles revolved around an abusive relationship with her partner) how she found being in prison, this was her response: "I like it. (laughs) At least it's safe for a while. (laughing) Nobody's pestering me." Tina also found that her health improved while in prison, as her blood pressure went down to normal levels.

In these various ways, prison has proved to be a benefit to some women, but often with great costs—not the least of which is to their children's well being. Twenty of the twenty-four women I met with were mothers of young children. Some of the women made arrangements to have relatives care for their children. Sometimes this option was unavailable—or unwise. Margret, for instance, spoke about how her children had returned from visits with relatives with evidence of abuse on their bodies:

> The last time [my son] came back he had bruises here, from someone pinching him like this. I took him to a doctor. I didn't know what the hell it was, but I knew either somebody had hit him or someone was pulling at his ears.... That was twice that happened to him out there. Like, a second time he came back and, um, he had burn marks right here? From coffee—coffee burns. And I didn't know about it.... We took him to CPU [Child Protection Unit] and I got it reported right away. 'Cause I didn't want Welfare to think I was doing it, you know?

Lacking other alternatives, children would be placed in foster care. This became an issue of concern for women like Christine, whose own experience of foster care had been far from the ideal: "I told them I don't want him in a foster home 'cause I was really scared cause I was abused at foster homes."

Summing Up

The women whose voices have been heard here have been imprisoned for a wide range of actions and behaviours. While the pains of imprisonment may be augmented by fears for their children's safety, separation from family and other sources of support, or the prospect of a lengthy sentence, the experience of prisoning as a form of punishment is one which all the women shared. Yet, while many of the women expressed their desire to change, attempting to do so while imprisoned is a daunting task. Indeed, it would be ludicrous to expect one institution in society to provide the range of resources required to resolve women's troubles. It would be especially ludicrous to hold such expectations of an institution which has as its primary purpose the punishment of its clients. In this same context, one could argue that a basic component in the effort to meet the women's needs is the provision of facilities and resources which would enable their empowerment. The majority of these women have histories of physical and sexual abuse. One of the key features of abuse is the taking of control from the person subject to it. For women to begin to heal from those experiences, they need to gain control over their lives. How is this possible in an institution which, by its very nature, endeavours to control the women's lives in almost every detail?

Noting that women's prisons "appear to accomplish the opposite of what is intended," the Aboriginal Justice Inquiry of Manitoba recommended that the prison "is an inappropriate facility and should be closed" (Hamilton and Sinclair 1991:501, 503). While the Commissioners were critical of the existing programs and the remote location of the prison, the women's accounts of their prison experience suggest that the problems are more systemic. No matter how well intentioned the staff may be or how adequate the programs offered, the fact remains that this is a prison—with all the discipline and control inherent in a "total institution." In this respect, prisoning—like abuse generally—represents the taking of control from the woman who experiences it. That some of the women have begun to resolve their troubles while incarcerated has, in large part, been *in spite of* rather than *because of* their experiences of confinement.

Looking to the Future?

It has been seven years now since I met with the women at the prison. Since that time, there have been a number of developments which lead me to be very sceptical about the prospects of realizing a sea change in how we respond to the situation of women in trouble. Some of these developments are broader ones. The cutbacks to social programs and community resources have continued to have their effects, undermining the vitality of local communities and people's ability to cope with hardship. Life is getting harsher; anger and frustration are mounting. For many inner-city kids in Manitoba, gangs have become an attractive solution for meeting their social needs. Meanwhile, talk of "getting tougher on crime" seems to be the main political response to allaying the public's heightening fears.

Women in Trouble came off the press in April of 1996. Just a few weeks later, a riot broke out at the Headingly Jail, the main provincial institution for men in Manitoba. Prisoners set fires and destroyed one wing of the prison, causing $3.5 million in damages. Seventeen guards and thirty-one inmates were injured. The subsequent report blamed the riot on a "systemic malaise" within the prison system and called for increased spending on social and economic development to alleviate the poverty which is at the root of crime (Krueger 1996:A4). Nevertheless, one of the immediate outcomes of the riot was the transfer of all women from the Remand Centre in Winnipeg in order to make room for the men while the prison was being repaired. This led to severe overcrowding at the women's prison, as the number of women rose to over seventy.

Conditions at the women's prison have not improved since that time, and the situation is not expected to ease until at least October of 2000 when new facilities for male prisoners will be ready. The overcrowding has meant that many of the programs offered to the women in 1992 are now unavailable, as staff resources are devoted to managing the more immediate needs of the women (such as the scheduling of mealtimes and finding enough places for them to sleep). Because of concerns over rivalling gangs (who identify by their clothing), the prison has instituted uniforms for the women (green for the general population and pink for the women who work in the kitchen), and the women are not allowed to mix.

By the spring of 1999, things were looking even worse. The Native Elder had retired, the woman who ran a program on Sunday evenings had taken ill, the Elizabeth Fry Society was in the midst of a funding shortage and disillusioned staff were asking for transfers to other (men's) institutions. In response, I offered to organize a book drive and to visit the prison every two weeks with two of my graduate students. Our offer was welcomed by both the prison staff and the women prisoners. Given the absence of programming, the idea was to give some respite from the everyday monotony for the women. At their suggestion, we played bingo. The prizes (funded by royalties from the book) were items the women needed—shampoo, socks, hair brushes, tooth brushes and the like.

While bingo may have helped in the short term, it obviously is not going to solve the long-term, systemic problem confronting the imprisonment of women in the province: the overcrowding, the inadequate prison conditions, the overworked and harried staff, the lack of programming. To a large extent, women in prison continue to remain invisible. Yet, while fixing the current problems may make prison a "better" place, it is questionable whether the actual experience of prisoning will be altered. Ultimately, the sources for change involve giving women in trouble access to choices and opportunities that exist outside the prison walls; it is in their own communities where real, substantive changes need to occur. As Eileen commented to me in 1992, prison may have provided her with the resources she needed to resolve her troubles, "but I shouldn't have to come to jail to get it." And she is right. That prisoning marks their first access to resources for resolving troubles tells us how socially impoverished life is for these women.

Notes

1. Pseudonyms are used throughout this discussion to maintain confidentiality. I have used the names of women with whom I share close relationships (my daughter, mother, sisters, friends) in an effort to combat the "othering" of women in prison.
2. These included: drug and alcohol counselling (Alcoholics Anonymous and Narcotics Anonymous), Adult Basic Education courses, community work programs, a parenting skills course and courses on anger management and assertiveness training. A Native Elder conducted a sharing circle and sweet grass ceremonies and was available for individual counselling. Church services, religious teaching and individual counselling were provided by the prison chaplain. Caseworkers in the prison worked with the women to develop their individualized programs and pre-release plans, and the Elizabeth Fry Society would visit the prison regularly to meet with the women on a one-to-one basis. There was a full-time nurse on staff and a psychiatrist who attended the prison one morning a week. One of the caseworkers ran a program called "Abuse Hurts," which consisted of two parts: a one-day information session and a group which met one evening a week for seven weeks. Women could also request a referral to meet with one of the workers from the local women's shelter.

Women in the "Hole"
The Unquestioned Practice of Segregation[1]
Joane Martel

Nowadays, segregation is a prison practice used for separating and isolating a prisoner from the general inmate population for various reasons ranging from safety (administrative segregation) to punitive purposes (disciplinary segregation). This model of imprisonment was developed by the Quakers of Pennsylvania in the late eighteenth century. Since then, solitary confinement has become a pivotal component of prisons' institutional framework in North America, being institutionalized as a habitual practice. In other words, through its repeated use, segregation has become entrenched in prisons as a frame of reference to the point where it is now an unquestioned way of doing things in prison, to the point where it has developed its own "regime of truth" (Garland 1990:4). This regime constantly reaffirms the rightness of the carceral framework by obscuring all evidence of its counter-productive effects. This regime has created a sense of its own inevitability, as if prisons could not possibly be envisaged without segregation cells.

Today, the apparent permanence of segregation as an assumed way of doing things in prison has relieved us of the need to reflect deeply on it. As a matter of fact, very few studies have recently been conducted on segregation (some of the few exceptions are Canada 1997; Motiuk and Blanchette 1997; Zinger and Wichmann 1999), especially on the segregation of women prisoners. Another notable exception is Shaylor (1998) who studied the conditions of solitary confinement for African American women in a U.S. prison. Apart from the meager research, policy-making endeavours pertaining to the segregation of women prisoners have also been rather scarce. The Correctional Service of Canada (CSC) has only recently started to consider the impact of segregation on federally sentenced women. This interest is closely tied to its current efforts at implementing the "women-centred" correctional philosophy (TFFSW 1990).

To partially fill this gap, a recent field study was undertaken with twelve women who experienced segregation while in federal or provincial prisons in the Canadian Prairies (Martel 1999). The findings indicate that the women in our sample spent more time in segregation in provincial prisons (the average for all women interviewed is approximately thirteen months of cumulated "stays" in segregation) than in federal institutions (an average of eight months). In spite of its limited sample, this difference raises several concerns about segregation in provincial prisons. First, incarceration in provincial prisons is relatively short (less than two years) and, second, it is generally imposed for minor offences, often for first-time offenders. Third, all women go through the provincial carceral system before sentence or while waiting for an appeal and, fourth, most women incarcerated in provincial prisons are held in maximum-security conditions (Finn et al. 1999). Finally, many more women serve their sentence in such prisons rather than in federal facilities. In 1996–97, while 182 women were admitted to federal institutions, 9,720 were sentenced admissions[2] to provincial or territorial institutions (Canada 1998a:53).

In view of the fact that women's imprisonment in provincial prisons in Canada has generally been neglected in the literature (some of the few exceptions are Imbleau 1987; Shaw 1994b; Comack 1996), and since a large majority of our participants have experienced segregation in provincial prisons at one point, a more systematic look at this issue is a pressing matter. In this paper, I will document several aspects of the practice of segregation in provincial and federal prisons in the Canadian Prairies as well as the women's experiences of this practice. Specifically, I will examine living conditions in segregation, how women resist these conditions, and the impact of segregation on women. In the concluding remarks, I will argue not only that the practice of segregation with women prisoners ought to be abolished in provincial prisons, but also that segregation has no place in the new federal women's prisons.

Conditions of Segregation

It is altogether difficult to access the rationales on which segregation is based today, especially if one strictly looks to the institutional framework for answers. In the Quakers' original prison model, the primary objective of solitary confinement was clearly to emphasize and promote meditation and repentance for prisoners. It was hoped that if left to themselves with little or nothing to distract them, prisoners would eventually reflect on their crime and feel remorse. Today, segregation has two legislated purposes in federal corrections. The objective of *administrative* segregation is to prevent an individual from interacting with the general prison population. It may be ordered on four possible grounds: 1) for the security of the institution; 2) for the safety of any person within the institution; 3) for the prisoner's own safety or; 4) if the prisoner's presence in the general inmate population interferes with an ongoing investigation that could lead to a criminal or disciplinary charge. *Disciplinary* (punitive) segregation, on the other hand, is a practice said to be exclusively used as a sanction for prisoners found guilty of committing disciplinary offences such as damaging property, fighting, gambling, disobeying a justifiable order, refusing to work or provide a urine sample or for being disrespectful (CCRA 1992, sect. 40). This form of segregation is reserved solely in cases of serious disciplinary offences and for no more than thirty consecutive days[3] (CCRA 1992, sect. 44.1(f)).

The women in our sample have indeed mentioned being segregated for motives like fighting, lighting fires or tampering with a prisoner's personal care products. But they also reported being confined to segregation for reasons not explicitly enumerated in the legislation, such as "being in a condition other than normal," being in possession of forbidden items like a deck of cards or little packs of salt and pepper, swearing, tattooing or self-injurious activities.[4]

Generally, segregation conditions in provincial prisons are reported to be considerably more oppressive than in federal facilities. In the best scenarios, women are forbidden access to a variety of things like telephone calls, cigarettes, personal belongings, undergarments, grooming items (like toothbrush, shampoo, toilet paper) and programs. In the worst scenarios, they have to cope with such conditions as cold temperatures, dampness, insects, contraband drugs, sleeping on mattresses on the floor with wet blankets or being chained to their bed (if they are allowed a bed). Of more concern is that women are repeatedly subjected to degrading and sexually humiliating practices such as camera monitoring, harassment from staff (e.g., flirting), or being denied a sufficient quantity of feminine hygiene products (e.g., sanitary pads), which forces them to repeatedly request additional supplies. In addition, they are often the target of sexualized behaviours (e.g., masturbation, indecent exposure) on the part of men prisoners, who are often segregated on the same unit.

Not surprisingly, the most significant feature of the women's experience of segregation is loneliness. Segregation appears to exacerbate the rupture of emotional links with close ones, which is found to be a corollary of imprisonment (Macleod 1986; Pollock-Byrne 1990; Shaw et al. 1991). Indeed, segregated women are often completely cut off from the sources of support they count on either in the community, or internally within the prison (e.g., friends, lovers, Aboriginal Elders). Moreover, segregated women are often deprived of opportunities to engage in the most basic verbal interaction with others, even on a daily basis. According to a majority of the women, in several federal institutions verbal contacts are, at worst, non-existent and, at best, sporadic. Contacts with staff are often reduced to the bare minimum stipulated in law (e.g., with health professionals, the warden or deputy warden). Besides "screaming," "talking through the wall" or "yelling underneath the [cell] door" to have some semblance of human communication with other segregated prisoners, women appear to be virtually silenced by their general lack of access to quality or sustained human contact. As Charlotte[5] said: "you're just in there and that's it." This silencing increases their social invisibility as women in general, and as prisoners in particular, as property of the State.

Overall, living conditions in segregation seem to engender profound feelings of seclusion and desolation for the women. They disclose feeling "lost," being "out of touch with what was going on" around them, being "nowhere but at the same time somewhere very far removed from humanity," or being "put on a different planet," or in "a cocoon." They also express feeling "ignore[d] like [they] don't exist" or feeling like "everybody hated [them] totally." In sum, segregation is most often lived in overwhelming solitude, which is generally experienced as rejection or abandonment, as a form of dehumanization, as a total invisibility or a general lack of acknowledgment of their existence. "I felt helpless, hopeless, full of fear, isolated, desolated, and extremely punished" concludes Emily.

Moreover, women of Aboriginal ancestry were over-represented in seg-regation at two thirds of our sample.[6] In general, the over-representation of Native women imprisoned in Canadian prisons has been amply documented (Canada 1988; LaPrairie 1993). This disproportion is particularly problematic in the western parts of Canada taken that, altogether, Western Canada comprises 53 percent of the total Aboriginal population (Norris 1996:191). In fact, of the total number of individuals sentenced to provincial and federal custody in the Prairie provinces, 74 percent are Aboriginal in Saskatchewan, while 58 percent of Manitoba's prisoners and 39 percent of Alberta's are of Native descent (Canada 1998a:17). In Alberta, for example, 56 percent of all adult women admitted in provincial prisons in 1998–99 (1525 out of 2716) were of Aboriginal ancestry. In this regard, female young offenders do not fare much better. Over one third (39 percent or 355) of the 900 female admissions in Alberta's young offenders correctional centres, in that same year, were Native.[7] It would appear, then, that the over-representation of Aboriginal women in segregation cells is greater than their general over-representation in provincial prisons in the Prairie provinces.

Not only are Native women disproportionately segregated but, once in segregation, they report being subjected to "racial comments" by other seg-regated prisoners and by staff and being subjected to situations different than other women, "Native girls" were refused access to the shower, for example, after being "tear gassed and maced." Some also report being confined in the basement section of a segregation unit while the "girls that were white" were held upstairs in better lit, ventilated and heated cells. It would appear, then, that segregation practices are racialized, and that segregation may be a physical and symbolic space reserved for particular women. It is reserved for those who, on the basis of their assumed racial characteristics, do not fit into stereotypical conceptions based on white femininity held within the institutional framework of prisons. For example, Native women report being sent to, or maintained in segregation, for reasons such as "throwing things around" and being "mouthy" or "argumentative." The model of femininity that is reproduced here supports and perpetuates stereotypical notions of women as inherently polite, docile, and submissive. This is further perpetuated if "proper" (feminine) behaviour results in the granting of privileges (e.g., being considered for release from segregation) or, conversely, if "improper" (unfeminine) behaviour leads to an unfavourable outcome (e.g., when being "mouthy" leads to disciplinary charges and additional time in segregation). In such cases, structural racism translates into determined paths, determined kinds of *troubles* an Aboriginal woman is likely to encounter when she is imprisoned.

Resisting Segregation

With the limited means they have at their disposal, however, women resist the repressive and dehumanizing conditions of segregation. As Shaylor (1998) previously documented, women are generally kept idle in segregation. In light of the nearly total absence of programs and recreational activities, women use whatever means at their disposal to alleviate the monotonous pace of time, be it by sleeping or doing trivial and mindless busywork (e.g., cleaning their cell, pacing back and forth, doing puzzles). Idleness and boredom are also alleviated by engaging in pretend games, for example, by making stuffed dummies out of their clothing and pretending they are talk show hosts like "David Letterman ... interview[ing a] guest."

Lessening the dullness of segregation by seeking an *other* with whom to engage in some semblance of human contact may provide women with a sense of their own validation as human beings, a way to reduce the invisibility resulting from their seclusion. To resist the helplessness of segregation, women also resort to a variety of other tactics, such as reading the Bible, calling or writing the media, pleading or using persuasion to be released from segregation, vandalizing their cell, assaulting staff, "closing down" their mind and body by putting thoughts in neutral, or engaging in self-induced starvation to trigger half consciousness. Furthermore, segregation may also mean intentionally resorting to self-injurious actions in the hope of being transferred out of the segregation area to the health services unit within the prison or to the community hospital. Several women report deliberately slashing their face or wrists, stabbing themselves, eating "screws and knobs off radios," setting their pants on fire or burning themselves with cigarettes or matches for that purpose: so they "wouldn't have to be left there," so the prison administration "would have to move [them] somewhere else."

Consequences of Segregation

Although one would hope that this disavowing of women's existence may cease once released from segregation, it does not appear to be the case. Beyond segregation, women still struggle with some long lasting effects, even after release from prison. Henceforth portrayed as a fragile, disturbed, suicidal or violent individual, the segregated woman who is returned to the general prison population may face paternalistic attitudes and their corollary behaviours, on the part of staff for example. For some women this translates into frequent inquiries or checks to verify how they are doing. Another woman reports that "staff members want to smother [her]" every time she is released from segregation. Albeit likely well intentioned, such reactions frequently result in maintaining and perpetuating the same feelings of inadequacy that women often had to cope with in segregation. Moreover, it is unlikely that segregation would elicit such reactions toward men prisoners in men's prisons. In sum, the seclusion constitutive of segregation policies continues well beyond confinement in segregation.

One of the most recurrent after-effects of segregation is certainly that of experiencing various levels of discomfort in open or public spaces which, as the literature suggests, may often lead to social withdrawal (Haney 1993; Brodsky and Scogin 1988; Grassian and Friedman 1986). Indeed, half of the women interviewed experienced difficulties being in crowded or noisy rooms. These difficulties range from mild but manageable discomfort or irritation, to "anxiety" reactions, "paranoia," "fear" or utter "hate" of being around people, especially soon after being re-introduced in the general prison population. Many other women choose to seclude themselves willingly from the rest of the prison population. This self-imposed segregation takes on different forms, be it not engaging mentally in any type of interaction, physically isolating themselves when they feel they "cannot cope" with something or "cut[ting] themselves off" from their children and "push[ing] them away."

Endured isolation from human contact also leads the women in our sample to experience feelings of "invasion" of their personal space when in the presence of unsolicited or intimate human contact. For example, being kept alone for so long in segregation may mean an inability to eat in front of people, or a general dislike of physical contact, especially sexual intimacy. Once released from prison, such difficulties are sometimes carried over into women's private lives. Some feel their "space" is "invaded" whenever someone knocks on the door of their home. This impression is especially exacerbated in the presence of men or in elevators or taxi-cabs for example. Such overpowering feelings of inadequacy ultimately contribute to re-shaping women's self-image. In this regard, the women in our sample are quite cognizant of the ways in which their self-esteem has indeed been "damaged" by their experience of segregation, and confide that they now struggle with negative views of themselves. Several of them have an acute sense of themselves as angry persons, while others fight against profound feelings of disrespect for themselves. Following segregation, numerous women now see themselves as "isolated," "loner[s]" who feel "disjointed and separated from [their] own body." "[I] feel so, so, so segregated still from everybody," says Charlotte in this regard. "I'm hopeless.… look what they did to me," adds Flora.

Conclusion: Questioning the Unquestioned

Examining the practice of segregation with women prisoners is a pressing issue especially in view of the current trend in Canadian criminal justice toward escalating punitiveness toward women. On the one hand, the ratio of women admitted to federal institutions has risen from 2 percent of the total adult admissions in 1986–87, to 5 percent in 1997–98. For their part, women admitted to provincial prisons in 1997–98 accounted for a total of 9 percent of adult admissions, an increase of two percent compared to 1986–87 data (Finn et al. 1999). Boritch (1997:183) asserts that, overall the rate of incarceration for women in provincial prisons has risen by 102 percent since the 1980s. On the other hand, several of the new regional facilities for federally sentenced women have been operating at full capacity, while others have already experienced over-crowding. As a result, some of these facilities are well engaged in the process of expanding. In view of this trend, a serious questioning of the practice of segregation is warranted, especially knowing that in other countries (e.g., Finland, Scotland), the segregation of women prisoners is used considerably less, or is set in better living conditions (Bertrand 1996) than women endured here.

Indeed, in segregation women are secluded, inactive, lonely, voiceless, fearful and emotionally destabilized. They are negated and marginalized on a daily basis. Segregation leaves women with a precarious self-image and rather fatalistic attitudes about their overall ability to counteract that image. Far from empowering women—and even further from rehabilitating them—segregation accentuates their marginalization and perpetuates it above and beyond actual confinement to segregation cells. Segregation denies them personality, recognition and full adult status. In this sense, it replicates—and participates in the maintenance of—the societal status quo in which women have historically been marginalized.

Moreover, both regimes of segregation (administrative and disciplinary) seem to be practised and experienced in conditions that do not appear to be vitally indispensable to achieving the legislated goals of segregation. It is doubtful whether sleeping on a mattress on the floor, being deprived of personal belongings, being subjected to degrading and humiliating practices, being kept in forced idleness and solitude and/or resorting to self-harming actions are necessary to prevent association with others or to foster behaviours that are compliant with the "good order" of prisons. Moreover, women's experiences of segregation indicate that confinement in such conditions seems to engender repercussions likely to be detrimental to any attempts at rehabilitation or, as the new Canadian correctional philosophy for federally sentenced women intends it, healing. Thus, the rationales behind the current and persistent use of segregation are by no means clear.

The new "women-centred" philosophy[8] as well as the Arbour Report (1996), both resulted in important changes in segregation policies designed to improve overall conditions in segregation. However, it seems that current practices are far removed from these empowering policies. Indeed, approximately half of our participants indicated having experienced harsh conditions in segregation in the federal prison system in the 1990s, which is *after* the implementation of the "women-centred" philosophy. Most of these women were segregated as recently as 1996, 1997 and 1998, which is *after* the majority of the new regional facilities for federally sentenced women had opened in Canada. It may be argued, then, that the official discourse surrounding the "progressive evolution" of penal regimes in Canada—especially as embodied in the new philosophy for federally sentenced women—is a deceitful teleology. In light of the "women-centred" principles, the continuing practice of segregating women prisoners, especially in the conditions reported here, becomes highly questionable in terms of its evident inconsistency with the new correctional philosophy. The "women-centred" model of incarceration is no less punitive than its predecessor. As far as the provinces are concerned, the problem of segregation remains in its entirety because none of the provinces, except Nova Scotia for a brief period, really adopted a "women-centred" correctional philosophy. As evidenced in nineteenth-century prison systems (Howe 1994), women still continue to be subjected to a tight disciplinary regime.

Under conditions such as those described here, the use of segregation with women prisoners may be seen as a rather oppressive institutional practice. To what extent, then, does the practice of segregation remain indispensable? Perhaps it is perceived as *indispensable* because within prisons' institutional framework it is thought to be *irreplaceable*. However, studies indicate that women incarcerated in Canada have committed less serious crimes than men, and that they are better parole risks and generally pose very little threat to society (Boritch 1997). In light of this, one must question whether segregation, and the conditions in which it is experienced, is an appropriate practice with women prisoners.

In all fairness, there is a pressing need for broader research on women's experiences of segregation in Canada in order to give more social legitimacy to a critique of the use of segregation. However, on the basis of the dire experiences of our participants, one might suggest that there is a need for a complete and swift eradication of segregation practices with incarcerated women in Canadian federal *and* provincial prisons, and that discussing anything else but elimination (e.g., reviewing segregation policies to reduce their negative impact) would amount to diluting the harsh reality of these experiences.

Notes

1. The author would like to thank Margaret Shaw, Kelly Hannah-Moffat, Yves Gendron, Wayne Antony and Dorothy Chunn, the external reviewer, for their invaluable comments on previous drafts of this paper.
2. Sentenced admissions do not include the significant number of women remanded in custody.
3. With a possibility of extending it to a total of forty-five days in cases of consecutive sanctions of segregation (*Commission of Inquiry Into Certain Events at the Prison for Women in Kingston* Arbour1996:120).
4. It is important to note that many of these reasons for segregation would rarely elicit such a reaction in men's prisons (Solicitor General Canada 1998).
5. To protect their identity, all women participants were given pseudonyms.
6. This is consistent with findings of a recent Canadian study showing that 60 percent of women segregated at the time of their study were of Aboriginal ancestry (Solicitor General Canada 1998).
7. Data received from Alberta Justice's Community Corrections and Division Support Services. Letter dated August 25, 1999.
8. See the editors' introductory account of the creation and implementation of the "women-centred" correctional philosophy for federally sentenced women.

Personal and Political Musings on Activism
A Two-Way Interview
Karlene Faith and Kim Pate

When, in 1997, Margaret Shaw and Kelly Hannah-Moffat invited us to submit a "two-way interview," we said "Sure." It sounded easy. But because Kim lives in Ottawa and Karlene lives in Vancouver, the logistics proved difficult. What follows is constructed from conversations in California and in Vancouver, and from e-mail, letters, and fax and telephone communications. KF & KP, June 1999.

KF: Over the years you and I have worked together in various Canadian locations coast to coast giving talks or taking part in panel discussions at Simon Fraser University (SFU), University of British Columbia (UBC), Carleton University, your Elizabeth Fry Annual General Meetings and other conferences, the Arbour Commission inquiry, the Gatineau Gatherings, Strength in SISterhood (SIS) meetings and so on. It's fitting that the only time we've found to get started on this interview is at the end of a long day at the International Critical Resistance conference (10 p.m., September 25, 1998). Here we are in our cheap, shared motel room in Berkeley, energized by what we've heard all day from others who oppose the growth of prison industries. I'm in awe of the courage of some of the former prisoners in the U.S. who are speaking out. Angela Davis [one of the organizers, along with Nancy Stoller, Eli Rosenblatt, Ellen Barry and many others] serves as a symbolic link who connects us all to one another, generating trust through all our differences—almost three thousand of us, from far reaching locations.

Of course, you're out of town almost as much as you're home. For starters, you have twenty-four Elizabeth Fry Societies scattered throughout Canada that require your coordinating attentions. With the five new federal prisons for women in the country, Burnaby Correctional Centre for Women, and the placement of women in segregated maximum-security units in men's prisons to boot, there are weeks when you will be meeting with women on both coasts and the Prairies in between. Crises will invariably intervene with your best-laid plans. You need to have meetings with officials at the prisons to remind them that prisoners do have certain human rights and to serve advocacy for specific women undergoing particular traumas. You will also be frequently contacted by the media, whose reporters will ask you infuriating and groundless questions like, "Why are so many more women committing crimes of violence?" Through this maze of emotion, stolid bureaucrats, sensation-hungry journalists and co-activists seeking your counsel, you will remain calm on the exterior, but friends in your midst will have to remind you to do things like eat.

My favourite image of you is when you arrived at my apartment door one day with a beautiful plant for me from the prison floral shop in one hand, your cell phone to your ear with your other hand and somehow juggling your laptop and your over-stuffed briefcase. You were in the midst of a phone conversation with a woman who had been drugged and placed in an isolation cell in a maximum-security men's prison in Saskatchewan.

KP: Yeah, well, let's talk about you now.

KF: From the late 1960s to the early 1980s, when I was doing prison work in California, life was a constant juggling of the needs of my four kids, working, being a student, worrying about whether the car would hold up, whether I would be able to pay the phone bill.… It became clear to me during those years that prisons as we know them would have no place in any truly civilized society. As a "mature student," I was engaged with the civil rights movement, the anti-war movement, the women's movement.… My first anti-prison project was to organize a buddy program for kids on probation, matching them one-on-one with university students who tutored them, played ball with them and otherwise tried to perk up their lives and keep them out of jail.

While working endless odd jobs, taking care of the kids and sleeping little, I moved quickly through the B.A. and into the graduate program, at which point I was invited to teach with Dr. Rafael Guzman at the maximum-security Soledad prison in Santa Cruz. I discovered how little significant others knew of the whereabouts of women who were locked up—even when it was their mothers, aunts, sisters or wives. At this time I was also teaching university classes and being flown by government plane (with my young boys along for the ride) to other cities every week to teach criminology classes for social service employees, police officers, prison guards and wardens and even the FBI. Many of the people in the classes were African–American or Chicano. One class was made up entirely of men, and they initially resented being taught by a woman. An important aspect of this work was confronting not only the sexism, but also the racism that permeated the criminal justice system.

KP: Misogyny and racism still permeate the system. Is this what moved you to start working with women in particular?

KF: As a researcher, I was a participant observer, did life history interviews with 100 of the 600 women then in the prison (now about 2,000, despite a string of new state prisons for women). I took notes on hundreds of "rap sheets," administered questionnaires and immersed myself in the institution. I was in awe of the women's resilience and optimism for their futures. I felt an affinity with the problems they faced as single parents. I knew poverty. It was easy to understand their situations. I felt myself to be among friends.

At the women's request I co-taught women's studies courses with a partner, Jeanne Gallick, and then we recruited volunteer coordinators, teachers from many disciplines, community activists and performers, to develop a full program; for four years, several hundred people from all over the state were involved in the Santa Cruz Women's Prison Project. The women worked very hard, and were stimulated and motivated by what they learned in the courses. Many went on to earn degrees. When they were released on parole, one by one, they were often able to get support in the process of re settling from one of their former teachers. Many of these former prisoners became activists, and they were important speakers at rallies, in the media and in public education settings. These years, the seventies, produced an accelerated, sustained commitment by many to create alternatives to retributive "justice." At one point our group helped organize conferences inside the prison, attended by both prisoners and outsiders, including a successful one on "Alternatives to Prison." Since then I've attended many conferences on that theme, but that was the most powerful because it was inside, with prisoners talking.

In 1979, I attended the SFU-organized international conference on women in prison, where Jean-Jacques Blais, then the Solicitor General, gave us false hope when he promised that the Prison for Women (P4W) would be closing. I met Claire Culhane there, who had just recently gotten involved in prison work, and we organized a radical caucus. She also interviewed me for community television, and we kept in touch from then on. Not long before she died [Claire passed away April 28, 1996], we reminded each other that just because there are more people than ever in prison, our work has not been for naught. The prison abolition movement continues to grow. At the same time that the carceral industry is growing, people are catching on to the implications of taking money from education and social services to invest it in prisons.

In 1981, I finally finished my Ph.D., and with my youngest son, then sixteen, came home to Canada, where I've continued to be active: visiting women inside; helping organize Strength in Sisterhood (SIS, a parolee support network); consulting; setting up meetings between prisoners and students; participating in conferences and inquiries; speaking at rallies and to the media; arranging for former prisoners to speak at the university; and so on. At Simon Fraser University's School of Criminology I have the privilege to exercise freedom of speech—in my teaching, researching, writing and community work—and I take advantage of this. As an activist and academic, it gives me a good feeling to watch students develop their own commitments to human rights work, whether or not it's specific to prison.

KP: What does it mean to you when you call yourself an activist academic?

KF: It means taking a position and staying grounded, integrating theory and practice. Research, publishing and teaching are all potentially radical activities. By providing empirical evidence supporting their positions, intellectual activists may seek to persuade the reader or student of a particular perspective and analysis which supports human rights. I observe that many academics do remain in an ivory-towered detachment from the subjects of their research. Others disseminate data and theories that support social change. Still others engage in participatory-action research, and get deeply involved in the communities which they research and with which they are also socially, culturally and/or politically aligned.

* * *

[When Kim and I were in Berkeley, she was five months pregnant. Her daughter, Madison Haika, was born January 27, 1999. Within a month, Kim was back on the prison circuit, the baby with her, just as big brother Michael has been cheerfully accompanying his mother in her work since he was a wee boy. On May 11, 1999, when Madison was three-and-a-half-months old, Kim brought her to Vancouver and we picked up where we left off while the baby slept in her basket. KF]

KF: Let me ask you…. In what ways do you think class background might affect one's approach to human-rights work in prisons?

KP: I think this is one of the keys to the way I approach my work. The struggles are about our liberty and the liberty interests of our families, friends and allies, as much as they are about the women in prison. The "issues" are rooted in our realities and/or the [imprisoned] women's realities. This means that no policy or legislative provision is a mere abstraction, they are always rooted in the realities of the women. Growing up working class, with parents (neither of whom had a high school education) and with the life experiences, both positive and negative, which accompany such a childhood and adolescence, were good preparation for this work.

I think a feminist analysis also has a profound impact on the work. I am always amazed when I meet people, especially women, working with women in prison, who are totally devoid of any sort of feminist or equality-based analysis. Most common, of course, amongst this crowd are the social workers, the people-fixers, and the do-gooders. It is a mystery to me how so many people get involved in this work, sometimes working in and around prisons for decades, yet are devoid of *any* contextualized analysis. They individualize the issues, rather than recognize the social and economic construction of crime, the racialized, gendered, heterosexist application thereof. Some recognize some of the contextual issues but employ sexist attitudes regarding women in prison.

KF: You and I agree that most women who are incarcerated should not be in prison in terms of public safety or in terms of addressing the inequalities that result in criminalization of certain lawbreakers. Ole Ingstrup (the Commissioner of "corrections" in Canada), members of the parole board, mental health workers in the prison, probation and parole officers and even wardens and guards routinely agreed in the 1990s, in the press and in our presence, that we need "restorative" or transformative justice instead of imprisonment and retributive justice. But the state keeps investing more money in the custodial and security functions of prisons, with ever more elaborate technological hardware. You came to the Canadian Association of Elizabeth Fry Societies (CAEFS) just a year or so after the government had tabled the report of the Task Force on Federally Sentenced Women (TFFSW), entitled *Creating Choices*. What was it like for you, inheriting that legacy?

KP: Thanks Karlene. Now how do I answer that here? As you know, I have written a lot about what has happened to *Creating Choices*. When I started with CAEFS in January of 1992, the die was cast to a great extent. While CAEFS had participated fully in the work of the Task Force (indeed, my predecessor, Bonnie Diamond, co-chaired the Working Group), CAEFS was not part of the National Implementation Committee struck by the Correctional Service of Canada (CSC) to breathe life into the report, despite a recommendation and significant lobbying after tabling the report.

In the year following the tabling of the report, CAEFS pushed the government for funds to compensate for Bonnie's anticipated active future role in the implementation process as a member of the external advisory committee. Instead, CAEFS was permitted to sit on one or two program sub-committees (e.g., the mother–child program sub-sub-committee of the programming sub-committee of the National Implementation Committee) and was given the nominal chair to an external advisory committee, which consisted of two other parties, the Native Women's Association of Canada (NWAC) and a representative from Status of Women Canada. NWAC was also integrally involved in the development of the plans for the healing lodge, and Status of Women, as a government department, was involved in much of the internal program, staffing and policy planning process. CAEFS had no other government-initiated access into the implementation process. Consequently, without the requisite resources to coordinate meetings and monitor processes, CAEFS' involvement was quickly marginalized and the organization was relegated to the margins of the government's implementation process.

From that point forward, it has been an incredible struggle to have the voices of the women heard, much less incorporated, in the planning process. In addition, we have witnessed the appropriation of feminist language, ideas and principles. This has also happened in conjunction with the continuing decontextualizing of women's experiences and life situations. Furthermore,the CSC has developed a distressing trend toward the conversion of women's needs into criminogenic risk factors. For instance, they have commissioned researchers to study the women in prison for linkages between self-injury and violent offending. Given that approximately half of the women in prison are in for offences involving violence, most of which is reactive and/or defensive in nature, and many self-injure while in prison, obviously it is possible to link these two factors in women's lives. Given the clearer and more consistent linkages between histories of sexual and physical abuse and self-injury, however, it seems irresponsible to do research that does not at least contextualize such realities.

It was no doubt with much hope and *naïveté* that CAEFS entered into the Task Force partnership with the CSC more than ten years ago. Records from the time show that there was considerable deliberation and trepidation about the potential impact of the Task Force partnership on the organization's work and mandate. As prison abolitionists and in response to the final report, *Creating Choices*, it is clear that some of our members questioned the advisability of replacing one prison for women with six new ones. It is also clear that many believed that the vision of developing community-based women-centred "facilities" would be realized.

Having come to CAEFS with the experience of being a tiny cog in the then eight-year-old struggle to implement the *Young Offenders Act* (YOA), I undoubtedly appeared very cynical to the CAEFS network. The dismal results achieved by the much larger and well-resourced YOA implementation machinery left little doubt in my mind that, given that resources were only earmarked for the bricks and mortar of the project (despite the fact that *Creating Choices* clearly articulated a strong community base), we were not likely to see the development of the promised community half of the Task Force recommendations. Most of those working on the Task Force seemed unaware of the YOA or other parallels. As a result, some of the most likely probabilities became subsequent realities, although they were not, in fact, anticipated and therefore not planned for by the Task Force.

KF: Was the report itself a disappointment to you, or was it the problem of implementation?

KP: Good faith and compromises for the feminist reformers typify the work and recommendations of the Task Force on Federally Sentenced Women. To most of the non-governmental participants, the report was a compromise and bottom-line position, not the visionary document that the CSC now describes it to be. In retrospect, a number of participants have indicated that the mandate, recommendations and subsequent consequences, intended and unintended, have exacted far too great a toll. On the one hand, we now have federally sentenced women imprisoned in ten federal prisons. Those in British Columbia, on the other hand, have no choice but to serve their federal sentences in a provincial jail. The number of women being imprisoned is escalating at alarming rates, especially in the Atlantic and Prairie provinces, due at least in part to the construction of new, well-promoted prisons in those regions. Ten years after the tabling of the TFFSW report, we still do not have a coherent community-release action plan, much less the actual resources promised by the CSC in *Creating Choices*.

In short, there have been many unintended consequences as a result of the work of the TFFSW . This is the case in almost any new venture, although some problems should presumably be more predictable and preventable than others. It is painfully clear that the CSC was ill-equipped to implement recommendations that were predicated upon an understanding that the Task Force partnership of corrections and the Aboriginal and feminist communities would persist throughout the implementation period. As one woman at the CSC advised me during my first weeks at CAEFS, the CSC felt that because they had so few First Nations staff they needed to retain the involvement of Aboriginal women in the planning of the healing lodge, but they did not need to continue the CAEFS partnership, as they had a growing number of non-Aboriginal women on staff. The early success of the Okimaw Ohci Healing Lodge underscored the value and importance of feminist, community-based leadership to the implementation process. Similarly, more recent issues at the Lodge parallel the reduced role of such leadership and the increasingly insidious injection of traditional (i.e., male-based) correctional norms and staff.

Would all this have happened anyway if CAEFS and other feminist groups had not been involved? Maybe, maybe not. There is no doubt that many women prisoners felt that the closure of the Prison for Women in Kingston and moving women closer to their homes were important and worthwhile goals. There is also no doubt that the intransigence of the CSC during the TFFSW process, the implementation and dismantling of the recommendations, and the Arbour Commission of Inquiry, reveal how difficult it is to change correctional culture.

KF: What is most evident is that the progressive rhetoric couldn't be further from the reality of what's happening, and it's hard to challenge the contradictions with all the changes in political tides. Nevertheless, let's see if we can set forth a set of guiding principles for potentially effecting change.... [The following combines our perspectives on activism, based on our respective and shared experiences.]

1. Recognize that Prisons are a Growth Industry
We all must recognize the dangers to human rights of the runaway growth of prison industries in most industrialized nations, especially in the United States. Canada seems to keep chasing the U.S.A. when it comes to jailing its citizenry and furthering the expansion of the prison industrial complex. As activists, we need to make linkages and work with feminist and social justice groups regionally, nationally and internationally. Unless we do so, we will continue to see the increased criminalization of the most marginalized. We cannot afford the human nor the financial costs of continuing on this trajectory.

2. Always Do Our Homework
Unless we know the history, players, facts, context, legislation, policy and procedures that pertain to concerns that originate in prison, we cannot fully

engage in a discussion about, or even address, issues that arise. Activists need to know and have strong alliances with other activists, prisoners and community supports. It also helps if they know how to work in and around the criminal justice system and its players.

3. Recognize the Nature of Collateral Damage Caused by Prisons

It is vitally important that activists become informed about and actively resist all attempts at net-widening damage caused by the proliferation of prisons (e.g., when prison rather than community sentences are imposed for minor offences, as well as the damage caused by the proliferation of prisons). The increased focus upon the use of lengthy periods of imprisonment is accompanied by a corresponding devastating decrease in government resourcing of social, health and educational services. Such cutbacks serve to exacerbate class, race and gender inequalities, which, in turn, serve to further marginalize and jeopardize the ability of those who are affected by such policies and practices. The end result is an ever-expanding group of the dispossessed. When social safety nets are eviscerated, those who fall through tend to be caught by and confined in the criminal (in)justice system, the only system that cannot refuse more "clients." The increased criminalization of the dispossessed is resulting in a corresponding expansion of the numbers of poor and racialized people who are being imprisoned. This damage is further exacerbated by punitive experiences in prison, as well as the prevailing trend toward diminishing access to social, health and educational services for those who are released from prison.

4. Communicate to Others What You Learn from Reliable Resources

Activists must ensure that they receive and address accurate information. Consequently, in addition to the prisoners with and for whom they advocate, it is important that activists recruit and retain linkages with institutional as well as community-based correctional staff and resources, in order to encourage staff to initiate and corroborate information about issues, especially illegalities and human-rights violations that arise in the prisons. It is on the foundation of reliable information that our credibility as advocates and activists is built.

5. Ensure All Parties are Invested

When working with other parties or individuals on issues it is essential that everyone involved, be they paid staff or volunteers, work as a team, but also that each have her own individual and equal voice. Each person or party should also have a clear and full, preferably equal, investment in the outcome. Obviously, on too many issues, prisoners will have the far greater investment in the result. If all those involved had an equal stake in the success of an intervention, we would likely see very different approaches employed by service providers and supervisors alike. We would also expect to see a relative improvement in the long-term success of services and approaches. For instance, it is increasingly true that correctional and paroling authorities focus upon the imposition and monitoring of behavioural restrictions, as opposed to the provision of support and assistance to those released from prison. In addition to standard restrictions that stipulate that parolees may be returned to prison if they fail to "keep the peace" and "be of good behaviour," or follow the instructions of their parole officers, the majority of parolees are also restricted from associating with others who have criminal records, have curfews and are subject to routine and/ or random analysis of their urine. Relatively little time tends to be devoted to providing support and assistance to parolees. If the evaluation and remuneration of parole-board members, prison wardens and parole supervisors was based upon the timely and successful release and community integration of prisoners, correctional authorities would be far more likely to be invested in the provision of supports designed to facilitate the successful release and community integration of prisoners.

6. Amplify and Echo Women's Voices
Activists must always aim to bring women's voices straight from the prison. Particularly, when trying to raise the public profile and, given the importance of issues, activists must recruit and utilize the most reliable reporting methods. The goal must always be to ensure that we create opportunities and the means by which imprisoned and formerly imprisoned women can speak directly to and via the media and public meetings. When such direct representation is not possible, we have the responsibility to ensure that we are accurately and effectively representing the issues and concerns of the women and that we remain accessible and accountable to the women with and on behalf of whom we speak.

7. Honour the Voices of the Women
Activists must avoid the construction of strategies or tactics which by-pass the experiences and opinions of imprisoned and formerly imprisoned women. Theirs is the first voice of authority in effective anti-prison work. In their absence and without their voice, we run the risk of constructing, entrenching and therefore perpetuating hierarchies of "experts" whose expertise is accepted based upon their relative status and their perceived ability to speak for others.

8. Recognize the Centrality of Human Rights
It is essential that activists recognize and understand that prisoners' rights are human rights and that all work be done within the context of an anti-discriminatory framework. The discriminatory elements and patterns of human-rights abuses experienced by women in prison generally involve struggles against inequities bred from social divisions of class, race, ethnicity and gender. Consequently, it is important to develop tactics and strategies that address injustices in a manner that is as holistic as possible. It is also necessary to create, expand and/or link up with grassroots coalitions which utilize strategies encompassing interests in the quality of life of the majority of the population, including prisoners.

9. Forge Linkages with the Media

It is extremely important that activists develop working relationships with media contacts, especially interested and progressive reporters. These contacts should represent all forms of media, from print to television. Activists need to keep such contacts well informed and up to date on current statistics as well as political and contextual realities in order to encourage thoughtful and progressive human rights, equality and social justice analyses, rather than facile and reactionary "crime" reporting. Activists must also cultivate allies within social services and criminal justice agencies, in order to enhance opportunities for collaboration to promote a progressive feminist agenda.

10. Contextualize the Role of the "Victim"

Given the histories of abuse that are common to most women prisoners, especially First Nations women, any advocacy with and on behalf of them must necessarily contextualize the actions of the woman *vis-à-vis* her "victim(s)" history. Understanding the context of the "crime" when working with and for women convicted of crimes that cause harm to others is extremely important. This usually involves having a full awareness of women's own histories of victimization and their influence on the commission of offences. It also necessitates an understanding of the relationship of the criminalized act to the criminal justice intervention.

11. Promote Revolutionary Reforms

When designing and organizing particular programs or projects to address the needs of women inside or newly out, activists must be fully cognizant of the potential consequences and unintended outcomes of various interventions. In so doing, activists need to ask themselves such questions as: If it works, who benefits? Prisoners? Women at large? The correctional establishment and other social control agencies? Antonio Gramsci, writing as a prisoner of the Fascists, spoke of reformist reforms versus revolutionary reforms. The first reinforces the status quo; the second is liberatory.

On the way to liberation, many activists working to reduce prison populations are working against recidivism. An outline of significant community-release issues raised in Canada in the 1990s by a diverse Solicitor General Task Force, the Canadian Association of Elizabeth Fry Societies (CAEFS) and community groups such as SIS (Strength in Sisterhood) follows for your information.

1. There is an urgent need for residential options that assist women to make the transition to the community when they exit prison. Such options could and should provide community-based alternatives to prison for sentencing purposes. These options need to include transitional or halfway houses, cooperative and/or supported, independent-living placements, private-home placements and other women and child-friendly accommodations.

2. It is fundamentally inappropriate to force women to live in men's prisons and/or community residences. Women are currently imprisoned in segregated maximum-security units in four men's prisons in Canada: Saskatchewan Penitentiary in Prince Albert, Saskatchewan; Regional Psychiatric Centre in Saskatoon, Saskatchewan; Ste. Anne des Plaines in Quebec; and Springhill Institution in Nova Scotia. In addition, in the Atlantic and Prairies regions, which account for seven of the ten provinces, and in the three territories, most women released from prison are forced to enter the community through men's halfway houses.

3. Residential options for women on parole must reflect the diversity of the women and their needs. For example, in addition to having access to culturally appropriate services in any community-release options, First Nations women should be permitted to return to their home communities. Sections 81 and 84 of the *Corrections and Conditional Release Act* (CCRA) provide mechanisms for the CSC to contract with and fund Aboriginal communities to provide correctional and community-release options for prisoners. Despite the interest of some women and their reserves to enter into such arrangements with corrections, to date, no s. 81 or s. 84 agreements have been signed for women. In addition to the needs of First Nations, Métis and Inuit women, there are growing numbers of older women in prison, largely as a result of the increased number of those serving long sentences. As a result of the evisceration of health, social and economic services in communities, there are increasing numbers of women being imprisoned who have serious mental or physical health needs and capacities and/or other special challenges.

4. Given that approximately two-thirds of women in prison are mothers, prisons and other "correctional" and community-release facilities must accommodate and nurture mother–child relationships.

5. In order to ensure that adequate and appropriate resources exist for women, funds should be diverted from the "correctional" industry to resource-based community residences and programs. Such a funding arrangement should also be accompanied by a corresponding diversion of women from prison to the community.

6. Services are needed to facilitate women's post-prison access to permanent housing, social assistance, child care, counselling, education, vocational training and a variety of employment opportunities. Such services must accommodate and be individually guided by each woman's needs and the particular circumstances of her financial and other resources, skills and interests.

7. Women in and out of prison rely upon their peers for support and assistance. In order to facilitate their ability to assist each other, peer-support groups for newly released women should be supported both practically and financially. It is also crucial that such groups are led by former prisoners.

8. The pervasive incidence among imprisoned women of prior physical and sexual abuse (82 percent of all women and 90 percent of Aboriginal women serving sentences of two years or more) must not only be acknowledged, their needs must be addressed through women-directed support and treatment options.

9. Any and all community-based initiatives must exercise caution and avoid the pull or push by corrections to construct deeper, wider and stickier nets of social control. Instead, the focus must always be on the encouragement and enhancement of supports and services that provide legitimate access to resources and recognize the realities of women's lives. In short, it is vital that approaches increase women's ability to be independent, responsible and accountable, in order to assist women to heal, habilitate and successfully integrate in our communities.

10. Prisons cause much harm. If we seek to live in a healthy society, we must all work to radically reduce the numbers of people who are incarcerated, while simultaneously ensuring a corresponding radical increase in community-based resources.

* * *

KP: The first time I met Gayle Horii, she introduced me to the words of Lilla Watson, an Aboriginal woman from Australia who I had the incredible privilege of speaking to when I was in Australia three years ago. I think the following words epitomize this area of activism for me.

> If you have come here to help me,
> you are wasting your time.
> If you have come here because
> your liberation is bound up with mine,
> then let us work together.
> (Watson, cited in Horii 1992)

References

Aboriginal Justice Inquiry of Manitoba. 1991. *Report of the Aboriginal Justice Inquiry of Manitoba*. Winnipeg: Queen's Printer.

Adelberg, E. 1985. *A Forgotten Minority: Women in Conflict with the Law*. Ottawa: Canadian Association of Elizabeth Fry Societies.

Adelberg, Ellen, and Claudia Currie (eds.). 1987. *Too Few to Count: Canadian Women in Conflict With the Law*. Vancouver: Press Gang Publishers.

_____. 1993. *In Conflict with the Law: Women and the Canadian Justice System*. Vancouver: Press Gang Publishers.

Allen, Hilary. 1987a. *Justice Unbalanced: Gender, Psychiatry and Judicial Decisions*. Milton Keynes: Open University Press.

_____. 1987b. "Rendering Them Harmless: The Professional Portrayal of Women Charged with Serious Violent Crimes." In P. Carlen and A. Worrall, (eds.), *Gender, Crime and Justice*. Milton Keyes: Open University Press.

Andrews, D.A. 1989. "Recidivism is Predictable and Can Be Influenced: Using Risk Assessments to Reduce Recidivism." *Forum on Corrections Research*. 1(2): 11–17. Ottawa: Correctional Service of Canada.

_____. 1996. "Criminal Recidivism is Predictable and Can Be Influenced: An Update." *Forum on Corrections Research*, 8(3): 42–44.

Andrews, D.A., J. Bonta and R.D. Hoge. 1990. "Classification for Effective Rehabilitation: Rediscovering Psychology." *Criminal Justice and Behavior* 17: 19–52.

Andrews, D.A., I. Zinger, R.D. Hoge, J. Bonta, P. Gendreau and F.T. Cullen. 1990. "Does Correctional Treatment Work? A Clinically Relevant and Informed Meta-analysis." *Criminology* 28: 369–404.

Arbour Commission, Public Hearings. 1995. *Transcript of Proceedings: Commission of Inquiry into Certain Events at the Prison for Women in Kingston*. (Phase II-B.C. 1995-608; volume 4).

Arbour, the Honourable Justice Louise, Commissioner. 1996. *Commission of Inquiry into Certain Events at the Prison for Women in Kingston*. Ottawa: Solicitor General.

Axon, Lee. 1989a. *Criminal Justice and Women: An International Survey*. Ottawa: Corrections Branch, Ministry of the Solicitor General. User report 1989-11.

_____. 1989b. *Model and Exemplary Programmes for Female Inmates: An International Review*. Task Force on Federally Sentenced Women. Companion Report #4.

Backhouse, Constance. 1991. *Petticoats and Prejudice: Women and Law in Nineteenth Century Canada*. Toronto: Women's Press.

Balfour, Gillian. 1994. "A Qualitative Study of Feminist Therapy at the Prison for Women." Master's Thesis. Ottawa: University of Ottawa.

Bannerji, Himani. 1995. "In the Matter of X: Building Voice into Sexual Harassment." In *Thinking Through: Essays on Feminism, Marxism and Anti-Racism*. Toronto: Women's Press.

Barak-Glantz, I.L. 1983. "Who's in the 'Hole'?" *Criminal Justice Review* 8: 29–37.

Barry, A.T., T. Osbourne, N. Rose. 1996. *Foucault and Political Reason: Liberalism, Neo-liberalism and Rationalities of Government*. Chicago: University of Chicago Press, 37–64.

Beattie, J.M. 1977. *Attitudes Towards Crime and Punishment in Upper Canada, 1830–1850: A Documentary Study*. Toronto: University of Toronto, Centre of Criminology.

Benjamin, T.B., and K. Lux. 1975. "Constitutional and Psychological Implications of the Use of Solitary Confinement: Experience at the Maine State Prison." *Clearinghouse Review* 9: 83–90.

Benson, M. 1968. "Special Problems Related to the Adult Female Offender." *Canadian Journal of Corrections* 10:206–16.

Berkovits, J.G. 1995. "Material Influence: Inmate Culture in the Andrew Mercer Reformatory for Women, 1980–1915." Unpublished discussion paper, Dept. of History, University of Toronto.

Bertrand, M.A. 1967. "The Myth of Sexual Equality before the Law." *Proceedings of the Fifth Research Conference on Delinquency and Criminality*. Montreal: Quebec Society of Criminology.

_____. 1994. "From *La Donna Delinquente* to a Postmodern Deconstruction of the 'Woman Question' in Social Control Theory." *The Journal of Human Justice* 5(2): 43–57.

_____. 1996. "Women in Prisons: A Comparative Study." *Caribbean Journal of Criminology and Social Psychology* 1(1): 38–58.

_____. 1998. *Prisons pour femmes*. Montreal: Editions du Méridien.

Berzins, L., and R. Collete Carrière. 1979. "La femme en prison: Un inconvénient social!" *Santé mentale au Québec* 4(2): 87–103.

Berzins, L., and S. Cooper. 1982. "Political economy of correctional planning for women." *Canadian Journal of Criminology* 24: 399–416.

Berzins, L., and B. Hayes. 1987. "The Diaries of Two Change Agents." In E. Adelberg and C. Currie.

Bindman, Stephen. 1990. "Antiquated Women's Prison to Close Doors." *Vancouver Sun* Sept. 26.

Biron, L. 1992. "Les Femmes et l'incarceration. Le temps n'arrange rien." *Criminologie* XXV(1): 119–34.

Blanchette, Kelly. 1997a. "Classifying Female Offenders for Correctional Interventions." *Forum on Corrections Research* 9(1): 36–41.

_____. 1997b. *Risk and Need Among Federally Sentenced Female Offenders: A Comparison of Minimum-, Medium-, and Maximum-Security Inmates* (Report No. R-58). Ottawa: Correctional Service of Canada.

_____. 1997c. "Comparing Violent and Non-Violent Offenders on Risk and Need." *Forum on Corrections Research* 9(2): 14–18.

Blanchette, K., and L. Motiuk. 1995. "Female Offender Risk Assessment: The Case Management Strategies Approach." Paper presented at the Annual Convention of the Canadian Psychological Association, Charlottetown, P.E.I.

_____. 1996. *Female Offenders with and without Major Mental Health Problems: A Comparative Investigation* (Report No. R-46). Ottawa: Correctional Service of Canada

_____. 1997. *Maximum-Security Female and Male Federal Offenders: A Comparison* (Report No. R-53). Ottawa: Correctional Service of Canada.

Bloom, B., C. Lee and B. Owen. 1995. "Offence Patterns among Women Prisoners: A Preliminary Analysis." Paper given at Annual Meetings of the American Society of Criminology, Boston, M.A.

Boin, R.A., and M.J. Van Duin. 1995. "Prison Riots as Organizational Failures: A Managerial Perspective." *The Prison Journal* 75(3):357–79.

Boisseau, N. (ed.). 1988. Entre les mures, entres les lignes: Ecrire l'incarceration. Montreal: Société Elizabeth Fry de Montréal.

Bonta, James. 1997. "Do We Need Theory for Offender Risk Assessment?" *Forum on Corrections Research* 9(1): 42–45.

Bonta, J., B. Pang and S. Wallace-Capretta. 1995. "Predictors of Recidivism Among Incarcerated Female Offenders." *The Prison Journal* 75(3): 277–94.

Boritch, Helen. 1997. *Fallen Women: Female Crime and Criminal Justice in Canada.* Toronto: ITP Nelson.

Bosworth, M. 1998. *Confirming Feminity: Gender, Power and Punishment.* Paper given at annual American Society of Criminology Meetings, Washington, DC.

_____. 1999. *Resisting Identities: Agency and Power in Women's Prisons.* Aldershot: Ashgate Press.

Boyd, S. 1991. "Dislodging Certainties: Feminist and Postmodern Engagements with Criminology and State Theory." *Journal of Human Justice* 3(1): 113–23.

Boyd, Susan, and Karlene Faith. 1999. "Women, Illicit Drugs and Prison: Views from Canada." *International Journal of Drug Policy.*

Braun, Connie. 1998. "Colonization, Destruction and Renewal: Stories from Aboriginal Men at the Pe'Sakastew Centre." Master's Thesis, Saskatoon, University of Saskatchewan.

Brodsky, S., and F. Scogin. 1988. "Inmates in Protective Custody: First Data on Emotional Effects." *Forensic Reports* 1: 267–80.

Brody, C.M. 1987. *Women's Therapy Groups: Paradigms of Feminist Treatment..* New York: Springer Publishing Company.

Brown, J. 1975. "Influences Affecting the Treatment of Women Prisoners in Toronto, 1880 to 1890." MA Dissertation, Wilfred Laurier University.

Brown, L. 1992. "A Feminist Critique of the Personality Disorders." In L. Brown and M. Balou, (eds.), *Personality and Psychopathology: Feminist Reappraisals.* New York: Guildford Press.

Brown, T. 1980. "Living With God's Afflicted: A History of the Provincial Lunatic Asylum at Toronto: 1830–1911." Ph.D. Dissertation, Kingston, Queen's University.

Burstow, Bonnie. 1992. *Radical Feminist Therapy: Working in the Context of Violence.* Newbury Park: Sage Publications.

Butler, S., and C. Wintram. 1992. *Feminist Groupwork.* London: Sage Publications.

Campbell, A. 1993. *Men, Women and Aggression.* New York: Basic Books.

Campbell, Gayle. 1990. "Women and Crime." *Juristat Service Bulletin* 10(20). Ottawa: Canadian Centre for Justice Statistics.

Canada. 1988. *Task Force on Aboriginal Peoples in Federal Corrections.* Ottawa: Solicitor General.

_____. 1997. "Administrative Segregation: Commitment to Legal Compliance, Fair Decisions, and Effective Results". Report of the Task Force to Review. Administrative Segregation. Ottawa, Ont.: Correctional Service of Canada.

_____. 1998a. *Adult Correctional Services in Canada, 1996–97.* Ottawa: Canadian Centre for Justice Statistics.

_____. 1998b. *Women Offenders: The Corrections and Conditional Release Act Five Years Later. Toward a Just, Peaceful and Safe Society.* Ottawa: Solicitor General Canada.

Canadian Association of Elizabeth Fry Societies (CAEFS). 1989. *Executive Director's Report,* October/November CAEFS, 3. Ottawa: CAEFS.

_____. 1995. "Position Paper on Proposed Security Management System for Federally Sentenced Women." March 17. Ottawa: CAEFS.

_____. 1998a. "Position of CAEFS Regarding the Carceral Placement of Women Classified as Maximum Security Prisoners." March 10. Ottawa: CAEFS.

_____. 1998b. "Five Year Review of the Corrections and Conditional Release Act." September. Ottawa: CAEFS.

Canadian Corrections Association. 1969. "Brief on the Woman Offender." *Canadian Journal of Corrections* 11 (1): 26–60.

Canadian Sentencing Commission. 1987. *Sentencing Reform: A Canadian Approach*. Ottawa: Supply & Services.

Carlen, P. 1983. *Women's Imprisonment: A Study in Social Control*. London: Routledge.

_____. 1985. "Law, Psychiatry and Women's Imprisonment. A Sociological View." *British Journal of Psychiatry* 146: 618–21.

_____. 1986. "Psychiatry in Prisons: Promises, Premises, Practices and Politics." In P. Miller and N. Rose, (eds.), *The Power of Psychiatry*. London: Polity Press.

_____. 1988. *Women, Crime and Poverty*. Milton Keynes: Open University Press.

_____. 1990a. "Women, Crime, Feminism, and Realism." *Social Justice* 17(4): 106–23.

_____. 1990b. *Alternatives to Women's Imprisonment*. Milton Keynes: Open University Press.

_____. 1994. "Why Study Women's Imprisonment? Or Anyone Else's?" *British Journal of Criminology* 34 Special Issue: 131–40.

_____. 1998. *Sledgehammer. Women's Imprisonment at the Millennium*. Basingstoke: Macmillan Press.

Carlen, P., D. Christina, J. Hicks, J. O'Dwyer and C. Tchaikovsky. 1985. *Criminal Women*. Cambridge: Polity Press.

Carlen, P., and C. Tchaikovsky. 1996. "Women's Imprisonment in England at the End of the Twentieth Century: Legitimacy, Realities and Utopias." In R. Matthews and P. Francis, (eds.), *Prisons 2000: An International Perspective on the Current State and Future of Imprisonment*. New York: St. Martin's Press.

Carlen, P., and A. Worrall (ed.). 1987. *Gender, Crime and Justice*. Milton Keynes: Open University Press.

Carrigan, D.O. 1991. *Crime and Punishment in Canada, A History*. Toronto: McClelland & Stewart.

Castel, R. 1991. "From Dangerousness to Risk." In G. Burchell, C. Gordon and P. Miller, (eds.), *The Foucault Effect: Studies in Governmentality*. London: Harvester Wheatsheaf.

Chalke Report. 1972. *The General Program for the Development of Psychiatric Services in Federal Correctional Services in Canada*. Ottawa: Solicitor General Canada.

Chesler, P. 1972. *Women and Madness*. New York: Avon Books.

Chesney-Lind, M. 1995. "Preface." In N.H. Rafter and F. Heidensohn.

Chunn, D.E., and R. Menzies. 1990. "Gender, Madness and Crime: The Reproduction of Patriarchal and Class Relations in a Court Clinic." *The Journal of Human Justice* 1 (2): 33–54.

_____. 1998. "Out of Mind, Out of Law: The Regulation of 'Criminally Insane' Women inside British Columbia's Public Mental Hospitals, 1888–1973." *Canadian Journal of Women and the Law* 10(2): 306–337.

Clarke, R.A., M.J. Fisher and C. McDougall. 1993. "A New Methodology for Assessing the Level of Risk in Incarcerated Offenders." *British Journal of Criminology*, 33: 436–48.

Clement, Grace. 1996. *Care, Autonomy, and Justice: Feminism and the Ethic of Care*. Boulder: Westview Press.

Cohen, S. 1985. *Visions of Social Control*. Cambridge, U.K.: Polity Press.

Collin, Ginette. 1997. "Legal Aspects of Inmates' Security Classification." *Forum On Corrections Research* 9(1): 55–57.

Comack, E. 1993. *Feminist Engagement with the Law: The Legal Recognition of the Battered Women Syndrome*. The CRIAW Papers No. 31. Ottawa: Canadian Research

Institute for the Advancement of Women.

_____. 1996. *Women in Trouble.* Halifax: Fernwood Publishing.

_____ (ed.). 1999. *Locating Law: Race/Class/Gender Connections.* Halifax: Fernwood Publishing.

Commission on Systemic Racism in the Ontario Criminal Justice System. 1994. *Racism Behind Bars.* Interim Report.Toronto: Queen's Printer for Ontario.

_____. 1995. Report of the Commission on Systemic Racism in the Ontario Criminal Justice System. Toronto: Queen's Printer for Ontario.

Committee Appointed to Inquire into the Principles and Procedures Followed In the Remission Service of the Department of Justice. 1956. Report. Ottawa: Queen's Printer.

Committee of Inquiry into the Personality Disorder Unit, Ashworth Special Hospital. *Expert Evidence on Personality Disorder. Volume II.* London: HMSO.

Cooke, D.J. 1989. "Containing Violent Prisoners: An Analysis of the Barlinnie Special Unit." *British Journal of Criminology* 29(2):129–43.

_____. 1991. "Violence in Prisons: The Influence of Regime Factors." *Howard Journal of Criminal Justice* 30(2):95–109.

Cooper, S. 1987. "The Evolution of the Federal Women's Prison." In E. Adelberg and C. Currie.

_____. 1993. "The Evolution of the Federal Women's Prison." In E. Adelberg and C. Currie.

Correctional Service of Canada (CSC). 1980. *Steering Committee on Mentally and Behaviourally Disordered Inmates.* Ottawa: Correctional Service of Canada.

_____. 1988. *Management Officer's Perceptions Concerning the Prevalence of Mental Disorders: Identification, Needs and Resources in Minimum Security Institutions and on Conditional Release.* Ottawa: Corrections Services Canada, Offender Policy and Program Development Sector.

_____. 1993. *Healing Lodge—Final Operating Plan.* Ottawa: Correctional Service of Canada.

_____. 1994. *Correctional Program Strategy for Women.* Ottawa: Correctional Service of Canada.

_____. 1995a. *Substance Abuse Program for Women.* Ottawa: Correctional Service of Canada.

_____. 1995b. *Board of Investigation—Major Disturbance and Other Related Incidents—Prison For Women from Friday April 22 to Tuesday April 26, 1994.* Ottawa: Correctional Service of Canada.

_____. 1996a. *Interim Commissioner's Directive.* September. Ottawa: Correctional Service of Canada.

_____. 1996b. *Major Inmate Disturbance: NOVA Institution, September 5, 1996.* Ottawa: Correctional Service of Canada.

_____. 1997a. *Board of Investigation into the Disturbance on the Federally Sentenced Women Unit, Saskatchewan Penitentiary July 12, 1997.*

_____. 1997b. *Administrative Segregation: Commitment to Legal Compliance, Fair Decisions, and Effective Results.* Report of the Task Force to Review Administrative Segregation. Ottawa: Correctional Service of Canada.

_____. 1997c. *Board of Investigation into the Disturbance on the Federally Sentenced Women's Unit, Saskatchewan Penitentiary, July 12, 1997.* August 5. Ottawa: Correctional Service of Canada.

_____. 1997d. *Board of Investigation into a Suicide on February 29, 1996, and Other Major Incidents at Edmonton Institution for Women.* August 20. Ottawa: Correctional Service of Canada.

_____. 1997e. *Board of Investigation into Alleged Inappropriate Application of Use of Force by the Cell Extraction Team on a Female Inmate at Springhill Institution From March 1, 1997–March 9, 1997.* September 23. Ottawa: Correctional Service of Canada.

_____. 1997f. *csc Action Plan.* Nov. 26 (Protected).

_____. 1998a. *Board of Investigation into Allegations of Mistreatment by a Former Inmate at the Prison for Women Between March 22, 1960 and August 1, 1963.* Ottawa: Correctional Service of Canada.

_____. 1998b. "Offender Management System." Unpublished statistics February 1998. Ottawa: Correctional Service of Canada.

_____. 1999a. News Release. "National Strategy for High Need Women Offenders in Federal Institutions." September 3, 1999. http://www.csc-scc.gc.ca/text/releases/99-09-03_e.shtml.

_____. 1999b. News Release. "Backgrounder—What is the Strategy?" September 3, 1999. http://www.csc-scc.gc.ca/text/releases/99-09-03str_e.shtml.

_____. n.d. Major Inmate Disturbance: NOVA Institution, September 5, 1996. Board of Investigation into the Disturbance on the Federally Sentenced Women Unit, Saskatchewan Penitentiary.

Coulson, G.E., and V. Nutbrown. 1992. "Properties of an Ideal Rehabilitative Program for High-Needs Offenders." *International Journal of Offender Therapy and Comparative Criminology* 36(3): 203–08.

Crenshaw, K. 1992. "Whose Story Is It, Anyway? Feminist and Anti-Racist Appropriations of Anita Hill." In T. Morrison, (ed.), *Race in Justice, Engendering Power.* Pantheon.

Cruikshank, Barbara. 1993. "Revolutions within Self-government and Self-esteem." *Economy and Society* 22(3) August: 327–43.

_____. 1994. "The Will to Empower: Technologies of Citizenship and the War on Poverty." *Socialist Review* 93(4): 29–55.

Crump, Judy. 1995. *Literature Review on Women's Anger and other Emotions.* Ottawa: Correctional Service of Canada.

Culhane, Claire. 1972. *Why is Canada in Vietnam?* Toronto: NC Press.

_____. 1979. *Barred from Prison: A Personal Account.* Vancouver: Arsenal Pulp Press.

_____. 1985. *Still Barred from Prison.* Montreal: Black Rose Books.

_____. 1991. *No Longer Barred from Prison.* Montreal: Black Rose Books.

Daly, K., and M. Chesney-Lind. 1988. "Feminism and Criminology." *Justice Quarterly* 5(4): 101–43.

Daly, K., and L. Maher. 1998. *Criminology at the Crossroads: Feminist Readings in Crime & Justice.* Oxford: Oxford University Press.

Daubney, David, M.P., Chairman. 1988. *Taking Responsibility. The Report of the Standing Committee on Justice and Solicitor General on its Review of Sentencing, Conditional Release and Related Aspects of Corrections.* Ottawa: Queen's Printer, issue no. 65.

Dell, Anne, and Roger Boe. 1998. *Adult Female Offenders in Canada: Recent Trends.* Ottawa: Correctional Service of Canada, Correctional Research Branch.

Deurloo, B., and C. Haythornthwaite. 1990. *Task Force on Mental Health. Sub-Task #12. Special Needs of Female Offenders.* Ottawa: Correctional Service of Canada.

Dickie, I., and L. Ward. 1997. "Women Offenders Convicted of Robbery and Assault." *Forum on Corrections Research* 9(2): 29–32

Dobash, R.E., and R.P. Dobash. 1992. *Women, Violence and Social Change.* London: Routledge.

Dobash, R.E., R. P. Dobash and S. Gutteridge. 1986. *The Imprisonment of Women.* New

York: Routledge.

Dougherty, J. 1993. "Women's Violence against Their Children: A Feminist Perspective." *Women and Criminal Justice* 4(2): 91–114.

Douglas, M. 1992. *Risk Acceptability According to the Social Sciences*. London: Routledge and Kegan Paul.

Dowden, C., and K. Blanchette. 1999. *An Investigstion into the Characteristics of Substance Abusing Women Offenders: Risk, Need and Post-Release Outcome*. Report No. R-81. Ottawa: Correctional Service of Canada.

Doyle, A., and R.V. Ericson. 1996. "Breaking into Prison. News Sources and Correctional Institutions." *Canadian Journal of Criminology* 38(2): 155–90.

Duggan, Lisa. 1992. *Voice Literary Supplement*. Comments during a conference on "Queer Theory." Rutgers, Nov. 1991.

Ekstedt, J.W., and C.T. Griffiths. 1984. *Corrections in Canada. Policy and Practice*. Toronto: Butterworths.

Elizabeth Fry Society of Edmonton. 1994. *Common Threads: Women Who have Been in Conflict Tell their Stories*. Edmonton: Elizabeth Fry Society of Edmonton.

Elizabeth Fry Society of Edmonton and the Women's Program of the Secretary of State Dept. of Canada. 1993. *Building Pathways. The Employment Needs of Provincially Sentenced Women*. October.

Evans, Monica J. 1995. "Stealing Away: Black Women, Outlaw Culture and the Rhetoric of Rights." In R. Delgado, (ed.), *Critical Race Theory: the Cutting Edge*. Philadelphia: Temple University Press.

Eveson, M. 1964. "Research with Female Drug Addicts at the Prison for Women." *Canadian Journal of Corrections* 6: 21–27.

Ewick, Patricia, and Susan Silbey. 1995. "Subversive Stories and Hegemonic Tales: Toward a Sociology of Narrative." *Law and Society Review* 29(2): 197–226.

Fabiano, E., F. Porporino and D. Robinson. 1990. *Rehabilitation through Clearer Thinking: A Cognitive Model of Correctional Intervention*. Ottawa: Research and Statistics Branch, Correctional Service of Canada.

Faith, Karlene. 1989. "Justice: Where Art Thou? And Do We Care?" *Journal of Justice* J(1): 77– 98.

_____. 1991. "Gender, Power, and Foucault." *Institute for the Humanities* 4(2) Spring.

_____. 1993a. *Unruly Women: The Politics and Confinement of Resistance*. Vancouver: Press Gang Publishers.

_____. 1993b. "Media, Myths and Masculinization: Images of Women in Prison." In E. Adelberg and C. Currie.

_____. 1995. "Aboriginal Women's Healing Lodge: Challenge to Penal Correctionalism?" *Journal of Human Justice* 6(2) Spring/Autumn: 79–104.

_____. 1999. "Transformative Justice vs. Re-entrenched Correctionalism: The Canadian Experience." In S. Cook and S. Davies, (eds.), *Harsh Punishments*. Boston: Northeastern Press.

Faith, Karlene, and Mary Gottfriedson, Cherry Joe, Wendy Leonard and Sharon. 1990. "Native Women in Canada: A Quest for Justice." *Social Justice* 17(3): 1.

Fauteaux Commission, Canada. 1956. *Report on a Commission Appointed to Inquire into the Principles and Practices Followed in the Remission Service of the Department of Justice*. Ottawa: Department of Justice.

Federally Sentenced Women Program (FSWP). 1994. Literature Review. Ottawa: Correctional Service of Canada.

Feeley, M., and J. Simon. 1992. "The New Penology: Notes on Emerging Strategy for

Corrections and Its Implications" *Criminology* 30(4): 49–74.

_____. 1994. "Actuarial Justice: The Emerging New Criminal Law." In D. Nelken, (ed.), *The Futures of Criminology*. London: Sage.

Findlay, Susan. 1987. "Facing the State: The Politics of the Women's Movement Reconsidered." In J.H. Maroney and M. Luxton, (eds.), *Feminism and Political Economy: Women's Work, Women's Struggles*. Toronto: Methuen.

Finn, Anne, Shelley Trevethan, Gisèle Carrière and Melanie Kowalski. 1999. "Female Inmates, Aboriginal Inmates, and Inmates Serving Life Sentences: A One-Day Snapshot." *Juristat* 19(5). Ottawa, ON: Canadian Centre for Justice Statistics.

Flint, M. 1960. "An Experiment in the Rehabilitation of Women Offenders." *Canadian Journal of Corrections* July: 240–54.

_____. 1964. "Narcotic Addiction in Women Offenders." *Canadian Journal of Corrections* 6: 246–65.

Foucault, M. 1977. *Discipline and Punish: The Birth of the Prison*. London: Allen Lane.

_____. 1978. "About the Concept of the 'Dangerous Individual' in 19th Century Legal Psychiatry." *International Journal of Law and Psychiatry* 1: 1–18.

_____. 1991. "Governmentality." In G. Burchell, C. Gordon and P. Miller, (eds.), *The Foucault Effect: Studies in Governmentality*. Chicago: University of Chicago Press.

Fraser, Nancy. 1989. "Struggle Over Needs: Outline of a Socialist-Feminist Theory of Late Capitalist Political Culture." In *Unruly Practices: Power, Discourse and Gender in Contemporary Social Theory*. Minneapolis: University of Minnesota Press.

Fraser, Nancy, and Linda Gordon. 1997. "A Genealogy of 'Dependency': Tracing a Key Word of the U.S. Welfare State." In Nancy Fraser, (ed.), *Justice Interruptus: Critical Reflections on the "Postsocialist" Condition*. New York: Routledge.

Freedman, E. 1981. *Their Sisters' Keepers: Women's Prison Reform in America 1830–1930*. Ann Arbour: University of Michigan Press.

Freire, Paulo. 1982. *Pedagogy of the Oppressed*. NY: The Continuum Publishing Corp.

Friedland, Martin L. 1986. *The Case of Valentine Shortis. The True Story of Crime and Politics in Canada*. Toronto: University of Toronto Press.

_____. 1988. *Sentencing Structure in Canada: Historical Perspective*. Research Reports of the Canadian Sentencing Commission. Ottawa: Department of Justice.

Frigon, S. 1997. "Sexe, Mensonge et Vidéo." *Journal of Prisoners on Prisons* 8(1 & 2): 105–12.

_____. 1999. "Une Radioscopie des événements survenus à la Prison des Femmes de Kingston en Ontario en Avril 1994: La Construction d'un corps dangereux et d'un corps en danger." *Canadian Women Studies/Les cahiers de la femme* 19(1&2). Toronto: York University Publications.

Garland, D. 1985. *Punishment and Welfare: A History of Penal Strategies*. Brookfield: Grower Publishing Co.

_____. 1990. *Punishment and Modern Society: A Study in Social Theory*. New York: Oxford University Press.

_____. 1996. "The Limits of the Sovereign State: Strategies of Crime Control in Contemporary Society." *British Journal of Criminology*. 36(4): 445–71.

Geertz, Clifford. 1988. "Us/Not Us" In Clifford Geertz *Works and Lives: The Anthropologist as Author*. Stanford: Stanford University Press.

Gelsthorpe, Loraine, and Allison Morris. 1990. *Feminist Perspectives in Criminology*. Milton Keynes: Open University Press.

Genders, E., and E. Player. 1986. "Women's Imprisonment: The Effects of Youth Custody." *British Journal of Criminology* 26(4): 357–71.

Gendreau, P. 1981. "Treatment in Corrections: Martinson was Wrong." *Canadian Psychology* 22: 332–38.

Gendreau, P., and D.A. Andrews. 1990. "Tertiary Prevention: What the Meta-Analyses Tell us about 'What Works'." *Canadian Journal of Criminology* 32: 173–84.

Gendreau, P., and C. Goggin. 1996. "Principles of Effective Correctional Programming." *Forum on Corrections Research* 8 (3): 38–41.

Gilbert, N. 1987. "Advocacy Research and Social Policy." In M. Tonry, (ed.), *Crime and Justice*. Vol. 22. Chicago: University of Chicago Press.

Gilmore, N., and M.A. Somerville. 1998. *A Review of the Use of LSD and ECT at the Prison for Women in the Early 1960s*. Ottawa: Correctional Service of Canada.

Gleason, M. 1997. "Psychology and the Construction of the 'Normal' Family in Postwar Canada, 1945–60." *The Canadian Historical Review* 78(3): 442–77.

_____. 1999. *Normalizing the Ideal. Psychology, Schooling and the Family in Postwar Canada*. Toronto: University of Toronto Press.

Globe and Mail. 1999. "Ottawa Makes Plans to Close Aging Prison." September 4: A5.

Goff, C. 1999. *Corrections in Canada*. Cincinnati: Anderson Publishing Co.

Gordon, Jody K. 1992. "The 'Fallen' and the Masculine: A Feminist Historical Analysis of the B.C. Industrial Home for Girls, 1914–1946." Unpublished Honours Thesis. School of Criminology, Simon Fraser University.

Gorsuch, N. 1998. "Unmet Needs among Disturbed Female Offenders." *The Journal of Forensic Psychiatry*, 9(3): 556–70.

Grassian, S. 1983. "Psychological Effects of Solitary Confinement." *American Journal of Psychiatry*, 140: 1450–54.

Grassian, S., and N. Friedman. 1986. "Effects of Sensory Deprivation in Psychiatric Seclusion and Solitary Confinement." *International Journal of Law and Psychiatry*, 8: 49–65.

Greenland, Dr. Cyril. 1987. "Twenty Years of Research in the Field of Dangerousness." *Liaison* (May).

Greenspan, M. 1983. *A New Approach to Women and Therapy*. New York: McGraw Hill.

Griffiths, C.T., and A. Cunningham. 2000. *Canadian Corrections*. Scarborough: Nelson.

HM Chief Inspector of Prisons. 1997. *Women in Prison: A Thematic Review*. London: Home Office.

Habermas, J. 1987. *The Philosophical Discourse on Modernity: Twelve Lectures*. Cambridge, Massachusetts: Massachusetts Institute of Technology.

Hamelin, M. 1989. *Femmes et prison*. Montreal: Méridien.

Hamilton, A.C., and C.M. Sinclair. 1991. *The Justice System and Aboriginal People: Report of the Aboriginal Justice Inquiry of Manitoba*. Winnipeg: Queen's Printer.

Haney, C. 1993. " 'Infamous Punishment': The Psychological Consequences of Isolation." *The National Prison Project* 3–21.

Hannah-Moffat, Kelly. 1991. "Creating Choices or Repeating History: Canadian Female Offenders and Correctional Reform." *Social Justice* 8(3): 184–203.

_____. 1994. "Unintended Consequences of Feminism and Prison Reform." *Forum on Corrections Research*. Ottawa: Correctional Service of Canada.

_____. 1995. "Feminine Fortresses: Women-centred Prisons?" *The Prison Journal* 75(2): 135–64.

_____. 1997. "From Christian Maternalism to Risk Technologies: Penal Powers and Women's Knowledges in the Governance of Female Prisons." Ph.D. dissertation. Toronto: University of Toronto, Centre of Criminology.

_____. 1999. "Moral Agent or Actuarial Subject: Risk and Canadian Women's Imprisonment." *Theoretical Criminology* 3(1): 71–94.

_____. 2000. Forthcoming. "Prisons that Empower: Neoliberal Governance in Canadian Women's Prisons." *British Journal of Criminology* Winter.

_____. Forthcoming. "Punishment in Disguise: Penal Governance in Canadian Women's Prisons. Toronto: University of Toronto Press.

Hannah-Moffat, K., and M. Shaw. Forthcoming. *Gender and Diversity Issues in Risk and Classification Management*. Report of a study for Status of Women, Canada.

Harding, S. 1986. *The Science Question in Feminism*. Milton Keynes: Open University Press.

_____. 1987. *Feminism and Methodology*. Bloomington, IN.: Indiana University Press.

_____. 1991. *Whose Science? Whose Knowledge?: Thinking from Women's Lives*. Ithaca: Cornell University Press.

Hargreaves, D. 1967. *Social Relations in a Secondary School*. London: Routledge and Kegan Paul.

Haslam, P. 1964. "The Female Prisoner." *Canadian Journal of Corrections* 7: 338–50.

Hatch, Alison J., and Karlene Faith. 1989–90. "The Female Offender in Canada: A Statistical Profile." *Canadian Journal of Women and the Law*, 3(J): 433–56.

Hattem, T. 1984. *Le recours à l'Isolement cellulaire dans quatre établissements de détention du Québec*. Université de Montréal: Centre International de Criminologie Comparé.

_____. 1990. "L'histoire se poursuit…." Femme et Justice, Organe d'information de la Sociéte Elizabeth Fry de Montréal 5(5).

_____. 1991a. "Vive avec ses Peines." *Déviance et Société* 15(2): 137–56.

_____. 1991b. "Vive avec ses Peines: Les Fondements et les Enjeux de l'usage de Médicaments Psychotropes saisis à l'emprisonment à Perpétuité." *Criminologie* XXIV(1): 49–61.

Hayman, S. 1996. *Community Prisons for Women*. London: Prison Reform Trust.

Heidensohn, F. 1968. "The Deviance of Women: A Critique and an Inquiry." *British Journal of Sociology* 19(2): 160–75.

_____. 1985. *Women and Crime*. New York: New York University Press.

_____. 1992. "Sociological Perspectives on Violence by Women." Paper given at University of Montreal, February 1992.

_____. 1995. "Feminist Perspectives and their Impact on Criminology and Criminal Justice in Britain." In N.H. Rafter and F. Heidensohn.

Heney, Jan. 1990. *Report on Self-Injurious Behaviour in the Kingston Prison for Women*. Ottawa: Solicitor General.

Hester, M., L. Kelly and J. Radford (eds.). 1996. *Women, Violence, and Male Power*. Buckingham: Open University Press.

Hogan, T., and L. Guglielmo. 1985. *Mental Disorder Needs Identification Study*. Ottawa: Correctional Service of Canada.

hooks, bell. 1995. *Killing Rage: Ending Racism*. New York: Henry Holt and Company.

Hornblum, A.M. 1998. *Acres of Skin. Human Experiments at Holmseburg Prison*. London: Routledge.

Horii, Gayle. 1992. "The Art In/Of Survival." *Matriart: A Canadian Feminist Art Journal*, 3(J):1.

_____. 1993. "Healing the Past, Forming the Future." Address, National Association of Women and the Law Tenth Biennial Conference, Vancouver, February 19–21.

Horster, Detlef. 1991. *Habermas: An Introduction*. Philadelphia: Pennbridge Books.

Howe, Adrian. 1994. *Punish and Critique: Towards a Feminist Analysis of Penality*. London: Routledge.

Ignatieff, M. 1978. *A Just Measure of Pain*. London: Penguin Books.

Imbleau, Monique. 1987. Profession détenue. Cahier du GRAPPP (Groupe de recherche et d'analyse sur les politiques et les pratiques pénales). Montréal: Université du Québec à Montréal (Département de sociologie).

Immarigeon, R., and M. Chesney-Lind. 1992. *Women's Prisons Overcrowded and Overused*. San Francisco, CA: National Council on Crime and Delinquency.

Jackson, Michael. 1983. *Prisoners of Isolation: Solitary Confinement in Canada*. Toronto: University of Toronto Press.

Jackson, M., D. Hitchen and W. Glackman. 1995. *Corrections Branch Programs for Female Offenders: Perspectives and Visions*. Burnaby, B.C.: Simon Fraser University Criminology Research Centre.

Jaggar, A.M. 1989. "Love, Knowledge: Emotion in Feminist Epistemology." In A. Garry and M. Persall, (eds.), *Women, Knowledge and Reality: Explorations in Feminist Philosophy*. London: Unwin Human.

Johnson, H. and K. Rodgers. 1993. "Getting the Facts Straight." In E. Adelberg and C. Currie.

Joliffe, K. 1983. "An Examination of Medical Services at the Kingston Penitentiary, 1835–1856." M.A. Thesis, Kingston: Queen's University.

_____. 1984. *Penitentiary Medical Services, 1835–1983*. (Report No, 1984-19). Ottawa: Solicitor General Canada.

Kantrowitz, R.E., and M. Ballou. 1992. "A Feminist Critique of Cognitive-Behavioral Therapy." In L. Brown and M. Balou, (eds.), *Personality and Psychopathology. Feminist Reappraisals*. New York: Guildford Press.

Kelly, L. 1996. "When does the Speaking Profit Us?: Reflections on the Challenges of Developing Feminist Perspectives on Abuse and Violence by Women." In M. Hester, L. Kelly, and J. Radford.

Kendall, K. 1993a. *Program Evaluation of Therapeutic Services at the Prison for Women*. Ottawa: Correctional Service Canada.

_____. 1993b. Companion Volume I. Literature Review. *Program Evaluation of Therapeutic Services at the Prison for Women*. Ottawa: Correctional Service Canada.

_____. 1993c. Companion Volume II. Supporting Documents. *Program Evaluation of Therapeutic Services at the Prison for Women*. Ottawa: Correctional Service Canada.

_____. 1994a. "Therapy Behind Prison Walls: A Contradiction in Terms?" *Prison Service Journal* 96 (November): 2–11.

_____. 1994b. "The Discipline and Control of Women." Review essay. *The Journal of Human Justice* 6(1): 111–19.

_____. 1999a. "Beyond Grace: Criminal Lunatic Women in Victorian Canada." *Canadian Woman's Studies* 19(1&2): 110–15.

_____. 1999b. "The Rockwood Asylum and Criminal Lunatic Women in 19th Century Canada." *Forum on Corrections Research*. September.

Kershaw, Anne, and Mary Lasovich. 1991. *Rock-a-Bye Baby: A Death Behind Bars*. Toronto: McClelland & Stewart.

Kersten, J. 1990. "A Gender Specific Look at Patterns of Violence in Juvenile Institutions: Or are Girls Really 'More Difficult to Handle'?" *International Journal of Sociology and the Law* 18:473–93.

King, R. 1991. "Maximum-Security Custody in Britain and the U.S.A.: A Study of Gartree and Oak Park Heights." *British Journal of Criminology* 31(2):126–52.

King, R., and K. McDermott. 1990. "My Geranium is Subversive: Some Notes on the Management of Trouble in Prisons." *British Journal of Sociology* 41(4):445–71.

Klein, D. 1973. "The Etiology of Female Crime: A Review of the Literature." *Issues in Criminology* 8(2): 3–30.

Krueger, Alice. 1996. "Poor need help: Judge." *Winnipeg Free Press*. December 10: A5.

Kuhn, T. 1996. *The Structure of Scientific Revolutions*. Third edition. Chicago: University of Chicago Press.

Kupers, T. 1999. *Prison Madness. The Mental Health Crisis Behind Bars and What We Must Do About It*. San Francisco: Jossey-Bass Publishers.

Kutchins, H. and S.A. Kirk. 1997. *Making Us Crazy*. DSM-*The Psychiatric Bible and the Creation of Mental Disorders*. London: The Free Press.

LaChance, André. 1988. "Women and Crime in Canada in the Early Eighteenth Century, 1712–1759." In R.C. Macleod, (ed.), *Lawful Authority: Readings on the History of Criminal Justice in Canada*. Toronto: Copp Clark Pitman.

Laishes, J. 1997. *Mental Health Strategy for Women Offenders*. Ottawa: Correctional Service of Canada, Federally Sentenced Women Program.

Laishes, Jane and Sandra Lyth. 1996. *Intensive Healing (Mental Health) Program*. Ottawa: Correctional Service of Canada, Federally Sentenced Women Program.

LaJeunesse, T., and C. Jefferson. 1998. *Cross-Gender Monitoring Project, Federally Sentenced Women's Facilities—First Annual Report*. Ottawa: Correctional Service of Canada.

_____. 1999. *Cross-Gender Monitoring Project, Federally Sentenced Women's Facilities—Second Annual Report*. Ottawa: Correctional Service of Canada.

Lambert, L., and P. Madden. 1974. *Summary of the Vanier Centre for Women*. Research Report No. 1. An Examination of the Social Milieu. Ottawa: Ministry of Correctional Services.

LaPrairie, C. 1992. "Aboriginal Crime and Justice: Explaining the Present, Exploring the Future." *Canadian Journal of Criminology* 34(3–4):281–97.

_____. 1993. "Aboriginal Women and Crime in Canada: Identifying the Issues." In E. Adelberg and C. Currie.

Lavigne, B., L. Hoffman and I. Dickie. 1997. "Women who have Committed Homicide." *Forum on Corrections Research* 9(2): 25–29.

Lewis and Appleby. 1988. "Personality Disorder: The Patients Psychiatrists Dislike." *British Journal of Psychiatry* 153: 44–49.

Liebling, A. 1992. *Suicide in Prison*. London: Routledge.

_____. 1994. "Suicide among Women Prisoners." *Howard Journal of Criminal Justice* 33(1):1–9.

_____. 1995. "Vulnerability and Prison Suicide." *British Journal of Criminology* 35(2):173–87.

Liebling, A., and D. Ward (eds.). 1994. *Deaths in Custody: International Perspectives*. Bournemouth: Whiting & Birch.

Lindquist, C.A. 1980. "Prison Discipline and the Female Offender." *Journal of Offender Counselling, Services and Rehabilitation* 4(4):305–18.

Linehan, M. 1993a. *Cognitive Behavioral Treatment for Borderline Personality Disorder*. New York: Guildford Press.

_____. 1993b. *Skills Training Manual for Treating Borderline Personality Disorder*. London: Guildford Press.

Long, David and Ovide Dickason. 1996. *Visions of the Heart*. Toronto: Harcourt Brace (Second edition, forthcoming).

Los, M. 1990. "Feminism and Rape Law Reform." In L. Gelsthorpe and A. Morris.

Loucks, A., and E. Zamble 1994. "Some Comparisons of Female and Male Serious Offenders." *Forum on Corrections Research* 6(1):22–25.

_____. 1999. "Predictors of Recidivism in Serious Female Offenders. Canada Searches for Predictors Common to Both Men and Women." *Corrections Today* February: 26–28, 30–32.

Lowe, Mick. 1992. *One Woman Army.* Toronto: Macmillan.

Lupton, D. 1999. *Risk.* London: Routledge.

Lyons, Kris. 1996. "Barriers to Equality at British Columbia's Centre for Women: Can We Slash the Gordian Knot?" In M.A. Jackson and N.K.S. Banks, (eds.).], *Ten Years Later. The Charter and Equality for Women.* Burnaby: Simon Fraser University.

MacKinnon, C. 1982. "Feminism, Marxism, Method and the State: Towards Feminist Jurisprudence." *Signs* 8(4): 635–58.

MacLean, Brian D., and Harold E. Pepinsky (eds). 1993. *We Who Would Take no Prisoners.* Selections From the Fifth International Conference on Penal Abolition. Vancouver: Collective Press.

Macleod, Linda. 1986. *Sentenced to Separation: An Exploration of the Needs and Problems of Mothers who are Offenders and their Children.* Ottawa: Ministry of the Solicitor General.

Maden, T. 1997. *Women, Prisoners and Psychiatry: Mental Disorder Behind Bars.* London: Butterworth Heineman.

Maden, T., M. Swinton and J. Gunn. 1994. "Criminological and Psychiatric Survey of Women Serving a Prison Sentence." *British Journal of Criminology* 34(2): 172–91.

Mandaraka-Sheppard, A. 1986. *The Dynamics of Aggression in Women's Prisons in England and Wales.* London: Gower.

Mann, C. 1988. *Female Crime and Delinquency.* Birmingham: University of Alabama Press.

Marron, K. 1996. *The Slammer: The Crisis in Canada's Prison System.* Toronto: Doubleday.

Martel, J. 1999. *Solitude and Cold Storage: Women's Journeys of Endurance in Segregation.* Elizabeth Fry Society, Edmonton, Alberta: ACI Achievement Communications Inc.

Mason, Karen. 1992. "Familial Ideology in the Courts: The Sentencing of Women." Master's Thesis, School of Criminology, Simon Fraser University.

Mason, T., and D. Mercer. 1999. *A Sociology of the Mentally Disordered Offender.* London: Longman.

Mathiesen, T. 1974. *The Politics of Abolition: Essays in Political Action Theory.* Oxford: Martin Robertson.

Mayhew, Jo-Anne. 1992. "Truro: Women Delivered to a Pork Barrel Decision." *Matriart: A Canadian Feminist Art Journal* 39(1):15.

McConnell, Moira. 1993. "Feminist Analysis as the Embodiment of Marginalization." A presentation for the WILIG Panel, *Developing a Feminist Theory of International Law.* Washington. April 3.

McConney, Denise. 1999. "Differences for our Daughters: Racialized Sexism in Art, Mass Media and Law." *Canadian Woman Studies* 19(1&2):209–14.

McDonagh, D. 1999. *Federally Sentenced Women Maximum Security Interview Project: "Not Letting the Time Do You."* Ottawa: Correctional Service of Canada.

McGovern, Constance M. 1986. "The Myths of Social Control and Custodial Oppression: Patterns of Psychiatric Medicine in Late Nineteenth-Century Institutions." *Journal of Social History* 20(3): 3–23.

McGrath, A. 1992. "Mental Health Services for Women." *Healthsharing* Spring/Summer: 27–30.

McLean, J. 1995. "The Power of Feminist versus Other Critical Perspectives in the Analysis

of North American Prisons for Women." Ph.D. dissertation. University of Montreal.
McMahon, M. 1999a. *Women On Guard: Discrimination and Harassment in Corrections.* Toronto: University of Toronto Press.
_____. 1999b. "Assisting Female Offenders: Art or Science" Chairperson's Commentary on the 1998 Annual Conference of the International Community Corrections Association, September 27–30, Arlington, Virginia.
Melossi, Dario, and Massimo Pavarini. 1981. *The Prison and the Factory: Origins of the Penitentiary System.* London: Macmillan.
Menzies, R. 1987. "Cycles of Control: The Transcarceral Careers of Forensic Patients." *International Journal of Law and Psychiatry* 10(3):233–49.
_____. 1991. "Psychiatry, Dangerousness and Legal Control." In N. Boyd, (ed.), *The Social Dimensions of Law.* Scarborough, Ontario: Prentice-Hall.
Menzies, R. and D.E. Chunn. Forthcoming. "The Gender Politics of Criminal Insanity: 'Order-In-Council' Women in British Columbia, 1888-1950." *Social History.*
Menzies, R., D.E. Chunn and C.D. Webster. 1992. "Risky Business: The Classification of Dangerous People in the Canadian Carceral Enterprise." In K.R.E. McCormich and L.A. Visano (eds.), *Canadian Penology: Advanced Perspectives and Research.* Toronto: Canadian Scholars' Press.
Messerschmidt, J.W. 1995. "From Patriarchy to Gender: Feminist Theory, Criminology and the Challenge of Diversity." In N.H. Rafter. and F. Heidensohn, (eds.), *International Feminist Perspectives in Criminology: Engendering a Discipline.* Buckingham: Open University Press.
_____. 1997. *Crime as Structured Action: Gender, Race, Class and Crime in the Making.* Thousand Oaks, CA: Sage.
Mitchinson, W. 1991. *The Nature of their Bodies: Women and their Doctors in Victorian Canada.* Toronto: University of Toronto Press.
Monture-Angus, Patricia. 1995a. *Thunder in My Soul: A Mohawk Woman Speaks.* Halifax: Fernwood Publishing.
_____. 1995b. "Roles and Responsibilities." In *Thunder in My Soul: A Mohawk Woman Speaks.* Halifax: Fernwood Publishing.
_____. 1996. "Lessons in Decolonization: Aboriginal Over-Representation in Canadian Criminal Justice." In D. Long and O. Dickason.
_____. 1999a. *Journeying Forward: Dreaming First Nations Independence.* Halifax: Fernwood Publishing.
_____. 1999b. "The Justice Report of the Royal Commission on Aboriginal Peoples: Breaking with the Past?" Prepared for Building the Momentum: A Conference on Implementing the Recommendations of the Royal Commission on Aboriginal Peoples, April 22–24, 1999 at Osgoode Hall, Toronto, Ontario.
_____. 1999c. "Standing against Canadian Law: Naming Omissions of Race, Culture, and Gender." In E. Comack.
_____. 1999d. "Women and Risk: Aboriginal Women, Colonialism and Correctional Practice." *Canadian Woman Studies* 19(1&2): 24–29.
Moran, J.E. 1998. "Insanity, the Asylum and Society in Nineteenth Century Quebec and Ontario." Unpublished Ph.D. Dissertation, Toronto, York University.
Moran, P. 1999. *Antisocial Personality Disorder: An Epidemiological Perspective.* London: Gaskell.
Morgan, R. 1994. "Minimizing Risk of Suicide in Custody." In A. Liebling and D. Ward.
Morin, S. 1999. *Federally Sentenced Aboriginal Women in Maximum Security: What Happened to the Promises of "Creating Choices"?* Ottawa: Correctional Service

of Canada.

Morris, A. 1987. *Women, Crime and Criminal Justice*. Oxford: Basil Blackwell.

Morris, A., and A. Wilczynski. 1993. "Rocking the Cradle: Mothers who Kill their Children." In H. Birch, (ed.), *Moving Targets: Women, Murder and Representation*. London: Virago Books.

Motiuk, Larry. 1997. "Classification for Correctional Programming: The Offender Intake Assessment (OIA) Process." *Forum on Corrections Research* 9(1): 18–22.

Motiuk, Larry, and Kelly Blanchette. 1997. *Case Characteristics of Segregated Offenders In Federal Corrections* (Report No. R-57). Ottawa: Correctional Service of Canada.

_____. 1998. "Assessing Female Offenders: What Works?" Paper Presented at the Annual Conference of the International Community Corrections Asociation, September 27–30, Arlington, Virginia.

Naffine, N. 1987. *Female Crime: The Construction of Women in Criminology*. Sydney: Allen & Unwin.

Naylor, B. 1995. "Women's Crime and Media Coverage: Making Explanations." In R.E. Dobash, R.P. Dobash and L. Noakes, (eds.), *Gender and Crime*. Cardiff: University of Wales Press.

Nesbitt, C. and A.R. Argento. 1984. *Female Classification: An Examination of the Issues*. College Park Maryland: American Correctional Association.

Newburn, T. and E. Stanko. 1994. *Just Boys Doing Business: Men, Masculinities and Crime*. London: Routledge.

Noonan, S. 1993. "Strategies for Survival: Beyond the Battered Woman Syndrome." In E. Adelberg and C. Currie, (eds.), *In Conflict With the Law: Women and the Canadian Justice System*. Vancouver: Press Gang.

Norris, Mary Jane. 1996. "Contemporary Demography of Aboriginal Peoples in Canada." In D.A. Long and O.P. Dickason, (eds.), *Visions of the Heart: Canadian Aboriginal Issues*. Toronto: Harcourt Brace.

Oakes, Larry. 1999. Personal interviews, April 27, 1999; August 3, 1999; and August 4, 1999.

O'Brien, Patricia. 1982. *The Promise of Punishment: Prisons in Nineteenth Century France*. Princeton: Princeton University Press.

Oliver, P. 1998. *Terror to Evil-Doers*. Toronto: The Osgoode Society for Canadian Legal History.

_____. 1994. "To Govern by Kindness: The First Two Decades of the Mercer Reformatory for Women." In J. Phillips, T. Loo and S. Lewthwaite, (eds.), *Essays in the History of Canadian Law: Crime and Criminal Justice* (volume v). Toronto: The Osgoode Society for Canadian Legal History.

O'Malley, Pat. 1992. "Risk, Power and Crime Prevention." *Economy and Society* 21(3): 252–75.

_____. 1994. "Penalising Crime in Advanced Liberalism." Melbourne: Department of Legal Studies, La Trobe University.

_____. 1996. "Risk and Responsibility." In A. Barry, T. Osbourne and N. Rose.

_____. 1998. *Crime and the Risk Society —The International Library of Criminology, Criminal Justice and Penology*. Australia: Ashgate Dartmouth.

Paglia, Camille. 1991. *Sexual Personae*. NY: Vintage Books.

Parent, C., and F. Digneffe. 1996. "A Feminist Contribution to Ethics in Criminal Justice Intervention." In T. O'Reilly-Fleming, (ed.), *Post-Critical Criminology*. Scarborough: Prentice Hall Canada.

Pate, Kim. 1994. "This Woman's Perspective on Justice: Restorative? Retributive? How about Redistributive?" *Journal of Prisoners on Prisons* 5(2):60–64.

_____. 1995. "CSC and the 2 percent solution." *Journal of Prisoners on Prisons* 6(2):41–61.

Pearson, P. 1997. *When She Was Bad*. Toronto: Random House.

Peers, Archbishop Michael, Primate. 1996. "Seek Penitence, Not Retribution." *Anglican Journal*. May.

Penfold, S., and G. Walker. 1983. *Women and the Psychiatric Paradox*. Montreal: Eden Press.

Phillips, M.S. 1979. "Historical Development of Forensic Psychiatry Service in Canada." Unpublished Paper. Toronto: Archives on the History of Canadian Psychiatry and Mental Health Services.

Pollack, Shoshana. 1993. "Opening the Window on a Very Dark Day: A Program Evaluation of the Peer Support Team at the Kingston Prison for Women." Master's Thesis. Carleton University School of Social Work, Ottawa.

Pollock-Byrne, J. M. 1990. *Women, Prison and Crime*. Pacific Grove, CA: Brooks/Cole Publishing Company.

Porporino, F. 1989. *Role of the Research Branch*. Ottawa: Correctional Service of Canada, Research Branch. Report No. R-5.

Pratt, J. 1997. *Governing the Dangerous*. Sydney: Federation Press.

_____. 1998. "Towards the 'Decivilizing' of Punishment." *Social and Legal Studies* 7(4): 487–515.

Proctor, D., and F. Rosen. 1994. *Chameleon. The Lives of Dorothy Proctor from Street Criminal to International Special Agent*. Far Hills, NJ: New Horizon Press.

Quinn, P. 1995. "Reflexivity Run Riot: The Survival of the Prison Catch-all." *Howard Journal of Criminal Justice* 34(4): 354–63.

Rafter, N.H. 1982. "Chastizing the Unchaste: Social Control Functions of a Woman's Reformatory." In S. Cohen and A. Scull, (eds.), *Social Control and the State: Historical and Comparative Essays*. Oxford: Martin Robertson.

_____. 1985. *Partial Justice: Women in State Prisons, 1800–1935*. Boston: Northeastern University Press.

_____. 1992. *Partial Justice: Women, Prison and Social Control*. New Brunswick, NJ: Transaction Publishers.

Rafter, N.H., and F. Heidensohn (eds.). 1995. *International Feminist Perspectives in Criminology*. Buckingham: Open University Press.

Razack, S. 1991. *Canadian Feminism and the Law*. Toronto: Second Story Press.

_____. 1994. "What is to be Gained by Looking White People in the Eye?" *Signs* 19(4): 894–923.

_____. 1998. *Looking White People in the Eye: Gender, Race and Culture in Courtrooms and Classrooms*. Toronto: University of Toronto Press.

Reiss, A.J., and J.A. Roth. 1993. *Understanding and Preventing Violence*. Washington DC: National Academy Press.

Reynolds, B. 1996. "Federally Sentenced Women in Canada" Paper presented at Commonwealth Corrections Administrators Conference, November 25–28, Australia.

Rice, M. 1990. "Challenging Orthodoxies in Feminist Theory: A Black Feminist Critique." In L. Gelsthorpe and A. Morris.

Rice, M., G.T. Harris, G.W. Varney and V.L. Quinsey. 1989. *Violence in Institutions*. Toronto: Hogrefe & Huber.

Richie, Beth E. 1996. *Compelled to Crime: The Gender Entrapment of Battered Black Women*. New York: Routledge.

Rivera, M. 1996. "Giving Us a Chance." Revised edition. *Needs Assessment: Mental*

Health Resources for Federally Sentenced Women in the Regional Facilities. Ottawa: Correctional Service of Canada.

Rock, P. 1986. *A View From the Shadows*. Oxford: Oxford University Press.

_____. 1996. *Reconstructing a Women's Prison; The Holloway Redevelopment Project 1968–88*. Oxford: Clarendon Press.

Rose, N. 1988. "Calculable Minds and Manageable Individuals." *History of the Human Sciences* 1(2): 179–200.

_____. 1993. "Government, Authority and Experts in Advanced Liberalism." *Economy & Society* 22(3):283–300.

_____. 1996. *Inventing Ourselves. Psychology, Power and Personhood*. Cambridge: Cambridge University Press.

_____. 1999. *Governing the Soul*. Second edition. London: Free Association Books.

Ross, R., and H.B. McKay. 1976. *Self-Mutilation*. Lexington, Mass.: D.C. Heath.

_____. 1978. "Behavioral Approaches to Treatment in Corrections: Requiem for a Panacea." *Canadian Journal of Criminology and Corrections* 20: 279–95.

_____. 1979. "Adolescent Therapists." *Canada's Mental Health* 24: 15–17.

Rostaing, Corrine. 1996. "Les relations entre surveillantes et détenues." In C. Faugeron, A. Chauvenet, Ph. Combessie, (eds.), *Approches de la Prison*. Paris/Bruxelles: De Boeck Université.

Rothman, D. 1980. *Conscience and Convenience: The Asylum and its Alternatives in Progressive America*. London: Scott Foresman & Company.

Royal Commission on Aboriginal Peoples. 1996a. *Bridging the Cultural Divide: A Report on Aboriginal People and Criminal Justice in Canada*. Ottawa: Supply and Services Canada.

_____. 1996b. *People to People, Nation to Nation: Highlights from the Report of the Royal Commission on Aboriginal Peoples*. Ottawa: Supply and Services Canada.

Royal Commission to Investigate the Penal System of Canada. 1938. *Report of the Royal Commission to Investigate the Penal System in Canada*. Ottawa: King's Printer.

Ruemper, W. 1994. "Locking Them Up: Incarcerating Women in Ontario 1857–1931." In L. Knaafla and S. Binnie, (eds.), *Law, Society and the State: Essays in Modern Legal History*. Toronto: University of Toronto Press.

Saidman, L., and F. Chato-Manchuk. (n.d.). "Intensive Treatment Program for Female Offenders." Burnaby Correctional Centre for Women (BCCW).

Sangster, J. 1999. "Criminalizing the Colonized: Ontario Native Women Confront the Criminal Justice System, 1920–60." *The Canadian Historical Review* 80 (1): 32-60.

Scott, G. 1982. *Inmate: The Casebook Revelations of a Canadian Penitentiary Psychiatrist*. Montreal: Optimum Publishing.

Scott, James C. 1991. "Domination, Acting, and Fantasy." In C. Nordstrom and J. Martin, (eds.), *The Paths to Domination Resistance and Terror*. Berkeley: University of California Press.

Seear, N., and E. Player. 1986. *Women in the Penal System*. London: Howard League.

Shaw, Margaret. 1990. *The Federal Female Offender: Report on a Preliminary Study*. Task Force on Federally Sentenced Women, Companion Report #2. Ottawa: Solicitor General.

_____. 1991. *The Federal Female Offender: Report on a Preliminary Study. User Report 1991–93*. Ottawa: Ministry of the Solicitor General.

_____. 1992. "Issues of Power and Control: Women in Prison and their Defenders." *British Journal of Criminology* 32(4): 438–52.

_____. 1993. "Reforming Federal Women's Imprisonment." In E. Adelberg and C. Currie.

_____. 1994a. *Ontario Women in Conflict with the Law: Community Programmes and Regional Issues.* Toronto: Ministry of the Solicitor General & Correctional Services.

_____. 1994b. "Women in Prison: A Literature Review." *Forum* (Special issue on Women in Prison) 6(1): http://198.103.98.138/crd/forum/e06/e061d.htm.

_____. 1995. "Conceptualizing Violence by Women." In R.E. Dobash, R.P. Dobash and L. Noakes, (eds.), *Gender and Crime.* Cardiff: University of Wales Press.

_____. 1996. "Is there a Feminist Future for Women's Prisons?" In R. Matthews and Peter Francis, (eds.), *Prisons 2000: An International Perspective on the Current State and Future of Imprisonment.* Basingstoke, U.K.: Macmillan Press.

_____. 1998. *Risking Your Reputation: Advocacy Research and Offending Women.* Paper presented at the annual meetings of the American Society of Criminology, Washington, D.C., Nov. 9–11.

_____. 1999. "Knowledge without Acknowledgement: Violent Women, the Prison and the Cottage." *Howard Journal of Criminal Justice* 38(3): 252–66.

Shaw, M., and S. Dubois. 1995. *Understanding Violence by Women: A Review of the Literature.* Ottawa: Correctional Service Canada.

Shaw, M. and K. Hannah-Moffat. 1999. "Women and Risk: A Geneology of Classification." Paper presented at the British Criminology Conference, Liverpool, July 13–16.

Shaw, M., K. Rodgers, J. Blanchette, T. Hattem, L.S. Thomas and L. Tamarack. 1991. *Survey of Federally Sentenced Women: Report to the Task Force on Federally Sentenced Women.* User Report 1991-4. Ottawa: Ministry of the Solicitor General.

_____. 1992. *Paying the Price: Federally Sentenced Women in Context.* Ottawa: Ministry of Solicitor General, Corrections Branch.

Shaylor, Cassandra. 1998. "'It's Like Living in a Black Hole': Women of Colour and Solitary Confinement in the Prison Industrial Complex." *New England Journal on Criminal and Civil Confinement* 24(2): 385–416.

Showalter, E. 1985. *The Female Malady: Women, Madness and Culture, 1830–1980.* New York: Pantheon Books.

Sim, J. 1990. *Medical Power in Prisons: The Prison Medical Service in England 1774–1989.* Milton Keynes: Open University Press.

Simon, Jonathon. 1994. "In the Place of the Parent: Risk Management and the Government of Campus Life." *Social and Legal Studies* 3:15–45.

Simon, J., and M. Feeley. 1995. "True Crime: The New Penology and Public Discourse on Crime." In T. Blomberg and S. Cohen, (eds.), *Punishment and Social Control.* New York: Aldine de Gruyter.

Simpson, S. 1991. "Caste, Class and Violent Crime: Explaining Difference in Female Offending." *Criminology* 29(1): 115–35.

Sims, C. 1981. "An Institutional History of the Asylum for the Insane at Kingston. 1856–1885." M.A. dissertation, Queen's University.

Smart, C. 1976. *Women, Crime and Criminology: A Feminist Critique.* London: Routledge & Keegan Paul.

_____. 1989. *Feminism and the Power of Law.* London: Routledge.

_____. 1990. "Feminist Approaches to Criminology or Postmodern Woman Meets Atavistic Man." In L. Gelsthorpe and A. Morris.

Snider, L. 1990. "The Potential of the Criminal Justice System to Promote Feminist Concerns." *Studies in Law, Politics, and Society* 10: 143–72.

_____. 1994. "Feminism, Punishment and the Potential of Empowerment." *Canadian Journal of Law and Society* 9(2): 75–104.

Solicitor General's Special Committee on Provincially Incarcerated Women. 1992.

Ten years after the publication of *Creating Choices*, a remarkable report on women's imprisonment in Canada, this book sets out to reflect on attempts to reform prison. In a series of critical essays, the contributors stimulate reflection and discussion. They explore the effects of punishment and penality on women's lives, the impact of feminist reforms on the lives of women in prison and the systemic barriers which limit change in the context of both provincial and federal prisons. Each of the authors has a personal and sometimes intimate knowledge of the recent history of women's prisons in Canada. Taking *Creating Choices* as a starting point, these essays question the role of prisons in our society, the importance of taking account of gender and its intersection with race and class, and the problems of both weak feminist models and the co-optation of feminist ideals and Aboriginal spirituality by correctional systems.

Contributors include: editors Kelly Hannah-Moffat and Margaret Shaw, Gillian Balfour, Elizabeth Comack, Karlene Faith, Stephanie Hayman, Gayle Horii, Kathleen Kendall, Joane Martel, Patricia Monture-Angus, Kim Pate and Shoshana Pollack

cover image: Gayle Horii

ISBN 978-1552660249

9 781552 660249

Fernwood Publishing
www.fernwoodpublishing.ca
ISBN 9781552660249